THESE STONES WILL SHOUT

A new voice for the Old Testament

by Mark Link, S.J.

Argus Communications A Division of **DLM,** Inc.
Niles, Illinois 60648 U.S.A.

ACKNOWLEDGMENTS

Scripture texts used in this work, unless otherwise indicated, are taken from the *New American Bible,* copyright © 1970 by the Confraternity of Christian Doctrine, Washington, D.C., and are used by license of said copyright owner. No part of the *New American Bible* may be reproduced in any form without permission in writing from the Confraternity of Christian Doctrine, Washington, D.C. All rights reserved.

Scripture texts marked Today's English Version are from the *Good News Bible.* Old Testament: Copyright © American Bible Society 1976. New Testament: Copyright © American Bible Society 1966, 1971, 1976. Reprinted by permission of the American Bible Society.

Excerpt from "The Trial That Rocked the Nation" by John T. Scopes, *Reader's Digest,* March 1961. Reprinted by permission.

Excerpt from "The Lutheran Pope," *Newsweek,* July 23, 1973. Copyright 1973 by Newsweek, Inc. All rights reserved. Reprinted by permission.

Excerpt from "Protestant Misuse of the Bible" by Charles Clayton Morrison. Copyright 1946 Christian Century Foundation. Reprinted by permission from the June 5, 1946, issue of *The Christian Century.*

Excerpts from "Dinosaurs Before Adam?" by Robert E. Gentet, *Tract #670.* Copyright 1963. Reprinted by permission of Ambassador College, Pasadena, California.

Excerpts from *Is the Bible Really the Word of God?* by the Watch Tower Bible and Tract Society of Pennsylvania. Copyright 1969. Reprinted by permission of the Watch Tower Bible and Tract Society of Pennsylvania.

Excerpt from "In Darwin's Century" by Loren Eiseley from *Adventures of the Mind,* reprinted from *The Saturday Evening Post.* © 1958 The Curtis Publishing Company. Reprinted by permission.

Excerpts from "Deadend for Expanding Universe?" by Ronald Kotulak, *Chicago Tribune,* 1973. Reprinted, courtesy of the *Chicago Tribune.*

Excerpts from "Creation" and "Noah Built the Ark" from *God's Trombones* by James Weldon Johnson. Copyright 1927 by The Viking Press, Inc., © renewed 1955 by Grace Nail Johnson. Reprinted by permission of Viking Penguin Inc.

Excerpts from *The Last Temptation of Christ* by Nikos Kazantzakis, trans. by P. A. Bien. Copyright © 1960 by Simon & Schuster, Inc. Reprinted by permission of Simon & Schuster, a Division of Gulf & Western Corporation, and Mrs. Helen Kazantzakis.

Excerpt from "Carbon Copy Man" by Bill Barry, *Chicago Sun-Times Midwest Magazine,* March 11, 1973. Reprinted by permission of Bill Barry.

Excerpt from ". . . Half Plant, Half Animal" by Ronald Kotulak, *Chicago Tribune,* March 21, 1976. Reprinted, courtesy of the *Chicago Tribune.*

Excerpt from *Strength to Love* by Martin Luther King, Jr. Copyright © 1963 by Martin Luther King, Jr. Reprinted by permission of Joan Daves.

Excerpt from "Man's a Born Killer . . ." by Arthur J. Snider, *Chicago Daily News,* September 1–2, 1973. Reprinted with permission from Field Enterprises, Inc.

Excerpt from *The Seven Storey Mountain* by Thomas Merton. Copyright © 1948 by Harcourt Brace & Company, Inc. Copyright renewed © 1976 by Trustees of the Merton Legacy Trust. Reprinted by permission of Harcourt Brace Jovanovich, Inc., and Curtis Brown, Ltd.

Excerpt from *Studs Lonigan* by James T. Farrell. Copyright © 1932, 1933, 1934 by Vanguard Press, Inc. Copyright renewed 1960, 1962, 1963 by James T. Farrell. Epilogue and author's introduction to epilogue copyright © 1978 by James T. Farrell. Reprinted by permission of Vanguard Press, Inc.

Continued on page 236.

PHOTO CREDITS

Gene Ahrens/Freelance Photographers Guild, Inc. 132

J. Baker/Shostal Associates, Inc. 226

The Bettmann Archive, Inc. 121

Biblical Archaeology Review 98, 109, 114

Courtesy of the Trustees of the British Museum 17, 40, 48L, 102, 146–47, 154, 155, 156, 164, 173, 175T, 193, 217

Brown Brothers 8, 9

Chicago Tribune 41

Robert deGast/Photo Researchers, Inc. 25

Diane Dybsky 141

Stephen L. Feldman/Photo Researchers, Inc. 204

Georg Gerster 120

Weems Hutto 180

Courtesy of the Israel Department of Antiquities and Museums 97T, 175B

Israel Government Tourist Office 51, 52, 84, 87, 89, 95B, 105, 117, 118, 119, 128, 129, 138, 152, 166, 197, 198, 200, 220

Israel Museum 95T, 96, 169, 178

Leo M. Johnson/Corn's Photo Service 23

Algimantas Kezys 37, 56

Ken Lambert/Freelance Photographers Guild, Inc. 136

H. Lanks/Freelance Photographers Guild, Inc. 125

Jean-Claude Lejeune 59, 81, 139

Archie Lieberman 11, 82, 163

Mark Link 26, 65, 88, 122

Llewellyn/Freelance Photographers Guild, Inc. 143

Alexander Lowry/Photo Researchers, Inc. 134

Margot Lubinski/Freelance Photographers Guild, Inc. 171

Tom McHugh/Photo Researchers, Inc. 28–29

David Muench/Freelance Photographers Guild, Inc. 210

Courtesy of the Oriental Institute, University of Chicago 34, 44–45, 48R, 49, 67, 97B, 158, 176, 184–85, 189, 190, 191, 194T, 195R, 196, 202

Photoworld, Inc. 29, 113

Curt Salonick 20

Raymond Schoder 6–7, 16, 18 (Courtesy of the Oriental Institute, University of Chicago, Statuette Orinst. A 7119), 19, 72R, 73TR, 73B, 77, 100–101, 104, 127, 130, 142, 165, 194–95, 203, 206, 209, 215, 222, 223

E. Streichan/Shostal Associates, Inc. cover

Arthur Tress/Photo Researchers, Inc. 159

James Vorwaldt 115, 212–13, 225

Wolfe Worldwide Films 47, 66, 68, 72L, 73TL

The Archives of the YIVO Institute for Jewish Research 43

CONTENTS

PREFACE

A New Voice for the Old Testament

John Henry Newman once said:
"I read the Bible to know what people ought to do,
and my newspaper to know what they are doing."
Paul Tillich made a similar observation.

We might add a further observation
made by Maurice Zundel: "You can understand
the Bible only on your knees."

These Stones Will Shout
tries to present the Jewish Scriptures
in a way that not only remains faithful to them,
but in a way, also, that relates them
to what people today are doing and thinking.

More importantly, *These Stones Will Shout*
tries to present the Jewish Scriptures
in a way that leads to a prayerful reflection
of them.

When *These Stones Will Shout* appeared in 1975,
the author said that his method and approach
grew out of a classroom teaching situation.
The same is true of this revised edition:
it represents nine years of classroom experience.

For those interested in teaching this book,
the following aids are available:
a highly detailed *Teacher Manual,*
a *Blackline Master Kit,* and a *Poster Activity Kit.*

The author concludes his observations
as he did his original edition.
He tried to follow the scholars at a distance.
With each page he wrote,
he saw the desirability to qualify something.

Yet, he knew that if he did
he would end up with just another scholarly effort—
a poor one at that.
And so he decided to risk all
for the pearl of great price.

If he has failed the scholars,
he begs their understanding.
If he has failed his readers,
he hopes another will succeed where he has not.
If he has failed the Bible,
he trusts in the forgiveness
of what he understands to be a forgiving God.

Easter, 1980   Mark Link, S.J.

5

MACEDONIA

Black Sea

PHRYGIA

Mt. Ararat

MESOPOTAMIA

Mediterranean Sea

JERUSALEM

EGYPT

Red Sea

Time Chart

5000 BC	walled town built at Jericho
5000	towns along the Nile
4500	towns in Mesopotamia
4241	first known date of history (calendar adopted in Egypt)
3500	rise of great civilization in Mesopotamia (Sumer)
3100	writing appears
2600	great pyramid built in Egypt
2000	ziggurat built at Ur

BIBLICAL PREHISTORY

Books

Genesis 1–11

1

The Confrontation

It all started rather harmlessly.
On March 21, 1925,
the Tennessee legislature passed this law:

*It shall be unlawful for any teacher
in any of the Universities, Normals,
and all other public schools of the state,
which are supported in whole or in part
by the public school funds of the State,
to teach any theory that denies the story of the
Divine Creation of man as taught in the Bible,
and to teach that man has descended
from a lower order of animals.*

No one expected much would come of the law.
It was merely in the books
to pacify those who interpreted the Bible literally.
Within days, however,
the American Civil Liberties Union
voted to test the constitutionality of the law.

John Scopes, a biology teacher
who taught evolution to his classes,
agreed to submit to arrest.
Clarence Darrow, the famous criminal lawyer,
agreed to defend Scopes without a fee.

On the other side of the fence,
the World's Fundamentalist Association
hired the renowned William Jennings Bryan
to assist the prosecution.

Darrow (left) and Bryan (right) pose at the Dayton trial.
Because of huge crowds and the July heat,
the judge moved several sessions out-of-doors.
Scopes was found guilty and fined $100.
Bryan collapsed and died in Dayton
a few days after the trial.

A fundamentalist and three-time nominee for
President on the Democratic ticket,
he would counter the prestige of Darrow.

THE TRIAL

On July 10, 1925, the trial began in Dayton.
To everyone's surprise, one of Darrow's first moves
was to call Bryan as a witness.
Here is a report of what happened.

The Trial That Rocked the Nation
JOHN T. SCOPES

Darrow read from Genesis:
"And the morning and the evening
were the first day."
Then he asked Bryan if he believed
that the sun was created on the fourth day.
Bryan said he did.

8

"How could there have been morning
and evening without any sun?" Darrow inquired.
Bryan mopped his bald dome in silence.
There were snickers from the crowd,
even among the faithful. . . .
"And you believe that God punished the serpent
by condemning snakes forever after
to crawl upon their bellies?"

"I believe that!"

"Well, have you any idea
how the snake went before that?"

The crowd laughed, and Bryan turned livid.
His voice rose
and the fan in his hand shook in anger.

"Your honor," he said, "I will answer
all Mr. Darrow's questions at once.
I want the world to know that this man who does
not believe in God is using a Tennessee court
to cast slurs on Him. . . ."

"I object to that statement," Darrow shouted.
"I am examining you on your fool ideas
that no intelligent Christian on earth believes."

STILL A PROBLEM

The dispute over the Bible is far from over.
It leaped back into the news in the mid-1970s
when Missouri Synod Lutherans
voted to adopt a stricter interpretation of the Bible.
The vote received a great deal of coverage
in the popular news media.

The Lutheran Pope
NEWSWEEK

It is now absolute dogma within the sect
that a man named Jonah
was swallowed by a whale and lived to tell the tale.
In addition, all the miracles in the Bible
occurred precisely as reported.
And Adam and Eve were real people created by God,
which means
that the theory of evolution is fantasy. . . .

For the moment, the future is uncertain
for at least one million Missouri Synod Lutherans
whose ideas of Christian orthodoxy
do not include Biblical literalism. . . .
As soon as the convention declared . . .
fundamentalism to be the standard for the church,
more than 400 delegates marched on the podium
to deposit their names in dissent.

Scenes like this gave the trial a carnival atmosphere.
Preachers held forth on street corners,
and peddlers hawked their wares among the crowds.
A local drugstore renamed itself
"Monkeyville Soda Fountain."

Who Decides?

The problem of biblical interpretation
is as old as the Bible itself.
Peter wrote concerning Paul's letters:

There are certain passages in them
hard to understand.
The ignorant and the unstable distort them
(just as they do the rest of Scripture)
to their own ruin.

2 PETER 3:16

Early Christians resolved major biblical disputes
by deferring to church leadership,
which they believed to be divinely guided.
This way of resolving disputes
ended for many Christians, however,
with the advent of the Protestant Reformation
in the 16th century.
The effects were far-reaching,
as this Protestant report explains.

Protestant Misuse of the Bible
CHARLES CLAYTON MORRISON

The conference of Luther and Zwingli . . .
to unify the German and Swiss Reformation,
broke down . . .
over the failure of the two leaders
to agree on the interpretation
of a single Biblical text: "This is my Body."

From that day on the misuse of the Bible
has vitiated the spirit of Protestantism . . .
and divided it into sects.

2
Literal Interpreter

Modern Bible readers split into two main groups.
For the sake of clarity,
we may refer to them as literal interpreters
and contextual interpreters.

Literal interpreters
focus primarily on the *text* of the Bible.

Contextual interpreters focus equally on the *text*
and *context* (historical, cultural, and literary)
in which the Bible developed.
Within each group there is some flexibility.

An example of flexibility among *literal* interpreters
is shown by the positions taken by
Jehovah's Witnesses and the Church of God
concerning the word *day* in the creation story.
Jehovah's Witnesses hold
you may interpret the word *day* to mean "era."
Church of God members hold
you must interpret it to mean 24 hours.

Thus, Church of God members,
following a strict biblical timetable,
hold that creation took place in the year 4004 B.C.
Moreover, they believe it took place
in the course of six 24-hour days.

People ask: "How can you hold
that creation took place about 6,000 years ago,
when science proves the earth is millions of years old?"
The literal interpreters answer: "Read your Bible!"

The earth became chaotic and void.

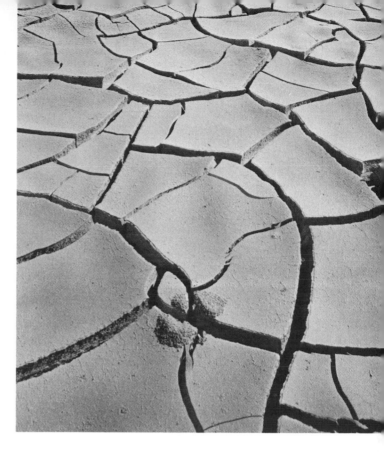

In the beginning,
when God created the heavens and the earth,
the earth was a formless wasteland,
and darkness covered the abyss,
while a mighty wind swept over the waters.
Then God said, "Let there be light."

GENESIS 1:1-3

Literal readers say the word *then* holds the key.
It shows that
"the heavens and the earth" already existed
before God began his six days of work.
The six days, therefore,
refer only to *preparing* earth for human habitation.

PREHUMAN ERA

But this still leaves a problem.
How do we explain the existence of fossils, ferns,
and dinosaurs that are millions of years old?
Shouldn't they also be 6,000 years old,
if God created them?

Again, the literalists feel they have an answer.
They believe the earth had a prehuman habitation—
an angelic civilization.

Dinosaurs Before Adam?
ROBERT E. GENTET

Ezekiel 28 and Isaiah 14 tell of the time
when the great archangel called Lucifer—
who ruled the earth before Adam's creation—
rebelled against his Creator and fought God's
loyal angels for control of the universe.
In his rebellion, he led away
one third of the angelic world (Revelation 12:4). . . .

It was at this time
the archangel Lucifer became Satan!

This great battle for control of the universe
caused great destruction upon the earth.

Animal and plant life of the types that then lived
were destroyed, rapidly buried, and fossilized.
The earth became chaotic and void. . . .
The first six days recorded in Genesis 1
describe the surface of the earth
being reformed out of a chaotic condition!

To support his theory,
Gentet cites Carl Dunbar's *Historical Geology,*
which notes that dinosaurs vanished suddenly,
not gradually, as the theory of evolution requires.

It was as if the curtain
were rung down suddenly on a stage . . .
and rose immediately
to reveal the same setting but an entirely new cast,
a cast in which dinosaurs do not appear . . .
and the leading parts are all played by mammals.

Gentet feels that his explanation fits the facts.
The *great battle* ended up in a global wipe-out:
total and sudden destruction of all forms of life
on the planet earth.

11

Indeed, this was the "curtain"
that came down suddenly on the stage.
It rose just as suddenly
when God decided to create a human civilization.

The literal interpreters also feel
they can answer Darrow's first question to Bryan:
"How could there have been morning and evening
without any sun?"

Here's how Jehovah's Witnesses respond.

Is the Bible Really the Word of God?
WATCH TOWER BIBLE AND TRACT SOCIETY

Genesis 1:1 shows that the "heavens,"
which include the sun, moon and stars . . .
were already created
before the "first day" even began.
Yet, prior to the "first day"
the earth itself was in darkness.

The Bible does not state
what prevented the sun's rays
from reaching the planet at that point. . . .

The Book of Job, in describing the earth's formation,
at one point speaks of it as having
"the cloud as its garment and thick gloom
as its swaddling band." (Job 38:4–9)

To illustrate:
One planet in our solar system, Venus,
is completely blanketed
by an unbroken layer of clouds.
Even with their powerful telescopes,
astronomers have never seen its surface.
Though Earth's "swaddling band"
may have been of different composition,
the present state of Venus at least illustrates
what may have been the condition of its neighbor
planet Earth up until the "fourth day."

One thing is certain: A notable change
took place in that fourth period. . . .
God evidently caused the "swaddling band"
high above the earth to become translucent,
thus dispelling the darkness beneath.
So, by God's creative force the sun, moon and stars
were now "made" to be visible
from within the earth's atmosphere.

CREATIONIST

Because they believe the creation story
took place as the Bible describes it,
the literal interpreters reject the theory of evolution.

They take a creationist view of life,
namely, that the various "kinds" of life on earth
came directly from the creative hand of God.
They do stress, however,
the importance of the word *kinds*.
The creationist does not rule out variations
within a specific kind.
Here is one statement of this position.

Why the New Creation-Evolution Controversy?
WILLIAM F. DANKENBRING

At a recent convention
of the National Association of Biology Teachers
in California, it was evident that evolutionists
assumed that the Genesis "kinds"
referred to every last species and variety
as being individually created. . . .

Simply because each "kind"
reproduces after its own kind
does not mean that there can be no variation
within an original Genesis kind.

There are many varieties of dogs, horses and cats.
Yet, each of these varieties
is still a member of the same original kind. . . .
These variations . . . are merely new varieties
arising within the original Genesis kind.

EVOLUTIONIST

Readers who interpret Scripture less rigidly
are open to the possibility of evolution.
Thus, they can read with serious reflection
this imaginative description of human origin.

In Darwin's Century
LOREN EISELEY

In all that prehuman world there had been
no animal capable of looking back or forward.
No living creature had wept over another's grave.
There had been nothing to comprehend the whole.

For three billion years that rule remained unbroken.
At the end of that period
there occurred a small soundless concussion. . . .
The event itself took place in silence,
the silence of cells multiplying at an enormous pace
under a small bone roof,
the silence of some great fungus
coming up at night in a forest glade. . . .

For three billion years,
until some ageless watcher
might have turned away in weariness,
nothing moved but the slime and its creations.
Toward the end of that time,
a small unprepossessing animal sat on his haunches
by a rock pile on a waste of open ground.
He clutched a stick
and chewed the end of it meditatively.
He was the first of the great explosion.
In his head was the first twinkle
of that tenuous rainbow bridge that stretches
between the earth and the city of the Gods.

Evolutionists suggest
that man is part of an evolutionary process
that has been going on for billions of years—
and still goes on.
Among evolutionists
there are both theists and nontheists.

Nontheistic evolutionists do not, necessarily,
see a God involved in this process in any way.
Some speak of a "life force" at work,
but it is in no way a *personal* God.

Theistic evolutionists, on the other hand,
see the process intimately linked to a personal God.
Strangely enough, Saint Augustine (fifth century)
seems to have had a sense of the process of evolution.
He suggested that God could have created
a primeval form or seed
from which our universe and life slowly emerged.

Though Augustine's theory was rejected in his time,
some modern scientists think along similar lines.

Deadend for Expanding Universe?
RONALD KOTULAK

Most astronomers believe in the "big bang" theory
of the creation of the universe.
According to this concept,
all of the matter in the universe was condensed
into a primeval fireball about 10 billion years ago.

The ball exploded [bang], and all the matter
has been expanding outward ever since,
forming the stars, planets,
and galaxies in the process. . . .

What has perplexed scientists, however,
is whether the universe
would continue to expand indefinitely
or if it would stop expanding at some point
and begin to come together again.

The only way it could contract would be
if there was sufficient matter in the universe
so that the collective gravity of this mass
would be strong enough to brake the expansion.
Like a ball
at the end of an outstretched rubber string,
all of the matter would then snap back
into another fireball. . . .

Scientists are divided
on the answer to this question.
Some think
there is enough matter in the universe
to reverse the expansion process.
Others think the discovery of "fossil" elements,
like deuterium (residue from the "big bang"),
suggests that the amount of matter
may not be sufficient.
If this is true,
the universe will continue to expand,
while slowing down gradually,
as great galaxies burn themselves out
to become giant graveyards of cooling cinders.

A second question perplexes scientists.
Ronald Kotulak puts it this way:

Astronomers are still stumped
by the imponderable question
of where the original fireball came from. . . .

For all their studies, scientists have not been able
to come up with a better answer than
that posed by many of the world's major religions:
At one point matter was created.

STILL OPEN-ENDED

Teilhard de Chardin, a priest-scientist,
accepts the possibility
that God could have created in the way described.

A paleontologist and theologian, he blends
both science and theology, discerning God
to be the author and destiny of the process.

In the final analysis, however,
we are dealing in theory.
When it comes to "earth's infancy,"
says J. H. Umgrove in *The Earth's Shifting Crust,*
we are still in the dark.
"Probably not a single step can be placed
on solid ground."

Creation "Fossils"?

All that the two scientists wanted to do
was to get rid of the "faint static"
from Bell Lab's big radio telescope in New Jersey.
They even got down on their hands and knees
and scrubbed pigeon dung from the big horn,
thinking the slight radiation it gave off
might be the culprit.

Then, a chance phone call to a Princeton professor
ignited a chain of events
that left the scientific community stunned.

End Only 100 Billion Years Away
RONALD KOTULAK

That nuisance static turned out to be a whisper
from space and ancient history.
It was a message

left over from the creation of the universe
about 18 billion years ago
and it confirmed the "big bang" theory
of how the universe was created.

The next step was to try to identify
the elements in space producing the static
and believed to be "fossils" from the "big bang."

The discovery of deuterium among the fossils
suggests insufficient matter in the universe
to brake its present outward motion
and cause the galaxies to rush together again
in what is known as the "big crunch."

Eventually, the universe will grind to a halt.
In the words of poet T. S. Eliot, "The world ends
not with a bang but a whimper."

3
Contextual Interpreter

Contextual interpreters view the Bible
differently than do their literal colleagues.
They believe the key to understanding it
lies not in adherence to the *text* alone.
Equally important is an understanding
of the historical and cultural *context*
in which the Bible developed and was written.

This is especially true of early accounts
that deal with *prehistory,*
that foggy period of time
between the appearance of humans on earth
and their first attempts to tell their story.

For example, when the Bible says
that Adam lived 930 years,
did the biblical writer intend this literally?
Or when the Bible says the snake talked to Eve,
did the biblical writer intend to teach us something
about the previous condition of snakes?

Or when the first chapter of the Book of Genesis
says that man was created last,
and the next chapter says that he was created first,
wasn't the biblical writer aware
that this report is contradictory, if taken literally?

The contextualists firmly believe
that the Bible is the word of God
but is expressed in the words of humans.
They believe that God inspired the biblical writers.
God, however, did not dictate what to say.

The biblical writer
was a person uniquely open to God's revelation
and uniquely inspired by God to express it
in the language and idiom of his time.

GO BACK IN SPIRIT

Contextual interpreters believe
that they must read the Bible within the context
of its historical times and cultural background.
This gives a better understanding
not only of the words, but also of the special meaning
certain words and symbols held in ancient times.
Pope Pius XII told Catholic biblical scholars:

*You must go back, as it were,
in spirit to those remote centuries of the East.
With the aid of history, archaeology, ethnology,
and the other sciences,
you must determine accurately what modes
of writing the ancient writers would likely use,
and in fact did use.*

In other words, scholars must approach the Bible
from the viewpoint of ancient times,
and not impose their own 20th-century viewpoint.
This is simple in theory but difficult in practice.

MODERN SCHOLARSHIP

In recent years, however, remarkable advances
have been made in biblical interpretation.
New sciences, like biblical archaeology,
have cast new light on passages and stories.
Never, since the biblical time itself,
has so much new information been available.

As a result,
a whole new understanding of the Bible is emerging.
The biblical scholar is like a person
who has been walking in the fog.
Now the fog is lifting,
and the scholar sees, in beautiful detail,
things once seen only in vague outline.
To illustrate, consider the Book of Genesis.

Biblical Archaeology

The science of biblical archaeology
selects from the remains of the past
any evidence that sheds light on the Bible.

Illustrations from Biblical Archaeology
D. J. WISEMAN

On the basis of this evidence,
it is now possible
to paint a picture of Old Testament times
on a canvas
which a hundred years ago was almost blank.

Archaeologists dig, sift, study, and catalog
every people-produced object they come across.
It is a tedious, painstaking task.

CREATION STORY

In the beginning,
when God created the heavens and the earth,
the earth was a formless wasteland,
and darkness covered the abyss,
while a mighty wind swept over the waters.

Then God said,
"Let there be light,"
and there was light.
God saw how good the light was.
God then separated the light from the darkness.
God called the light "day,"
and the darkness he called "night."
Thus evening came, and morning followed—
the first day.

Then God said,
"Let there be a dome
in the middle of the waters,
to separate one body of water from the other."
And so it happened:
God made the dome,
and it separated
the water above the dome
from the water below it.
God called the dome "the sky."
Evening came, and morning followed—
the second day.

Then God said,
"Let the water under the sky
be gathered into a single basin,
so that the dry land may appear."
And so it happened. . . .
God called the dry land "the earth,"
and the basin of the water he called "the sea." . . .
Then God said,
"Let the earth bring forth vegetation. . . ."
And so it happened. . . .
God saw how good it was.
Evening came, and morning followed—
the third day.

Then God said:
"Let there be lights in the dome of the sky,
to separate day from night. Let them mark the
fixed times, the days and the years,
and serve as luminaries in the dome of the sky,
to shed light upon the earth."
And so it happened: God made the two great
lights, the greater one to govern the day,
and the lesser one to govern the night;
and he made the stars. . . .
God saw how good it was.
Evening came, and morning followed—
the fourth day.

Then God said,
"Let the water teem with an abundance
of living creatures . . .
let birds fly beneath the dome of the sky."
And so it happened:
God created the great sea monsters
and all kinds of swimming creatures . . .
and all kinds of winged birds.
God saw how good it was,
and God blessed them. . . .
Evening came, and morning followed—
the fifth day.

Then God said,
"Let the earth bring forth all kinds of living
creatures: cattle, creeping things,
and wild animals of all kinds."
And so it happened. . . .
Then God said: "Let us make man in our image,
after our likeness". . . male and female he
created them. God blessed them, saying:
"Be fertile and multiply; fill the earth and subdue it.
Have dominion over the fish of the sea,
the birds of the air, and all the living things
that move on the earth.". . . And so it happened.
God looked at everything he had made,
and he found it very good.
Evening came, and morning followed—
the sixth day.

These clay tablet fragments found at Nineveh
are part of a series
that contain a Babylonian account of creation.
Although the Nineveh tablets
date from about the 7th century B.C.,
their story goes back to the 20th century B.C.
Scholars believe that the Babylonians
borrowed it from an earlier Sumerian story.

Thus the heavens and the earth
and all their array were completed. . . .
So God blessed the seventh day
and made it holy, because on it he rested
from all the work he had done in creation.

GENESIS 1:1–31; 2:1–3

This remarkable four-faced deity
was just one of many Babylonian gods.
Archaeologists retrieved it from the sandy grave
where it lay buried for nearly 4,000 years.

LITERARY PATTERNS

A careful analysis of the Genesis story turns up
something that many Bible readers miss.
Each day is described
in almost identically the same pattern:

> an introduction,
> a command,
> the accomplishment of the command,
> an affirmation of goodness,
> an identification of the day.

Going further, we discover
that the overall week also follows a fixed pattern:

FIRST DAY   God created light,
and separated it from darkness.

SECOND DAY   God separated the waters above
the dome from the waters below it.
(Hebrews viewed the sky
as a thin dome, holding back
the waters "above" [rain]
from the waters "below" [sea].)

THIRD DAY   God separated the waters below
from the dry land
and clothed the land with vegetation.

FOURTH DAY   God populated the sky
with sun, moon, and stars.

FIFTH DAY   God populated the air and sea
with birds and fish.

SIXTH DAY   God populated the land
with people and animals.

SEVENTH DAY   God celebrated. He blessed the
seventh day and made it holy,
because on it he rested.

This overall pattern emerges:

FIRST STAGE   Three days of separation
SECOND STAGE   Three days of population
THIRD STAGE   One day of celebration

LITERARY FORM

These fixed patterns warn us
that we are dealing with a special kind of writing,
not scientific description or an eyewitness report.
Rather, we are dealing with a poemlike story,
designed to aid memory and to teach. (Ancients
learned almost everything by word of mouth.)

What truths did the biblical writer intend to teach?
The truths emerge only if we "go back in spirit"
to the historical times in which the writer lived.

MANY GODS

When the biblical writer lived,
the worship of many gods was as widespread
as is the worship of one God today.

Almost every object in nature
was worshiped by some group or nation.
The biblical writer testified to this fact
when he warned:

Be strictly on your guard . . .
not to degrade yourselves by fashioning an idol
to represent any figure,
whether it be the form of a man or of a woman,
of any animal on the earth or of any bird . . .
or of any fish. . . .

And when you look up to the heavens
and behold the sun or the moon
or any star among the heavenly hosts,
do not be led astray into adoring them.

DEUTERONOMY 4:15-19

The biblical writer's point is this:
There is only one God!
He makes his point by having the "one" God create
the false gods that ancient peoples worshiped.

In the process of teaching this key truth,
the biblical writer touches upon another error
widespread among ancients.

Archaeology shows that Babylonian astrologers
believed the heavenly bodies controlled people.
The Genesis writer reversed this view.
He taught that God intended the heavenly bodies
to serve people,
to "mark" their seasons and to "light" their earth.

HAPHAZARD EVENT

Also widespread in biblical times
was the belief that the world came into being
through the haphazard act of feuding gods.
For example, a Babylonian creation story,
called *Enuma Elish,* expresses this belief.

Stone tablets of the Babylonian story
were found at Nineveh by archaeologists.
Some interpreters think the biblical writer
consciously set out to refute the Babylonian story.

The biblical writer
follows the Babylonian sequence of creation.
But he departs radically
when it comes to the creator.
He portrays God creating the world by design
and with loving care.

The Babylonian account describes the world
coming about after a bloody battle
between two rival gods: Marduk and Tiamat.
From the lacerated and slain body of Tiamat,
Marduk fashions the world.

The biblical writer's point is this:
God created the world not by whim or chance
but by loving design.

These Assyrian/Hittite gods,
in an apparent feuding posture,
turn back the clock of history
nearly 3,000 years.

EVIL MATTER

Next, many people in biblical times
believed that parts of creation were evil
because they were created by evil gods.
As late as the 12th century A.D.
this idea was still widely circulated.

Those who taught it maintained that people
were composed of two contradictory elements:
matter (from Satan) and spirit (from God).

Against these theories,
the Bible teaches that God created everything;
and everything God created is good!
The biblical writer makes this point
by having God affirm the goodness
of all that he creates, especially people.

GRAND FINALE

The key point about creation is left to last.
The biblical writer describes God
as blessing the last day and resting on it.
Why this conclusion?

First, he wants to teach that the Sabbath
should be observed in a special way.

Second, and more important, he wants to teach
that God, who created us in his image,
intends that we should enjoy creation with him
in a kind of eternal enjoyment, forever.
The reason God created us
is not that we should be his pawns
and the created world his personal chessboard,
but that we should be his children
and the created world our home—forever.

Biblical Singer

God's interest in people
excited the heart of the Hebrew psalmist.
Strolling out into the star-filled night,
he would climb a hill, face the sky, and sing:

O LORD, our Lord,
how glorious is your name over all the earth! . . .

When I behold your heavens,
the work of your fingers,
the moon and the stars which you set in place—
what is man that you should be mindful of him,
or the son of man that you should care for him?

You have made him little less than the angels,
and crowned him with glory and honor.
You have given him rule
over the works of your hands,
putting all things under his feet:
All sheep and oxen,
yes, and the beasts of the field,
the birds of the air, the fishes of the sea,
and whatever swims the paths of the seas.

O LORD, our Lord,
how glorious is your name over all the earth!

PSALM 8

4

The Bible God

Some people are surprised that chapter 1
of Genesis ends with the sixth day of creation.
Chapter 2 opens with the seventh day.

Chapter 2

1 *Thus the heavens and the earth*
   and all their array were completed.
2 *Since on the seventh day God was finished*
   with the work he had been doing,
   he rested on the seventh day
   from all the work he had undertaken.
3 *So God blessed the seventh day*
   and made it holy, because on it he rested
   from all the work he had done in creation.
4 *Such is the story of the heavens and the earth*
   at their creation.
   At the time when the LORD God
   made the earth and the heavens—
5 *while as yet there was no field shrub on earth*
   and no grass of the field had sprouted,
   for the LORD God had sent no rain upon the earth
   and there was no man to till the soil,
6 *but a stream was welling up out of the earth*
   and was watering all the surface of the ground—
7 *the LORD God formed man out of the clay*
   of the ground and blew into his nostrils
   the breath of life,
   and so man became a living being.
8 *Then the LORD God planted a garden in Eden,*
   in the east, and he placed there
   the man whom he had formed.
9 *Out of the ground the LORD God made various*
   trees grow that were delightful to look at
   and good for food.

HOW IT HAPPENED

Two questions arise.
Why put the chapter division after the sixth day?
Why a "second" creation story?

The biblical writers did not divide their works
into chapters and verses.
Later scholars did this to facilitate Bible study.

Some modern scholars feel
that some of the divisions were unfortunate.
For example,
they feel that the first chapter of Genesis
would better be called a "Preface to the Torah,"
not a chapter of Genesis.
They note that the early books of the Bible,
especially the first five books, called the Torah,
were passed on orally for centuries.
Only later were these oral traditions collected,
recorded, and edited in the form they now have.

Most scholars agree that the Torah
went through four major editing stages.
They identify them by the following names:

Yahwist (J)	around 900 B.C.
Elohist (E)	around 700 B.C.
Deuteronomist (D)	around 600 B.C.
Priestly (P)	around 500–400 B.C.

Scholarship shows that the "first" creation story
was written during the Priestly stage
as a kind of liturgical "Preface to the Torah."

It prepares us for all that follows.
It explains how God—

made all things,
planned them,
made them good,
intended us to enjoy them forever.

Thus, the main body of the Torah
actually begins with the "second" creation story,
which dates from the Yahwist stage.

Brother Star, Sister Earth

Occasionally, we are struck
with a special awareness of our unique kinship
with the rest of creation.
Here's one young person's experience.

The Brothers Karamazov
FEODOR DOSTOEVSKI

The vault of heaven, full of soft, shining stars,
stretched vast and fathomless. . . .
The mystery of earth was one
with the mystery of the stars. . . .

Alyosha stood, gazed,
and suddenly threw himself down on the earth.
He did not know why he embraced it. . . .
But he kissed it weeping,
sobbing and watering it with his tears. . . .
What was he weeping over?

Oh! in his rapture
he was weeping even over those stars,
which were shining to him from the abyss of space,
and "he was not ashamed of that ecstasy.". . .

He longed to forgive everyone and for everything,
and to beg forgiveness.
Oh, not for himself, but for all men,
for all and for everything. . . .
Something firm and unshakable
as that vault of heaven had entered into his soul.
It was as though some idea
had seized the sovereignty of his mind—
and it was for all his life and for ever and ever.

He had fallen on the earth a weak boy,
but he rose up a resolute champion,
and he knew and felt it suddenly
at the very moment of his ecstasy.
And never, never, all his life long,
could Alyosha forget that minute.

YAHWIST STORY

The Yahwist creation story
differs greatly in style from the Priestly "preface."
It is less formal and more earthy.
It portrays God as a potter,
molding man's body out of clay.

Underlying the story is an important teaching:
the intimacy that exists between God and people.

To begin with, man is described
as being created before all other creatures.
Second, he is described as being composed
of two elements: *clay* and the *breath* of God.

In the context of the story, *clay* points to
our kinship with the rest of God's creation.
The *breath* of God, on the other hand,
points to our kinship with God himself.
God and people are related as intimately
as a person is to his own breath.

REVOLUTIONARY TEACHING

The second creation story highlights a teaching
that makes the religion of the Bible
totally different from all other world religions.
Other religions may stress God's knowledge,
his infinity, or his power.
But the Bible stresses God's intimacy with people.

GOD'S OWN IMAGE

The God of the Bible is a "God of Intimacy."
He created people in his own "image" (first story)
and breathed into them
his own "breath" of life (second story).
God and people are related with an intimacy
that can be best explained
by comparing it to the intimacy
that exists between a parent and a child.

"LORD, I put my hope in you;
I have trusted you since I was young."
Psalm 71:5

*In times of trouble I pray to the Lord . . .
but I cannot find comfort.
When I think of God, I sigh;
when I meditate, I feel discouraged. . . .
I think of days gone by . . .
and this is what I ask myself:
"Will the Lord always reject us?
Will he never again be pleased with us?"*

PSALM 77:2–7*

*Sovereign LORD, I put my hope in you;
I have trusted in you since I was young.
I have relied on you all my life;
you have protected me since the day I was born.
I will always praise you. . . .
You have sent troubles and suffering on me,
but you will restore my strength. . . .
You will make me greater than ever;
you will comfort me again.*

PSALM 71:5–6, 20–21*

Relating to God

The Book of Psalms
is the prayerbook of the Old Testament.
More than any other book,
it lets us penetrate
the mind and the heart of the ancient Hebrew.

A recurring theme in the Book of Psalms
is the intimate relationship between God and people.
Sometimes the psalmist finds it a source of joy,
sometimes an occasion for concern,
but always a mystery.
Here are some of his reflections.

*LORD, you have examined me
and you know me.
You know everything I do;
from far away you understand all my thoughts.
You see me, whether I am working or resting;
you know all my actions.
Even before I speak,
you already know what I will say. . . .
Your knowledge of me is too deep;
it is beyond my understanding.*

PSALM 139:1–6*

*The LORD is my shepherd;
I have everything I need.
He lets me rest in fields of green grass
and leads me to quiet pools of fresh water.
He gives me new strength.
He guides me in the right paths, as he has promised.
Even if I go through the deepest darkness,
I will not be afraid, LORD,
for you are with me. . . .
I know that your goodness and love
will be with me all my life;
and your house will be my home as long as I live.*

PSALM 23:1–6*

*These psalm excerpts are from
Today's English Version.

23

5
Who Told Them?

Inspired by the Yahwist creation story,
poet James Weldon Johnson wrote "Creation."
A portion of it reads:

Then God walked around,
And God looked around
On all that he had made. . . .
He looked on his world
With all its living things,
And God said: I'm lonely still.

Then God sat down—
On the side of a hill where he could think;
By a deep, wide river he sat down;
With his head in his hands,
God thought and thought,
Till he thought: I'll make me a man!

Up from the bed of the river
God scooped the clay;
And by the bank of the river
He kneeled him down;
And there the great God Almighty
Who lit the sun and fixed it in the sky,
Who flung the stars to the most far corner
of the night,
Who rounded the earth in the middle of his hand;
This Great God,
Like a mammy bending over her baby,
Kneeled down in the dust
Toiling over a lump of clay
Till he shaped it in his own image;

Then into it he blew the breath of life,
And man became a living soul.

BIBLICAL INSPIRATION

How did God inspire the biblical writers?
Were these writers inspired the way a poet is?
Or did God inspire them in a more direct way?

Consider this imaginative scene
from a modern novel about biblical times.

The Last Temptation of Christ
NIKOS KAZANTZAKIS

Jesus took a long stride and entered the house.
He saw Matthew next to the lamp,
still holding the open notebook on his knees.
He stopped. Matthew's eyes were closed:
he was still submerged in all that he had read.

"Matthew," said Jesus,
"bring your notebook here.
What do you write?"

Matthew got up and handed Jesus his writings.
He was very happy.

"Rabbi," he said,
"here I recount your life and works,
for men of the future."

Jesus knelt under the lamp
and began to read.
At the very first words, he gave a start.

Kazantzakis then has Jesus confront Matthew,
asking him where he got all the information
he had put down in writing.

"The angel revealed it to me,"
Matthew answered, trembling.

"The angel? What angel?"

"The one who comes each night I take up my pen.
He leans over my ear and dictates what I write."

LED BY THE SPIRIT

There are many theories about how God
communicated *instruction* to priests,
counsel to the wise, and *messages* to the prophets
(Jeremiah 18:18).

Although the Old Testament gives no explanation,
we do find New Testament writers referring to it
in several places. Paul writes:

All Scripture is inspired of God. (2 Timothy 3:16)

Peter says:

*Prophecy has never been put forward by man's
willing it.*

*It is rather that men impelled by the Holy Spirit
have spoken under God's influence.* (2 Peter 1:21)

Jesus taught:

*"David himself, inspired by the Holy Spirit, said,
'The Lord said to my Lord: Sit at my right hand.'"*
(Mark 12:36)

ILLUMINATION

Basically, inspiration means
that the primary author of the Bible is God;
the human author is God's instrument.
From early times,
this was a firm and constant belief among Jews.
New Testament writers shared the belief,
and used the word *inspiration* to describe it,
but did not explain its meaning.

In the course of history,
there have been two extreme positions proposed
as to how God inspired the biblical writers.
The first is that God dictated to them,
much as a businessman dictates to his secretary.
The second is
that they were inspired in a "religious" way,
much as a songwriter is inspired in a musical way.

Modern scholars reject both extremes.
Generally, they hold that the biblical writers
were given some special illumination by God,
which enabled them to communicate faithfully
what God wanted them to convey.

The main concern of early Jews and Christians
was not *how* the biblical writers were inspired,
but *that* they were inspired.

The poet Samuel Taylor Coleridge
speaks for all believers when he says:

*I know the Bible is inspired
because it finds me at greater depths of my being
than any other book.*

6

Bone of My Bone

Oriental women go about their daily chores today much as they did in ancient times.

GOD   *It is not good*
for the man to be alone.
I will make a suitable partner for him.

NARRATOR   *. . . So the LORD God*
cast a deep sleep on the man,
and while he was asleep,
he took out one of his ribs
and closed up its place with flesh.

The LORD God
then built up into a woman
the rib that he had taken from the man.
Then he brought her to the man. . . .

MAN   *This one . . .*
is bone of my bones
and flesh of my flesh;
this one shall be called "woman.". . .

NARRATOR   *That is why a man leaves his father*
and mother and clings to his wife,
and the two of them become one body.

The man and his wife were both naked,
yet they felt no shame.

GENESIS 2:18–25

This colorful story of woman's origin
brings to a close the second creation story.
Inspired by its imagery,
Gordon Higham penned these words:

Woman was not taken
from man's head to be ruled by him,

nor from his feet to be trampled upon,
but from his side to walk beside him,
from under his arm to be protected by him,
and from near his heart to be loved by him.

CONTEXTUALIST VIEW

Hebrew society, like most ancient societies,
was dominated by men.
Women belonged to a depressed minority.
They existed primarily to bear children—
male children at that.

Contextualists interpret the story of woman's origin
as a rejection of this social situation.
By portraying woman
as coming from the same substance as man,
the biblical writer sought to teach
that man and woman are equal in dignity.

This idea was so revolutionary
that even later biblical writers struggled
to assimilate it into their human thought patterns.
The feminist movement of recent years
testifies that even modern man
has not fully understood this biblical teaching.

LITERALIST VIEW

Literalists hold that woman was created exactly as the biblical writer depicts the event.

Is the Bible Really the Word of God?
WATCH TOWER BIBLE AND TRACT SOCIETY

The creation of the first woman as recorded
in Genesis has been scoffed at by some. . . .
Yet they will read
with great interest and seriousness
an article such as appeared in Life *magazine*
of September 10, 1965. It dealt
with experiments on plant cells by biologists
and contained the following statement:

"It is not absurd
to imagine the day when a single tiny cell
taken from the skin of the world's greatest genius
might be grown into a second individual
who is in every respect identical."

Jehovah's Witnesses
refer to reports such as the following.
Though experimentation is still in early stages,
a few experts predict
that it may someday be realized at a human level.

Carbon Copy Man
BILL BARRY

A Clone is a human child
created from a single asexual body cell;
the child is the exact duplicate
of the person from whom the body cell was taken.
The simple, painless scraping of a human arm
produces enough healthy body cells
to make a thousand clones—
all perfect carbon copies of the man or woman
from whom they were created. . . .

If Cloning had been achieved twenty years ago:
John F. Kennedy, shot to death in Dallas
on November 22, 1963, could still be alive today,

in the person of his Clone—
not a son, but an exact copy of himself. . . .

In 1961, across the Atlantic at Oxford University,
zoologist J. B. Gurdon undertook
certain experiments with the African clawed frog.
From one frog, he extracted an unfertilized egg cell,
destroyed the nucleus with ultraviolet radiation,
and preserved the womb-like cytoplasm.
From a second frog's intestine,
he extracted the nucleus of a body cell,
and planted it in the preserved cytoplasm.

Soon after, a tadpole was born,
identical in every respect to the second frog,
from which the body cell had been taken.
Virgin birth had occurred in the animal kingdom. . . .

Nobel geneticist Joshua Lederberg . . .
suggests that Clones bred from one person
would be so similar neurologically,
they would communicate almost with the ease
of reading each other's minds.

The Mind
TIME

Another prospect is to alter genes
so that babies will be born with rote knowledge—
language skills, multiplication tables—
just as birds apparently emerge from the egg
with programs that enable them to navigate.

The Second Genesis
ALBERT ROSENFELD

When this kind of biochemical sophistication
has been attained . . .
man's powers will become truly godlike.
Just as man has been able, through chemistry,
to create a variety of synthetic materials
that never existed in nature,
so may he, through "genetic surgery,"
bring into being new . . . species of creatures
never before seen or imagined in the universe.

The development of creatures
"never before seen or imagined in the universe"
is no longer a biochemical dream.

_____ . . . Half Plant, Half Animal
RONALD KOTULAK

An organism
that nature hasn't dared create—
half plant and half animal—
has been produced
by a team of English scientists. . . .

The work of the British scientists
closely follows another genetic breakthrough
pioneered by California scientists.

Using newly discovered enzymes,
the California researchers
have been able to break the species barrier.
They can extract the genetic material
from one species and splice it into
the genetic code of another species.

And consider another recent report.

_____ Fierce DNA Debate
WILLIAM HINES

It is possible to "train" bacteria to make insulin,
an essential drug for many diabetics.
General Electric is working on a bacteria strain
that could "eat up" oil spills and die out
when there is no more oil to scavenge.
These are great promises.

But each could conceivably backfire. . . .
What if the insulin-producing bacteria
got loose and invaded human bodies,
throwing normal persons into insulin shock?
What if oil-eating bugs
got into natural crude deposits?

These scientific advances raise a question:
Is this the kind of *dominion*
God intended us to exercise over creation?

Uncreation

An anonymous poet
ponders the kind of dominion over creation
we have exercised so far.

In the beginning was the earth.
And it was beautiful.
And man lived upon the earth. And man said:
"Let us build skyscrapers and expressways."
And man covered the earth with steel and concrete.
And man said: "It is good."

On the second day,
man looked upon the clear blue waters of the earth.
And man said: "Let us dump our sewage
and wastes into the waters." And man did.
The waters became dark and murky.
And man said: "It is good."

On the third day,
man gazed at the forests on the earth.
They were tall and green. And man said:
"Let us cut the trees and build things for ourselves."
And man did. And the forests grew thin.
And man said: "It is good."

"Let us cover the earth . . ."

On the fourth day,
man saw the animals leaping in the fields
and playing in the sun. And man said: "Let us trap
the animals for money and shoot them for sport."
And man did. And the animals became scarce.
And man said: "It is good."

On the fifth day,
man felt the cool breeze in his nostrils.
And man said: "Let us burn our refuse
and let the wind blow away the smoke and debris."
And man did.
And the air became dense with smoke and carbon.
And man said: "It is good."

On the sixth day,
man saw the many kinds of people on the earth—
different in race, color, and creed.
And man feared and said: "Let us make bombs
and missiles in case misunderstandings arise."
And man did. And missile sites and bomb dumps
checkered the landscape.
And man said: "It is good."

On the seventh day, man rested.
And the earth was quiet and deathly still.
For man was no more.
And it was good!

"And man was no more . . ."

Something to Ponder

Dr. Martin Luther King wrote in *Strength to Love:*

*Our scientific power
has outrun our spiritual power.
We have guided missiles and misguided men. . . .*

*Science gives man knowledge which is power;
religion gives man wisdom which is control.*

7

Blaming the Snake

Man's a Born Killer . . .
ARTHUR J. SNIDER

*"Man has been violent since his remote ape-like ancestors descended from trees
and there is little prospect that his innate desire
to kill for dominance ever will change."*

*This gloomy assessment
was laid before anthropologists
gathered here from around the world. . . .*

*"We have to face the truth and accept one basic, unpleasant fact,"
warned Dr. Norman MacDonald. . . .
"Man being what he is, violence is forever."*

*"The only hope for humans to live in peace is to
first be honest with ourselves and accept the fact
that biologically man is a killer, the greatest
predator the world has ever known," he said.*

*"We deceive ourselves if we call murder inhuman,"
said Dr. MacDonald. "It is characteristic of man."*

"It may be inhumane, but it is not inhuman."

*"From the time he fashioned a club
as his first weapon, man has insisted on developing
more powerful weapons
so that now, instead of killing individuals or groups,
he can annihilate a planet."*

WHAT HAPPENED?

If the Bible is correct,
and God did make people "very good,"
what caused them to change so radically?
And if God and people are so intimately linked—
almost as a parent to children—
what happened to destroy that intimacy?

These questions cried for an answer in early times.
They still cry out for an answer today.
The biblical writer faced the question immediately
after he described the creation of woman.

NARRATOR *Now the serpent
was the most cunning of all the animals
that the LORD God had made.
The serpent asked the woman:*

SERPENT *Did God really tell you not to eat
from any of the trees in the garden?*

EVE *. . . It is only about the fruit of the tree
in the middle of the garden that God said,
"You shall not eat it
or even touch it, lest you die."*

SERPENT *You certainly will not die!
No, God knows well that the moment
you eat of it you will be like gods
who know what is good and what is bad.*

NARRATOR *So she took some of its fruit and ate it;
and . . . gave some to her husband. . . .
Then the eyes of both of them
were opened, and they realized
that they were naked.*

GENESIS 3:1–7

SYMBOL STORY

Contextualists interpret this as a symbol story.
Its purpose is to answer the question:
If God made people good,
how did evil enter their hearts?

The key symbol in the story is the snake.
Even in modern times,
the snake suggests an evil image for most people.
The snake was even more repulsive to Hebrews.

Archaeology reveals that snakes played a bizarre
role in the worship ceremony of the Canaanites,
Israel's ancient enemy. Thus the snake made an
ideal evil symbol for the biblical writer.

Another key symbol is the act of *eating*.
Recall that the snake promised:
If you eat from the tree,
you will be like gods, who *know* good and evil.

Eating is equated with *knowing*.
To know, for ancient peoples, was to discover
by experience, not to learn from books.
To eat is a symbolic way of saying Adam and Eve
learned evil by the experience of becoming evil.
They both shared in some derelict act.

What was this evil act?
Some literal readers think it was disobedience
to God's command "not to eat from the tree."
Others say it was pride: wanting to be like gods.
A few think it involved sex.

Contextual readers say the question lies outside
the biblical writer's intention.
The main point he wishes to communicate is this:
People broke faith with God in some way.
What they did is really irrelevant.

A second question is often asked:
Did the biblical writer intend the snake
to represent a real tempter apart from people,
or merely a temptation within people?
Again, Bible readers disagree.
Regardless of how you answer the question,
the writer's primary point remains unchanged:
People, freely, chose to break faith with God.
Thus, they are directly responsible
for the entry of evil into their lives.

SELF-ALIENATION

After Adam and Eve sinned, the Bible says
"they realized that they were naked" (Genesis 3:7).
Why this strange statement?

Archaeology shows
that nakedness was a sign of disgrace and defeat.
Excavations have uncovered stone slabs
showing enemy soldiers, defeated in battle,
marching naked before their conquerors.
The Genesis writer apparently took this idea
and gave it a deeper meaning.

An awareness of nakedness after sin
(not there before it) seems to imply
that a change took place in the consciousness
of the first couple as a result of sin.
Somehow, they are uneasy with themselves.
They are alienated from themselves,
no longer at peace with what they have become.

In modern times, a similar observation
has been made about contemporary man.

A Visit with India's High-Powered New Prophet
PAUL HORN

The main feeling you get today—
you can even see it in people's faces—
is that nearly everyone is uptight.
Tense vibrations are everywhere. . . .

Actually, they just reflect the sum
of conflicts and hostilities and tensions
on the individual level. . . .
Maharishi Mahesh Yogi of India . . .
believes such a tense atmosphere
and the wars that result from it
could never happen
in a world peopled by individuals
at peace with themselves.

He says, "For the forest to be green,
the trees must be green."

The Night I Prayed

Young Tom Merton
had just graduated from high school
and was traveling alone in Europe.
His father had died the year before,
and Tom was leading a wayward life.
One night, in the silence of his room,
he underwent a soul-stirring experience.
He describes it in his autobiography.

The Seven Storey Mountain
THOMAS MERTON

I was overwhelmed
with a sudden and profound insight
into the misery and corruption of my own soul . . .
I was filled with horror at what I saw,
and my whole being rose up in revolt
against what was within me,
and my soul desired
escape and liberation and freedom from all this
with an intensity and an urgency
unlike anything I had ever known before.

And now I think for the first time in my whole life
I really began to pray—
praying not with my lips and with my intellect
and my imagination,
but praying out of the very roots of my life
and of my being,
and praying to the God I had never known,
to reach down towards me out of His darkness
and to help me to get free
of the thousand terrible things
that held my will in their slavery.

GOD ALIENATION

The sin story continues:

NARRATOR   *When the couple heard the sound*
of the LORD God moving about in the
garden at the breezy time of the day,
the man and his wife
hid themselves from the LORD God
among the trees of the garden.

GOD   *Where are you?*

ADAM   *I heard you in the garden;*
but I was afraid, because I was naked,
so I hid myself.

GOD   *Who told you that you were naked?*
You have eaten, then, from the tree
of which I had forbidden you to eat!

ADAM   *The woman*
whom you put here with me—
she gave me fruit from the tree,
and so I ate it.

GOD   *[to Eve] Why did you do such a thing?*

EVE   *The serpent tricked me into it.*

GENESIS 3:8–13

Two points stand out in the sin dialogue.
First, Adam and Eve show an estrangement to God.
They conceal themselves, because they are naked.
Thus, another result of sin is implied:
alienation from God.

Second, when God questions Adam,
Adam immediately points his finger at Eve.
Eve, in turn, blames the snake.
Each attempts to shift the blame to the other.

The conclusion of the first sin story is this:
Evil did not enter the world through some force
over which people had no control.
People, themselves, are to blame for it.

8 Thorns and Thistles

Studs Lonigan
JAMES T. FARRELL

God, why do you permit men to starve,
hunger, die from syphilis, cancer, consumption?
God, why do you not raise one little finger
to save man from all the . . .
suffering on this planet?

Ancient peoples, also, cried out in anguish
about suffering and death in the world.
They asked their holy people:
If sin (moral evil) is the fault of the people,
who caused suffering and death (physical evil)?

NATURE ALIENATION

After the sin dialogue,
the biblical writer has God confront each involved.

TO SNAKE   *Because you have done this,*
            you shall be banned
            from all the animals . . . ;
            on your belly shall you crawl. . . .

            I will put enmity
            between you and the woman,
            and between your offspring and hers;
            he will strike at your head,
            while you strike at his heel.

TO EVE   *In pain*
            shall you bring forth children. . . .

TO ADAM   *Cursed be the ground*
            because of you! . . .
            Thorns and thistles
            shall it bring forth to you,
            as you eat of the plants of the field.
            By the sweat of your face
            shall you get bread to eat,
            until you return to the ground,
            from which you were taken;
            for you are dirt,
            and to dirt you shall return.

GENESIS 3:14–19

This conversation
between the Creator and his creatures
dramatizes a further alienation caused by sin.

Sin alienates one not only from God
and from oneself, but also from nature.
The earth
now resists human dominion over it.

One even loses dominion over one's own body.
It falls under the dominion of suffering and death.
Thus, the biblical writer answers the question:
How did suffering and death (physical evil)
enter the world?
They entered not through some defect in creation,
but through a sinful misuse of it.

Does the writer imply suffering and death
are punishment for sin?

Or are they the result of sin,
just as hunger is the result of not eating?
The writer seems to leave this question open.

Later books of the Bible, especially the Book of Job,
will probe more deeply the mystery of suffering.
For the present,
the biblical writer merely says this:
Suffering and death entered the world
not through a defect in creation,
but through a sinful misuse of creation.

SIGN OF HOPE

New Testament writers showed special interest
in God's remarks to the serpent.
They interpreted them as the first indication
of a savior for the human race.

Referring to the story, Jesus says:

*"The devil brought death . . .
from the beginning. . . .
He is a liar and the father of lies."* (John 8:44)

John says of Jesus:

*It was to destroy the devil's works
that the Son of God revealed himself.* (1 John 3:8)

In other words, enmity between people and evil
has existed from the beginning.
But people (in the offspring of Jesus)
will eventually crush evil.

END OF A DRAMA

The biblical writer brings down the curtain
on the first sin story this way:

*The LORD God therefore
banished him from the garden of Eden,
to till the ground from which he had been taken.
When he expelled the man,
he settled him east of the garden of Eden;
and he stationed
the cherubim and the fiery revolving sword,
to guard the way to the tree of life.*

GENESIS 3:23-24

Archaeologists have cleared up the confusion
that once surrounded these strange creatures.
Cherubim are legendary winged animals
with a human head.
Found at entrances to ancient buildings and cities,
cherubim were supposed to ward off evil intruders.

Paul-Emile Botta, a French archaeologist,
first unearthed them in the 1840s
while excavating the palace of Sargon II, an ancient
Assyrian king. Flanking the palace doorway,
they were carved in gigantic stone slabs.
Their discovery attracted worldwide attention.
The 16-foot slabs now reside
in the famous Louvre museum in Paris.

Similarly, archaeologists point out
that the tree of life is also an ancient symbol.
It refers to a legendary plant,
thought to confer immortality (freedom from death)
on those who had access to it.
It might be compared to the fountain of youth,
which legend says
Spanish explorers hoped to find in Florida.

When we connect these two symbols,
we understand the biblical writer's point.
Cherubim keep people away from the tree
in the garden
because people are no longer worthy to eat from it.
They are now subject to death.

LEVELS OF MEANING

Perhaps what is most striking in these stories
is the depth of meaning they contain.
Just as Jesus gave deeper meaning to his parables,
so Old Testament writers
gave deeper meaning to some of their narratives.

Obviously, there is the *literal* meaning—
the actual meaning of the words themselves.
For example, the story of the creation of woman
merely describes her as coming from man's side.

But beyond this literal meaning
is a deeper, *intended* meaning.
By describing woman
as coming from the same substance as man,
the biblical writer *intends* to teach
that man and woman are equal in dignity.

Legendary Watchdog

Standing an impressive 16 feet tall,
this colossal winged animal with human head
stood guard at the outer gate
of the 8th-century B.C. palace of Sargon II.

The Assyrian king's 209-room residence
was unearthed in the early 19th century
by French archaeologist Paul-Emile Botta.

The animal's fifth leg
was added by the ancient artist
for visual purposes.
When viewed from the front,
the creature appeared in perfect symmetry.
When viewed from the side,
it gave the impression of balance and motion.

9
And God Grieved

CAIN	*Let us go out in the field.*
NARRATOR	*When they were in the field, Cain attacked his brother Abel and killed him.*
GOD	*Where is your brother Abel?*
CAIN	*I do not know. Am I my brother's keeper?*
GOD	*. . . Your brother's blood cries out to me from the soil! . . .*
NARRATOR	*Cain then left the LORD's presence and settled in the land of Nod, east of Eden.*

GENESIS 4:8–10, 16

FURTHER ALIENATION

The main purpose of the Cain story
is to teach that when one breaks faith with God,
he soon breaks faith with others as well.

Thus, the story extends the biblical writer's theme
that sin alienates. Sin alienates not only

person from self   (Adam's nakedness),
person from God   (Adam's hiding),
person from nature   (curse), but also
person from person   (Cain's violence).

Cain's act of violence begins a tidal wave of sin
that now floods the world.

DISINTEGRATION

The biblical writer teaches this in a poetic way:
he lists two genealogies (family trees).

The first begins with Adam and ends with Noah.
Fantastic ages are assigned to the men named.

Adam lived 930 years.
Seth lived 912 years.
Lamech lived 777 years. (Genesis 5:1–32)

The second family tree starts with Shem,
Noah's son,
and ends with Terah, Abraham's father.

Shem lived 600 years.
Eber lived 464 years.
Terah lived 205 years. (Genesis 11:10–32)

The purpose of the family trees is twofold.

First, they build a literary bridge
between Adam, the father of all people,
and Abraham, the father of the Hebrew people.

Second, they advance the "sin" motif
in the Book of Genesis.
They do this by showing the steady decline
in human life spans
from the start of each family tree to its end.
Although the "pattern of decline" is not perfect,
the "decline" is definite and dramatic.

In brief,
the biblical writer uses the two family trees
as a literary device.

First, they establish the continuity of life
from Adam to Abraham.
Second, they show the disintegration of life
as it travels from Adam to Abraham.
Declining age spans are signs
not only of the spread of sin to all life,
but also of the disintegration of all life by sin.

CORRUPTION

A baffling report of marriages between the
"daughters of men" and the "sons of heaven"
appears in Genesis 6:1–4.
This episode is still the subject of much debate.

A few recent fundamentalist popularizers
have suggested that
the story is documentation
that ancient astronauts once visited Earth
and intermarried with its dwellers.

Some contextualists
interpret the narrative as another sin story.
Good people (sons of heaven)
and bad people (daughters of men) intermarry.
Good and evil intermingle
and become hopelessly entangled.
The disintegrating effect of sin spreads to everyone,
even the good.

Following this report, the biblical writer
portrays God looking down on the world
with a heavy heart.

When the LORD saw
how great was man's wickedness on earth,
and how no desire that his heart conceived
was ever anything but evil,
he regretted that he had made man on the earth,
and his heart was grieved.

GENESIS 6:5–6

Perhaps William Shakespeare
had this paragraph in mind when he wrote:

Man, proud man!
drest in a little brief authority . . .
Plays such fantastic tricks
before high heaven
As make the angels weep.

MEASURE FOR MEASURE

10

The Flood

"All the fountains of the great abyss burst forth,
and the floodgates of the sky were opened."
Genesis 7:11

Noah Built the Ark
JAMES WELDON JOHNSON

And a little black spot begun to spread,
Like a bottle of ink spilling over the sky;
And the thunder rolled like a rumbling drum;
And the lightning jumped from pole to pole;
And it rained down rain, rain, rain,
Great God, but didn't it rain!
For forty days and forty nights
Waters poured down and waters gushed up;
And the dry land turned to sea.
And the old ark-a she begun to ride;
The old ark-a she begun to rock;
Sinners came a-running down to the ark;
Sinners came a-swimming all round the ark;
Sinners pleaded and sinners prayed—
Sinners wept and sinners wailed—
But Noah'd done barred the door.

Even people who know little about the Bible
are familiar with the story of Noah and the Ark.

NARRATOR   *When God saw how corrupt*
the earth had become . . .
he said to Noah:

GOD   *I have decided to put an end*
to all mortals on earth. . . .
Make yourself an ark. . . .
Go into the ark,
you and all your household,
for you alone in this age
have I found to be truly just. . . .

NARRATOR   *For forty days and forty nights*
heavy rain poured down on the earth. . . .

The flood continued . . .
until all the highest mountains
everywhere were submerged.
GENESIS 6:12–14; 7:1, 12–19

Is this a factual story,
a symbolic story, or a combination of both?
By a combination of both,
we mean a symbolic story based on an actual flood.

37

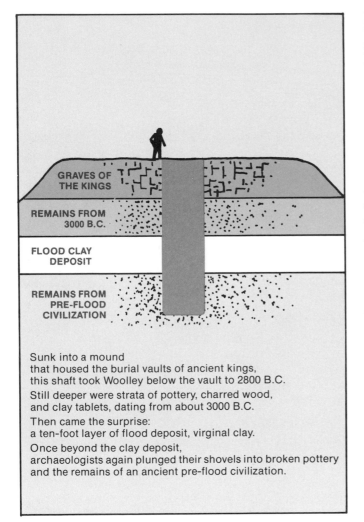

GRAVES OF THE KINGS

REMAINS FROM 3000 B.C.

FLOOD CLAY DEPOSIT

REMAINS FROM PRE-FLOOD CIVILIZATION

Sunk into a mound
that housed the burial vaults of ancient kings,
this shaft took Woolley below the vault to 2800 B.C.

Still deeper were strata of pottery, charred wood,
and clay tablets, dating from about 3000 B.C.

Then came the surprise:
a ten-foot layer of flood deposit, virginal clay.

Once beyond the clay deposit,
archaeologists again plunged their shovels into broken pottery
and the remains of an ancient pre-flood civilization.

LITERALIST VIEW

In his excavations in 1929, British archaeologist
Sir Leonard Woolley startled the world
with the news that he had discovered evidence
of a great flood that occurred about 4000 B.C.

Coinciding with the date of the biblical flood,
it was a layer of clay deposit about ten feet thick.

Following his discovery,
Woolley made digs
in other parts of Mesopotamia
to determine the extent of the clay deposit.

The Bible as History
WERNER KELLER

*Gradually, by a variety of tests,
the limits of the Flood waters could be established.
According to Woolley, the disaster
engulfed an area northwest of the Persian Gulf
400 miles long and 100 miles wide.
Looking at the map today,
we could call it a "local occurrence,"
but for the inhabitants of the river plains
it was, in those days, their whole world. . . .*

*A vast catastrophic inundation,
resembling the Biblical Flood . . .
had not only taken place but was, moreover,
an event within the compass of history.*

Later archaeologists are not so sure
that the tests prove adequately that the deposits
were as widespread as Woolley estimates.

The question returns. Did the biblical writer
intend his flood story to be a factual report?

The literal readers say "Yes!" Moreover,
they insist that the flood was worldwide.

Is the Bible Really the Word of God?
WATCH TOWER BIBLE AND TRACT SOCIETY

*If the Flood did not cover all the earth,
why bring animals and birds into the ark
to preserve all the different kinds?
Animals elsewhere could have survived.
And the birds could have easily escaped
by flying to another area.*

Literalists continue to sponsor expeditions
to Mount Ararat in Turkey, hoping to find
some evidence of the 450-foot ark.
Since 1961 over 30 forays have been attempted.
Recently, however, Turkish officials have said
"no" to further expeditions, because Ararat lies
in a politically touchy area on the Russian border.

Interest in the ark mounted in recent decades
because of two episodes in particular.
One was a U.S. Skylab photo taken in 1974
showing something "foreign" on the mountain.
The other was an L-shaped timber found in 1955
in an icy crevice 13,500 feet up the mountain.
The timber has been tested for dating.
A recent report sums up the results.

Science News
EDITORS

*Perhaps the last hope that the battered remains
of Noah's Ark exist on Mount Ararat
near the Turkish-Soviet border has been washed
away by a new wave of scientific evidence.
Recent tests at the University of California at
Los Angeles, La Jolla and Riverside all conclude
that a piece of timber found at the Ararat site
is only about 1,200 years old—
some 2,700 years younger
than the first known account of the Ark.*

Using carbon-14 dating, UCLA archaeologist
Rainer Berger confirmed earlier findings
"that the timber came from a tree
that was chopped down around A.D. 700."
In other tests, R. E. Taylor of Riverside
and Hans Seuss of La Jolla got similar results.

One theory is that the timber could be
the remnant of a shrine built by early monks
to celebrate the biblical account.
Meanwhile, interest in the ark continues
among literalist biblical interpreters.

CONTEXTUALIST VIEW

Contextualists see the flood story
as another link in the chain of symbolic sin stories.
A few feel that the story is totally symbolic,
designed to teach an important religious truth.

The majority, however,
feel the story is "factual-symbolic."
It is factual to the extent
that it is based on an ancient flood tradition.
It is symbolic in the sense that the writer
uses this tradition as a vehicle
to get across an important religious teaching.
Here's how one modern interpreter puts it.

Searching the Scriptures
JOHN J. DOUGHERTY

*Evidence of a flood has been found in excavations
at Ur and at Kish. It is not surprising
that there were floods in Mesopotamia,
the name meaning "the land between the rivers,"
the Tigris and Euphrates.
Archaeology . . .
does not supply evidence for a universal flood.*

*When all the relevant data are assembled
and weighed, the conclusion would seem to follow
that a popular tradition is common . . .
and that the inspired author used the popular
tradition to teach men a moral lesson.*

*The genre of Genesis 6–9 is therefore
didactic rather than historical,
and it is bootless to ponder such questions
as whether the flood covered the whole earth
or destroyed all men.*

Regardless of how you interpret the flood story,
its main point remains the same.
The biblical writer wishes to teach
that sin leads people down a one-way street:
destruction of themselves and the world.
God, alone, can save them.

Gilgamesh Epic

Archaeologists have found other flood stories
similar to the one in the Bible.
One such story
forms part of "The Epic of Gilgamesh,"
thought by many experts
to be the oldest recorded story.

Gilgamesh is a young king of Uruk.
He is plunged into deep sadness
when his closest friend, Enkidu, dies.
The sadness stems not only from the loss,
but also from the realization
that he too must die some day.

Then Gilgamesh learns of an ancestor
who lives in the "land of the immortals."
Of all human beings, he alone has cheated death.
But the land lies beyond the Bitter River—
outside the limits to the human world.

Gilgamesh sets out to find his relative.
After unbelievable ordeals,
the youth reaches the Bitter River
and crosses it into the land of the immortals.
There he finds his relative.

"I am Gilgamesh; you are my ancestor.
I have come far to seek your help.
I am told that you know the secret of life and death."

The old ancestor then tells his story.
He survived a great flood that covered the earth.
Because he survived,
the gods granted him immortality.
But no man can achieve this gift on his own.

But the old man tells Gilgamesh of a magic plant
that grows at the bottom of the Bitter River.
If a man could ever find it and eat it,
he would never die.

The youth starts back across the river.
Reaching midstream,
he strips and dives into the deep waters.

When he surfaces,
he holds the magic plant in his hand.

Now, Gilgamesh begins the long journey home.
One day he stops to bathe in a lake.
While he does,
a snake steals the magic plant.
Deeply saddened, Gilgamesh resumes his journey.

When the youth arrives home, he can find no rest.
His heart is troubled,
and he decides to set off on another journey—
this time to try to discover where Enkidu
resides in death.

Friendly gods direct him to the hidden
"gate to the underworld," inside which the youth
finds his friend and learns the fate of the dead.

Fearful, Gilgamesh starts to run away.
Then he stops. After several minutes of thought,
he walks over to his friend,
looks at him, and lies down beside him in death.

11

Still Falls the Rain

The chain of biblical sin stories
climaxes with the Tower of Babel incident.
This event takes place after Noah's descendants
have repopulated the earth. They say:

Come, let us build ourselves a city
and a tower with its top in the sky,
and so make a name for ourselves.

GENESIS 11:4

But the project stops before it can be completed.
God confuses the speech of the people,
and they are forced to stop work.
The biblical writer ends his story saying:

It was from that place
that God scattered them all over the earth.

GENESIS 11:9

FINAL ALIENATION

Again, archaeologists have illuminated this story.
The biblical writer has in mind a ziggurat.
The top of this pyramidlike structure
was intended as a meeting place for gods and people.

The writer uses the ziggurat as a pride-symbol
of people's desire "to be like the gods."
Recall the snake's promise to Eve.

Some think that the original purpose of the story
was to explain the origin of nations and languages.
But within the context of a sin-story sequence,

the biblical writer gives the story a deeper meaning.
Its purpose is to show that sin alienates not only

person from self (Adam's nakedness),
person from God (Adam's hiding),
person from nature (curse),
person from person (Cain's violence), but also
nation from nation (Babel story).

When we finish reading the chain of sin stories
of Genesis 3–11, we get this bleak impression.
People, individually and collectively,
are trapped in a giant whirlpool of sin.
Every person born, regardless of how noble,
is doomed to be caught
in its all-engulfing, destructive power.

This biblical picture is strikingly similar
to a newspaperwoman's impression
after her visit to a Nazi concentration camp.

Still Falls the Rain

You wouldn't expect
the dean of American psychiatry
to get up and start talking about sin.
But that's what Dr. Karl Menninger does
in his book *Whatever Became of Sin?*

Sin Comes Back on the Scene
GEORGE HIGGINS

Dr. Menninger
is deeply troubled about what he calls
"sin as collective irresponsibility."
He is bothered not only by individuals
who refuse to acknowledge personal sin,
but also by groups—even whole nations—
who refuse to admit "collective sins."

Discrimination,
war, polluting the environment,
ignoring the poor in ghettoes,
exploiting migrant workers—
these are some of the things that scare him.
He says that in "group sins,"
no single individual
considers himself responsible or guilty.

I kept thinking of that statement
as I was watching the CBS two-hour special
"The Autobiography of Miss Jane Pittman.". . .

A few days after the Jane Pittman show,
CBS scored again with a dramatic presentation,
written by playwright Tennessee Williams,
on the dreadful plight of migrant workers. . . .

Once again we were led
to think about "sin as collective irresponsibility"
and about our own personal involvement,
however indirect or marginal.

"When I surveyed Dachau," she said,
"my soul trembled within me."

What made her tremble was not just the memory
of the crimes that took place there.
Rather, it was the terrifying fact that
good prisoners helped commit these crimes.
Read her own words:

The Lesson of Dachau
DOROTHY THOMPSON

Does the world realize
that some of the worst crimes in these camps
were committed by inmates?

Reduce a man to the lowest level . . .
you can make him . . .
the executioner of his fellow victims . . .
the scientific experimenter on human bodies. . . .

The physicians who inoculated
concentration-camp victims with malaria . . .
were prisoners of the Nazis themselves. . . .
By assisting in the extermination
of their fellow prisoners,
they prolonged the lease on their own lives. . . .

They came into the camps because they believed . . .
in democracy, or communism, or because
they were patriots, loving Poland, or France. . . .

Under the pressure of life or death—
life for an extra week, or an extra day—
no beliefs of economic theories,
or physician's Hippocratic oaths,
or national affiliations were decisive.

Viktor Frankl, Europe's most noted psychiatrist,
and a prisoner of these camps himself,
makes one exception to Thompson's observations.

In *Man's Search for Meaning,*
he says that when a prisoner had a deep,
authentic faith, he was in touch with something
that enabled him to maintain his humanity.

Barbed-wire fence at Auschwitz.

The conclusion we draw from the sin stories
of Genesis 3–11 is this:
Given people as they are (vulnerable beings),
and given the world as it is (a corruptible power),
neither people nor the world can survive
unless God himself intervenes
in some drastic way to save them.

SITUATION TODAY

Four thousand years after Genesis,
a modern poet writes soberly:

_____ Still Falls the Rain
EDITH SITWELL

Still falls the Rain—
Dark as the world of man, black as our loss—
Blind as the nineteen hundred and forty nails
Upon the Cross. . . .

Still falls the Rain
In the Field of Blood where the small hopes breed and
the human brain
Nurtures its greed, that worm with the brow of
Cain. . . .

It Can Work

The light-hearted film *Oh, God!*
contains this thought-provoking scene.

_____ Oh, God!
AVERY CORMAN

GOD   *Looking back . . . I made a few mistakes.*
Giraffes. It was a good thought,
but it didn't really work out.
Avocados—on that I made the pit too big.
There are things that worked pretty good.
Photosynthesis is a big favorite of mine.
Spring is nice. . . .

AVERY   *But what about* Man? *. . .*
The future of the planet?

GOD   *It's a good question. . . . I don't get into that.*
Of course I hope you make it. I mean,
I'm a real fan. . . .

AVERY   *You're God. You can protect our future,*
alleviate suffering, work miracles! . . .
You have the power to intervene,
to help us in emergencies. . . .
So you've decided to just let us stumble
along and never do a thing to help? . . .

GOD   *Such a smart fella*
and you missed the point.
Now write this down, word for word. . . .
The thing is . . . God lives! . . .
If God was dead or never was,
then you should be plenty worried. . . .
But God is here
and He's giving you a guarantee.
I'm telling you that I set all this up for you
and made it so it can *work.*
Only the deal is you have *to work at it*
and you shouldn't look to me to do it for you. . . .
Tell them what I said. God says they got
everything they need—it's all built in,
and on that I give my word.

43

12
The Sheik Who Said "Yes"

BEHISTUN
A trilingual inscription on rock cliffs here
provided the key to decoding cuneiform writing.
It opened new doors to a world
long buried beneath the sands of history.

UR
Art objects and clay tablets
found here have been deciphered and bring alive
the world into which Abraham was born.

MARI
Archaeologists unearthed a palace library
of thousands of clay tablets here. The tablets
add new brush strokes to the picture of everyday life
in Abraham's time.

NUZI
Clay tablets found here clarify practices described,
but not explained, in the Bible—
e.g., Hagar and Abraham (Genesis 16:1–3).

SUSA
An inscribed stone pillar, the Law Code of Hammurabi,
was discovered at this location.
It describes the rights of citizens who traded
in the same marketplaces as did Abraham.

Adam's sin,
Cain's murder of Abel,
the declining ages of people,
the "sons of heaven" and the "daughters of man,"
the flood, the Tower of Babel—
when we finish reading these sin stories,
we get the impression that sin is spreading
like a cancer. People are doomed.

It is against this bleak backdrop
that the biblical writer introduces Abram in
chapter 12 of the Book of Genesis.
This desert sheik
is destined to be the father of a new people
who will be the vehicle
of a dramatic intervention by God in the world.

With Abram's appearance, the Book of Genesis
makes a dramatic switch in content and style.
The content of the first 11 chapters
is biblical prehistory or protohistory:
the origin of the world, life, people, good, evil.
The literary style of these chapters
is highly stylized and charged with symbolism.

Beginning with chapter 12,
the writing style and content change.
The literary style carries with it
the flavor of actual historical happenings.
The content takes on a historical continuity.
It begins with Abram in his native city of Ur.

This is the record
of the descendants of Terah. . . .
Terah took his son Abram, his grandson Lot . . .
and his daughter-in-law Sarai,
the wife of his son Abram,
and brought them out of Ur. . . .
But when they reached Haran, they settled there. . . .
Terah died in Haran.

GENESIS 11:27, 31–32

EXCAVATED GRAVEYARD

Abram's world is no longer a faceless world
buried under the debris of history.
Archaeologists have exhumed the cities
of Abram's time and made them retell their stories
and well-kept secrets.

Terah means "moon."
Since Ur was the center of a moon cult,
his ancestors were probably moon worshipers.

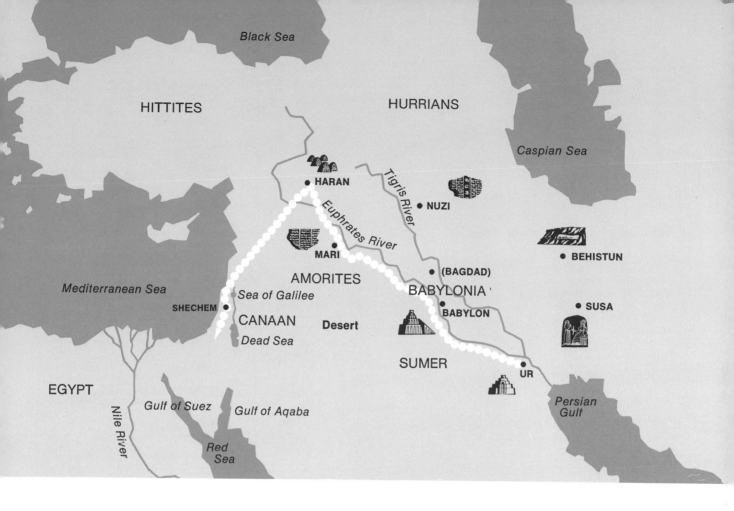

HITTITES

HURRIANS

Black Sea

Caspian Sea

● HARAN

Tigris River

● NUZI

Euphrates River

● MARI

● BEHISTUN

AMORITES

Mediterranean Sea

Sea of Galilee

(BAGDAD)

BABYLONIA

SHECHEM ●

● BABYLON

● SUSA

CANAAN

Desert

Dead Sea

SUMER

EGYPT

UR

Gulf of Suez

Gulf of Aqaba

Persian Gulf

Nile River

Red Sea

Archaeology shows
that Abram's moon-worshiping world of 2000 B.C.
bore similarities
to our moon-landing world of A.D. 2000.
It too was a period of radical change.
For one thing, Hurrians from the north
introduced new weapons of war—
the chariot and an improved fighting bow.

Second, seminomadic tribes, Amorites
("Westerners"), began to change their life-style.
They came in out of the desert
and began to settle in towns.
Abram's ancestors probably belonged to these
tribes before they settled in Ur.

Ur was once the capital of ancient Sumer,
where the first great civilization
was born over 5,000 years ago.
Today, Ur lies in an excavated graveyard

Once proudly called the "Hill of Heaven,"
this crumbling mound of brick is all that remains
of the beautiful ziggurat that marks the spot
where Abraham began his history-making journey.
Desert storms, scavengers, and amateur archaeologists
have wrecked its upper levels, once crowned
with a temple to the moon god, Nanna-Sin.

Writing began in Mesopotamia
out of a need to keep records.
The earliest writing on clay tablets
followed columns that read
from top to bottom and right to left.
The symbols stood for
concrete objects (picture writing).

Cuneiform writing
developed from picture writing
as a kind of early shorthand.
At first
the cuneiform symbols
stood for abstract ideas
and then for human sounds.
This Assyrian tablet,
pre-dating Abraham,
is an example of early
cuneiform writing.

near the northern tip of the Persian Gulf.
The Bagdad railroad still stops there
for history-minded tourists.
Towering over the site, like a giant tombstone,
are the crumbling remains of an ancient ziggurat.
Atop this man-made mountain of masonry
once stood a temple dedicated to the moon god.

Archaeologists began digging at Ur around 1845.
Not until the 1920s, however, did Ur come alive
under the excavations of Sir Leonard Woolley,
the British archaeologist.

Among his discoveries
was a tomb chamber dating from 2500 B.C.
It contained 74 skeletons, still ornately clothed,
teams of oxen, still in harness,
tableware, and musical instruments.
Apparently, the whole group was buried alive
to join their nobleman master in death.

STRANGE WRITING

Also found were thousands of clay tablets.
As early as 1800, similar tablets were discovered
by adventure seekers in the Near East.

At first, no one could read the odd wedge-shaped
(cuneiform) writing on these tablets.
Tourists and museum visitors jokingly referred to it
as "bird tracks on wet sand."

The dramatic breakthrough in translating it
came when similar "bird tracks" were found,
cut into a rock cliff at Behistun in Persia.
Paralleling the cuneiform inscription were two
other inscriptions, both in different languages.
Apparently, the same text
was repeated in three different languages,
a practice not uncommon among ancient peoples.

Whereas pictorial writing
was done with a pointed stylus
drawn across soft clay,
cuneiform writing
was done with a triangular stylus
pressed into the clay.
The result was a series
of wedge-shaped impressions.

The above impressions were made by rolling cylinder stones
across soft clay. The stones, from which these impressions
were made, are shown at the right.
They pre-date Abraham by over 1,000 years.

In 1835, Henry Rawlinson, a daring Englishman,
risked his life on the face of the 340-foot cliff
to make an exact copy of the three inscriptions.
Playing one against the other,
he broke the mysterious code 15 years later.
The inscription turned out to be
a report of the feats of Darius the Great,
the Persian king (521–486 B.C.).

At last the key to the wedge-shaped writing
was found.
Scholars began to read the tablets.
A library of Sumerian poetry, mythology,
and commercial documents leaped to life.
Suddenly, Ur and other Sumerian cities
burst into "living color."

There were even hundreds of clay tablets
which apparently had been used
by Sumerian schoolboys as copybooks.

The World of Abraham
SAMUEL NOAH KRAMER

*We have found hundreds of their practice tablets,
ranging from the sorry scratches of beginners
to the elegant copybooks of young men
about to "graduate." One delightfully human tablet
tells of a boy's bad day:*

*"When I awoke early in the morning,
I faced my mother and said to her,
'Give me my lunch, I want to go to school.'
My mother gave me two rolls and I set out. . . .
In school the monitor in charge said to me,
'Why are you late?'
Afraid and with pounding heart, I entered
before my teacher and made a respectful curtsy."*

*It did no good. A marked boy all day,
he took canings for talking, for standing,*

49

for poor stylusmanship.
We are quite sure of the rendering of caning,
since the sign consists of stick *and* flesh.

The clay tablets also tell us
that Sumerian mathematicians solved equations,
calculated square and cube roots,
and even the areas of circles and rectangles.
They also used our system
of the 360-degree circle and the 60-minute hour.
Abraham lived in this civilization.

MYSTERIOUS ENCOUNTER

Abram grew up in Sumer.
He walked along the streets of Ur
and bartered with its peddlers and merchants.

Eventually, however, Abram's father
moved his family up the Euphrates River to Haran.
At this city, which archaeologists have discovered,
Abram became the family head at his father's death.

At Haran, Abram underwent a religious experience
that rocked his own life and all history as well.
Here, for the first time in history,
a human being encountered the mysterious reality
that people now call God.

Abram's experience
was so profound and so unmistakable
that he responded to it without question.

The LORD said to Abram:
"Go forth from the land of your kinsfolk
and from your father's house
to a land that I will show you. . . ."

Abram went as the LORD directed. . . .
He took his wife Sarai,
his brother's son Lot,
all the possessions that they had accumulated,
and the persons they had acquired at Haran. . . .

When they came to the land of Canaan,

Abram passed through the land
as far as the sacred place at Shechem.

GENESIS 12:1–6

This experience is referred to as Abram's *call*.
It begins a pattern that repeats itself over and over
again in biblical history: certain people
experience an inner summons
to leave all and to embark upon a mission
that God reveals to them only gradually.
Abram was the first of a long line of people
called by God.

STORY OF SINHUE

When Abram pitched his tents at Canaan,
it was sparsely settled and controlled by Egypt.
The pattern of life Abram settled down to in Canaan
is described not only in the Bible,
but also in old Egyptian documents.

One fascinating record is the "Story of Sinhue."
Written in Egyptian script, it tells of a nobleman
who fled from Egypt to the hills of Canaan
to save his life.

Hiding in tall bushes,
Sinhue passed the Egyptian frontier at night.
In the desert, he nearly died of thirst.
His throat became "hot with the taste of death,"
but he was found and saved by a Bedouin chief.
Eventually, Sinhue reached Canaan and freedom.

The Sinhue story confirms with striking accuracy
many of the biblical details
about daily life in Canaan. Sinhue says:

It was a good land. . . .
Figs grew and so did grapes.
Wine was more available than water.
We had plenty of honey and olives.
There was every kind of fruit tree.

13

A Mystery Unfolds

Arab boy in Jerusalem.
He and his ancestors claim descendancy
from Ishmael, Abraham's son by Hagar.

Abram settled down to his new life in Canaan.
What lay ahead for him was shrouded in mystery.
All he could do was to wait for further revelation
from the strange "new God" he had encountered
in Haran.

At this point in Abram's life, his wife, Sarai,
was childless.
Sarai had, however, a maid servant called Hagar.
One day Sarai approached Abram.

SARAI   *The LORD has kept me from bearing*
        children, Abram.
        Have intercourse, then, with my maid;
        perhaps I shall have sons through her.

NARRATOR   *Abram heeded Sarai's request. . . .*
           Hagar bore Abram a son,
           and Abram named him Ishmael.

GENESIS 16:2, 15

Clay tablets found at Nuzi in Iraq
help us to understand this puzzling passage.
Among the tablets was an old marriage contract
stating that a sterile wife had to provide her husband
with a substitute wife for childbearing.
Thus Sarai, who appeared to be sterile,
merely carried out her obligation to Abram.

Sometime after this event, Abram experienced
a second encounter with the unknown God.

GOD   *Fear not, Abram!*
      I am your shield;
      I will make your reward very great. . . .
      Look up at the sky
      and count the stars, if you can.
      Just so, shall your descendants be. . . .

ABRAM   *O LORD GOD, how am I to know*
        that I shall possess it?

GOD   *Bring me a three-year-old heifer,*
      a three-year-old she-goat,
      a three-year-old ram,
      a turtledove, and a young pigeon.

NARRATOR   *Abram brought him all these,*
           split them in two,
           and placed each half opposite the other;
           but the birds he did not cut up.

51

*Birds of prey swooped down on the
carcasses, but Abram stayed with them.
As the sun was about to set,
a trance fell upon Abram, and a deep,
terrifying darkness enveloped him. . . .*

*When the sun had set and it was dark,
there appeared . . . a flaming torch,
which passed between those pieces.
It was on that occasion that the LORD
made a covenant with Abram, saying:
"To your descendants I give this land."*

GENESIS 15:1–18

Abram's second experience puts into focus
the purpose for which God called him.
He is to be the father of a people,
who will receive a land, grow into a great nation,
and enjoy a unique relationship to God.

The unusual ceremony
that is depicted as sealing this promise to Abram
was known as cutting a covenant.

Unlike modern nations and peoples,
ancients rarely signed treaties or contracts.
Rather, they solemnized important agreements
by a symbolic covenant rite.

The two parties split an animal down the middle.
Laying the two sides opposite each other,
they walked between them.

The meaning of this ancient rite is preserved
for us in the Bible.

*Thus says the LORD. . . .
The men who violated my covenant
and did not observe the terms . . .
I will make like the calf which they cut in two,
between whose two parts they passed.*

JEREMIAH 34:13, 18

The parties passing between the cut-up animal
signified that they would rather die a death
as violent as did the animal,
than break their agreement.

THIRD EXPERIENCE

Sometime later, Abram encountered God again.

GOD *I am God the Almighty.
Walk in my presence and be blameless. . . .*

*No longer shall you be called Abram;
your name shall be Abraham,
for I am making you
the father of a host of nations. . . .
I will maintain my covenant with you
and your descendants after you. . . .
I will be their God.*

*On your part . . .
circumcise the flesh of your foreskin,
and that shall be the mark
of the covenant between you and me.*

52

Moving from place to place and setting up camp
under open skies, this modern Sinai Bedouin
lives much in the same fashion as did Abraham over
3,500 years ago.

Throughout the ages, every male
among you, when he is eight days old,
shall be circumcised. . . .
As for your wife Sarai . . .
her name shall be Sarah.
I will bless her. . . .
Sarah is to bear you a son,
and you shall call him Isaac. . . .

NARRATOR *When he had finished speaking to him,*
God departed from Abraham.

GENESIS 17:1–22

Thus, by a series of progressive encounters,
God revealed himself to Abraham.

BIRTH OF ISAAC

Sarah became pregnant
and bore Abraham a son in his old age. . . .
Abraham gave the name Isaac to this son. . . .
When his son Isaac was eight days old, Abraham
circumcised him, as God had commanded. . . .
Isaac grew, and on the day of the child's weaning
Abraham held a great feast.

Sarah noticed the son whom Hagar the Egyptian
had borne to Abraham playing with her son Isaac;
so she demanded of Abraham:
"Drive out that slave and her son!". . .
Abraham was greatly distressed,
especially on account of his son Ishmael.
But God said to Abraham:

"Do not be distressed about the boy
or about your slave woman.
Heed the demands of Sarah,
no matter what she is asking of you;
for it is through Isaac
that descendants shall bear your name.
As for the son of the slave woman,
I will make a great nation of him also,
since he too is your offspring."

GENESIS 21:2–13

Names and Naming

Names were important in ancient times.
They did more than arbitrarily identify a person.
They said something significant about the person.

A change in a person's name
indicated an important change in the person.
God's action in the lives of Abram and Sarai
changed them so radically
that their original names no longer identified
the new persons they had become.

Similarly, the power to name
also indicated something important.
It symbolized control
over the person or thing named.
Recall the beautiful scene
in the second creation story in Genesis
where God parades the animals and the birds
before Adam to be named.

The LORD God formed out of the ground
various wild animals and various birds of the air,
and he brought them to the man . . . ;
whatever the man called each of them
would be its name.
The man gave names
to all the cattle,
all the birds of the air,
and all the wild animals.

GENESIS 2:19–20

Adam's naming of the animals and the birds
was symbolic.
It was the biblical writer's way of saying
that God intended Adam
to exercise dominion over them.

14
Trial By Fire

NARRATOR   *Some time after these events,*
God put Abraham to the test. . . .

GOD   *Take your son Isaac,*
your only one, whom you love,
and . . . offer him up as a holocaust
on a height
that I will point out to you. . . .

NARRATOR   *Thereupon Abraham took the wood*
for the holocaust
and laid it on his son Isaac's shoulders,
while he himself
carried the fire and the knife.

GENESIS 22:1–6

It is difficult for the modern mind to realize
that human sacrifice was not entirely unusual
in Abraham's time.
Here's how a modern novelist reconstructs
the atmosphere that surrounded the event.

The Source
JAMES A. MICHENER

The last child was a boy of nearly three . . .
he was old enough to understand . . .
and when they lifted him to the god
he screamed, trying to hold on to the stone fingers
and save himself,
but the priests pulled away his small, clutching hands,
and with a violent push
sent him tumbling into the flaming mouth.

As soon as the boy disappeared,
wailing in fiery smoke,

the mood of the temple changed.
The god Melak was forgotten;
his fires were allowed to die down
and his priests turned to other important matters.
Drums resumed their beat—
this time in livelier rhythms—and trumpets sounded.
The people of Makor,
satisfied that their new god would protect them . . .
gathered about the steps of the temple. . . .

[The people had adopted the new god]
partly because his demands upon them were severe,
as if this proved his power,
and partly because they had grown
somewhat contemptuous of their local gods
precisely because they were not demanding.
Melak, with his fiery celebrations,
had not been forced upon the town;
the town had sought him out
as the fulfillment of a felt need,
and the more demanding he became,
the more they respected him.

No recent logic in Makor was so persuasive as that
of the priests after the destruction of the town:
"You were content to give damaged sons to Melak
and in return he gave you damaged protection."
Equally acceptable
was the progression whereby Melak's appetite
had expanded from the blood of a pigeon
to the burning of a dead sheep
to the immolation of living children,
for with each extension of his appetite
he became more powerful and therefore
more pleasing to the people he tyrannized. . . .

Furthermore, the cult of human sacrifice
was of itself not abominable,
nor did it lead to the brutalization of society:
lives were lost
which could have been otherwise utilized,
but . . . excessive numbers were not killed,
nor did the rites in which they died
contaminate the mind.

In fact, there was something grave and stately
in the picture of a father willing to sacrifice
his first-born son as his ultimate gift
for the salvation of a community.

ABRAHAM OBEYS

Thus, the sacrifice of a son
was not a bizarre event in Abraham's time.
Still, it pained Abraham's heart
and confused his mind.
What about God's promise:
"It is through Isaac that you will have descendants"?
Nevertheless, Abraham obeyed.

NARRATOR *When they came to the place*
  of which God had told him,
  Abraham built an altar. . . .

MESSENGER *Abraham . . .*
  do not lay your hand on the boy. . . .
  I know now how devoted you are
  to God, since you did not
  withhold from me
  your own beloved son.

GENESIS 22:9–12

New Testament writers
explained Abraham's trial by fire this way:

By faith Abraham obeyed when he was called,
and went forth to the place he was to receive
as a heritage; he went forth, moreover,
not knowing where he was going. . . .
By faith Abraham, when put to the test,
offered up Isaac;
he who had received the promises
was ready to sacrifice his only son,
of whom it was said,
"Through Isaac shall your descendants be called."
Abraham reasoned
that God was able to raise from the dead,
and so he received Isaac back as a symbol.

HEBREWS 11:8, 17–19

Upon reflection, Abraham and his descendants
regarded the Isaac episode as revelation
that God did not want human sacrifice.
It could never be an option in Hebrew worship.

DYNAMIC OF BIBLICAL FAITH

Abraham's test of faith underscores
several key points concerning biblical faith.

First, it is not something totally intellectual,
like finding the answer to a math problem.
The old priest in *The Exorcist* came close
to the idea of biblical faith when he said:

I think belief in God is not a matter of reason at all;
I think it finally is a matter of love,
accepting the possibility that God could love us.

Biblical faith is loving trust in God—
even in the face of intellectual difficulties.
For example, Abraham's human reason
told him that Isaac was the vehicle
by which God's promise to him would be carried out.
But then he was told to sacrifice Isaac.
Abraham had to make a choice.
Had he relied solely on reason,
he would have set aside his trust.
But he did not. He chose to trust,
even in the face of deep intellectual turmoil.

Second,
because biblical faith involved loving trust,
it also demanded personal risk.
An everyday example illustrates this point.
When two people marry, neither is absolutely sure
the other will remain faithful,
should major difficulties arise.
In other words, they have no intellectual certainty.

Biblical faith was something like this.
It always involved a knowledge gap
that loving trust alone could bridge.

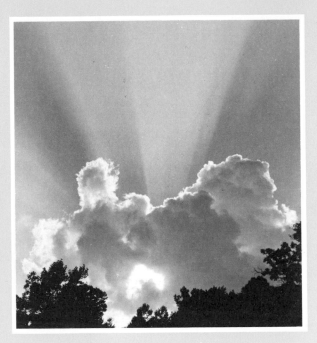

I Believe

On a cellar wall in Cologne,
an unknown World War II fugitive from the Nazis
left a beautiful testimony of faith.

Workers found the inscription
while clearing away debris and rubble
from a bombed-out house
that once stood on the cellar walls.
The inscription read:

I believe in the sun
  even when it is not shining.
I believe in love
  even when I do not feel it.
I believe in God
  even when he is silent.

Third,
biblical faith is pictured as an ongoing process.
The biggest mistake a person could make
was to think that some day he would "get the faith"
and never have any more questions about it.

Psychology makes an interesting observation here.
Consider this statement by a young man.

One day,
I decided to make God the center of my life.
This decision gave me unbelievable peace and joy.
But two days later,
I did something that no believer would ever do.
I was totally discouraged and concluded
that I had not really committed myself to God at all.
I had only psyched myself into believing I had.

But then I realized something important.
I realized that when we commit ourselves to God,
we commit only that part of ourselves
which we are aware of at the moment.
That's all any man can do.

Psychology tells us that the greater part of ourselves
lies below our consciousness.
It surfaces only gradually with each new experience.
This means that people constantly evolve
and change as persons.

Thus, faith-commitment is never achieved
by one decision on one occasion.
It is an ongoing process.

Finally, biblical faith involved periods of darkness.
It had a way of going in and out of focus.
Many modern believers report a similar experience.
There are times when their faith
seems to go behind a cloud, even seems lost.
They undergo a "dark night of the soul,"
a kind of "trial by fire" as Abraham experienced.

The agony this kind of experience can cause
has been graphically illustrated in a modern novel.

The Devil's Advocate
MORRIS WEST

How does one come back to belief? . . .
I tried to reason myself back to a first cause
and first motion, as a foundling might reason
himself back to the existence of his father.
He must have existed, all children have fathers.
But who was he?
What was his name? What did he look like?
Did he love me—
or had he forgotten me forever? . . .

I groped for Him and could not find Him.
I prayed to Him unknown and He did not answer.
I wept at night for the loss of Him.
Lost tears and fruitless grief.

Then, one day, He was there again. . . .
There are no words to record,
no stones scored with a fiery finger,
no thunders on Tabor.
I had a Father and He knew me
and the world was a house He had built for me. . . .
I had never understood till this moment
the meaning of the words "gift of faith."

Types and Figures

Alert readers note that Isaac resembles Jesus.
His father's only son, he carried the wood
of sacrifice on his shoulder, was to be sacrificed
on a hill, and was not defeated by death.

Are these resemblances coincidental?
Some say yes; others say no; many are not sure.
This much is certain.
New Testament writers occasionally drew parallels
between Old and New Testament events.
For example, Paul writes:

Just as in Adam all die,
so in Christ all will come to life again. . . .
Adam, the first man, became a living soul;
the last Adam has become a life-giving spirit. . . .
The first man was of earth . . .
the second is from heaven. . . .
Just as we resemble the man from earth,
so shall we bear the likeness of the man from heaven.

1 CORINTHIANS 15:22, 45–49

Jesus, himself, drew similar parallels to clarify
his mission of healing people
to save them from spiritual death. He said:

"Just as Moses
lifted up the serpent in the desert,
so must the Son of Man be lifted up,
that all who believe
may have eternal life in him."

JOHN 3:14–15

Jesus had in mind Numbers 21:6–9,
where Israelites were dying from serpent bites.
God tells Moses to mount a serpent on a pole.
Those who look on it and believe will not die.

An Old Testament person or event
that points to a New Testament person or event
is called a "type" or "figure."
Early Christians used "types"
to try to show Jews that Jesus was the person
toward whom the Old Testament was pointing.

Sand and Stars

The book *Letters from the Desert*,
by Carlo Carretto,
is exactly what the title says it is:
a journal of reflections by a person
who went into the desert to learn to pray.
Like Abraham,
Carlo felt an "inner call" to leave behind
his old life and to set out on a new one.
He writes:

God's call is mysterious;
it comes in the darkness of faith.
It is so fine, so subtle,
that it is only with the deepest silence within us
that we can hear it. . . .

Three times in my life I have been aware
of this call.

The first one brought about my conversion
when I was eighteen years old. . . .

In Lent a mission came to the town.
I attended it but what I remember most of all
was how boring and outdated the sermons were.
It certainly wasn't the words
which shook my state of apathy and sin.
But when I knelt before an old missionary—
I remember how direct his look was
and how simple. . . .

From that day on I knew I was a Christian,
and was aware that a completely new life
had been opened up for me.

The second time, when I was twenty-three,
I was thinking of getting married.
It never occurred to me
that I should do anything else. . . .

I was praying in an empty church where . . .
I heard the same voice that I had heard
during my confession with the old missionary.
"Marriage is not for you.
You will offer your life to me. . . ."

Many years passed. . . .

Then, when I was forty-four years old,
there occurred the most serious call of my life:
the call to the contemplative life.
I experienced it deeply. . . .

"Leave everything
and come with me into the desert.
It is not your acts and deeds I want;
I want your prayer, your love.". . .

I went into the desert.

Without having read the constitutions
of the Little Brothers of Jesus
I entered their congregation. . . .

When I reached El Abiod Sidi Seik
for the novitiate, my novice master told me
with the perfect calm of a man who had lived
twenty years in the desert:
"Il faut faire une coupure, Carlo."
I knew what kind of cutting he was talking about. . . .

In my bag I had kept a thick notebook,
containing the addresses of my old friends. . . .

I took the address book,
which for me was the last tie with the past,
and burnt it behind a dune. . . .

I can still see the black ashes of the notebook
being swept away into the distance
by the winds of the Sahara.

But burning an address is not the same thing
as destroying a friendship,
for that I never intended to do; on the contrary,
I have never loved nor prayed so much
for my old friends as in the solitude of the desert.

What is a life of prayer in the desert like?
Here are some insights from Carlo's book.

The first nights spent here
made me send off for books on astronomy
and maps of the sky;

and for months afterwards I spent my free time
learning a little of what was passing
over my head up there in the universe. . . .

Kneeling on the sand
I sank my eyes for hours and hours
in those wonders,
writing down my discoveries in an exercise book
like a child. . . .

Finding one's way in the desert is much easier
by night than by day. . . .
In the years which I spent in the open desert
I never once got lost, thanks to the stars.

Many times,
when searching for a Tuareg camp . . .
I lost my way
because the sun was too high in the sky.
But I waited for night and found the road again,
guided by the stars.

Elsewhere, Carlo writes:

Night came, and I could not sleep.
I left the cave, and walked under the stars
above the vast desert. . . .

How dear they were to me, those stars;
how close to them the desert had brought me.
Through spending my nights in the open,
I had come to know them by their names,
then to study them,
and to get to know them one by one.
Now I could distinguish their colour, their size,
their position, their beauty.
I knew my way around them, and from them
I could calculate the time without a watch.

Summing up his reflections on the night,
Carlo writes:

"Go forth . . .
to a land that I will show you."
Genesis 12:1

The friendly night is an image of faith. . . .

Faith is a gift of God but it needs effort
on our part if it is to bear fruit. . . .

David developed his faith by accepting to fight
against Goliath.
Gideon exercised himself in faith . . .
by going into battle
with a few soldiers against a stronger enemy.

Abraham became a giant in faith
by making the supreme act of obedience
which demanded of him the sacrifice of his son.

15

The Irreversible Word

NARRATOR   *Isaac was forty years old*
when he married Rebekah. . . .
Rebekah became pregnant. . . .
When the time of her delivery came,
there were twins in her womb.
The first to emerge was reddish . . .
so they named him Esau.
His brother came out next,
gripping Esau's heel;
so they named him Jacob. . . .

As the boys grew up,
Esau became a skillful hunter,
a man who lived in the open;
whereas Jacob was a simple man,
who kept to his tents.
Isaac preferred Esau,
because he was fond of game;
but Rebekah preferred Jacob. . . .
When Isaac was so old
that his eyesight failed him,
he called his older son Esau. . . .

ISAAC   *I am so old*
that I may now die at any time.
Take your gear, therefore—
your quiver and bow—
and go out into the country
to hunt some game . . .
that I may give you my blessing
before I die.

NARRATOR   *Rebekah had been listening. . . .*
So when Esau went out into the country
to hunt some game for his father,
Rebekah said to her son Jacob,

REBEKAH   *. . . Go to the flock and get me two choice*
kids. With these I will prepare
an appetizing dish for your father . . .
that he may bless you before he dies. . . .

NARRATOR   *So Jacob went and got them*
and brought them to his mother; . . .
with them she prepared an appetizing
dish, such as his father liked. . . .

JACOB   *Father!*

ISAAC   *Yes? Which of my sons are you?*

JACOB   *I am Esau. . . .*
Please sit up and eat some of my game,
so that you may give me
your special blessing.

ISAAC   *How did you succeed so quickly, son? . . .*
Are you really my son Esau?

JACOB   *Certainly.*

ISAAC   *Serve me your game, son. . . .*
[The game is served.]
Come closer, son, and kiss me.

NARRATOR   *As Jacob went up and kissed him,*
Isaac smelled the fragrance of his clothes.
With that, he blessed him. . . .
Jacob had scarcely left his father . . .
when his brother Esau came back
from his hunt. Then he too prepared
an appetizing dish. . . .

ESAU   *Please, father, eat some of your son's*
game, that you may then give me
your special blessing.

ISAAC   *Who are you?*

ESAU   *I am Esau, your first-born son.*

NARRATOR	*With that, Isaac was seized with a fit of uncontrollable trembling.*
ISAAC	*Who was it, then, that hunted game and brought it to me?* *I finished eating it . . .* *and I blessed him.* *Now he must remain blessed!*
NARRATOR	*On hearing his father's words,* *Esau burst into loud, bitter sobbing.*
ESAU	*Father, bless me too!*
ISAAC	*I have already appointed Jacob your master. . . .*
NARRATOR	*Esau bore Jacob a grudge* *because of the blessing* *his father had given him.*
ESAU	*When the time of mourning* *for my father comes,* *I will kill my brother Jacob.*
NARRATOR	*When Rebekah got news* *of what her older son Esau had in mind,* *she called her younger son Jacob.*
REBEKAH	*Listen . . .* *flee at once to my brother Laban* *in Haran.*

GENESIS 25:20–28; 27:1–43

HUMAN WORD

This episode highlights two key biblical ideas.
First, it shows how God dealt with biblical persons.
He did not dangle them from invisible puppet strings.
Nor did he program their actions.
Rather, he gave them autonomy
and worked through their free acts.

Second, Isaac's inability to withdraw his blessing
illustrates the biblical person's attitude
toward the spoken word.

Hebrews lived in a nonliterary culture.
The spoken word was important.
In business, it took the place of written contracts.
When a man gave his word,
nothing could excuse him from keeping it.

This was even more true with blessings or curses.
Once uttered, they could not be reversed.
Like an arrow shot from a bow,
they could not be stopped.

GOD'S WORD

God's word was even more powerful.
When God spoke,
nothing could keep his word from taking effect.
The creation story illustrates this:
God said, "Let there be light," and there *was* light.

We also see it in the lives of the prophets.
When God revealed his word to them,
they had to speak it. They could not hold it in.
Jeremiah says:

The word of the LORD . . .
becomes like fire burning in my heart . . . ,
I grow weary holding it in,
I cannot endure it.

JEREMIAH 20:8–9

The prophet Isaiah writes:

For just as from the heavens
the rain and snow come down
and do not return there
till they have watered the earth,
making it fertile and fruitful . . .
so shall my word be
that goes forth from my mouth;
it shall not return to me void,
but shall do God's will.

ISAIAH 55:10–11

New Testament writers portrayed God's word
as taking human form in Jesus.

The Word became flesh
and made his dwelling among us,
and we have seen his glory:
the glory of an only Son coming from the Father,
filled with enduring love.

JOHN 1:14

God's word and its power were present in Jesus.
John described Jesus' miracles as works of power;
Luke described power going out from Jesus
to cure sick people (Luke 8:46).

After Pentecost, Jesus' power continued to reside
in those who preached in his name.
Peter said to the crowd, after he cured a cripple:

"Why does this surprise you?
Why do you stare at us
as if we had made this man walk
by some power or holiness of our own?

"The God of Abraham, of Isaac, and of Jacob,
the God of our fathers,
has glorified his Servant Jesus. . . .
It is his name, and trust in this name,
that has strengthened the limbs of this man
whom you see and know well.
Such faith has given him perfect health,
as all of you can observe."

ACTS 3:12–16

Today, Christians still believe
that power goes out from Jesus' words in the Bible.
Consider this report
from a young man caught up in a life of evil.

The Confessions of Saint Augustine
SAINT AUGUSTINE

I threw myself on the ground
under a nearby fig tree and began to weep bitterly.
I cried out to God in words like this:
"And you, Lord! How long? How long will you
keep on being angry with me—forever?
How long will it be—tomorrow and tomorrow?

Why not now? Why not at this very hour
put an end to my evil life?"

I was crying out like this
when, suddenly, I heard the voice of a little boy
or a little girl—I couldn't tell which.
In sing-song fashion, the voice said:
"Take and read! Take and read!"

Immediately, my whole mood changed.
I asked myself if children at play
normally used such words.
I couldn't remember them ever doing so before.

I stood up. For the voice now seemed like
a divine command to open the Bible and read
the first passage that my eyes would fall upon. . . .
I got a Bible, opened it, and read:

"Let us live honorably as in daylight;
not in carousing and drunkenness,
not in sexual excess and lust,
not in quarreling and jealousy.
Rather, put on the Lord Jesus Christ
and make no provisions for the desires of the flesh."
(Romans 13:13–14)

Then I stopped. There was no need to go on.
My heart suddenly became flooded with light,
vanishing the dark doubts
and leaving me with a profound peace.

Ballads and Stories

After Jacob fled from Esau,
he went in the direction of Haran.

NARRATOR   *When he came upon a certain shrine,*
as the sun had already set,
he stopped there for the night.

Taking one of the stones at the shrine,
he put it under his head
and lay down to sleep. . . .
Then he had a dream:
a stairway rested on the ground,
with its top reaching to the heavens;
and God's messengers
were going up and down on it.
And there was the LORD
standing beside him.

GOD   *I, the LORD, am the God*
of your forefather Abraham
and the God of Isaac;
the land on which you are lying
I will give to you
and your descendants. . . .
In you and your descendants all the
nations of the earth shall find blessing.

GENESIS 28:11-14

Jacob settled in Haran.
Later, he returned to the site of his dream.
Again, he experienced God's presence.

GOD   *You whose name is Jacob*
shall no longer be called Jacob,
but Israel shall be your name. . . .
A nation . . .
shall stem from you,
and kings
shall issue from your loins. . . .

NARRATOR   *Then God departed from him.*
On the site
where God had spoken to him,
Jacob set up a memorial stone. . . .

Jacob named the site Bethel,
because God had spoken with him there.

GENESIS 35:10-15

The colorful stories of Abraham, Isaac, and Jacob
are referred to as patriarchal narratives.
That is,
they deal with the origin of the people of Israel.
Since the stories were passed on by word of mouth,
they took the form of folk history.

Folk history is not scientific history.
Rather, it is expressed in popular form:
short stories that could be easily remembered,
folk ballads that could be sung for entertainment
and instruction.

As a result, these narratives carry the authentic
flavor of the desert, the smell of the tents,
and the atmosphere of the tribal campfire.
They are very human documents about real people.

The ability to preserve history in folk story
has been confirmed by nonbiblical sources,
especially archaeology.

Origin Stories

A part of the folk history of any people
consists in dealing with such questions as

how a group got its name,
how it developed its customs,
why it celebrates certain holidays.

For example, a Hebrew boy might ask:
Why are we called Israel?
Why do our grandfathers pilgrimage to Bethel?
Why are we 12 tribes, rather than 10?

Modern scholars place some of the stories
of Abraham, Isaac, and Jacob in this category.
The biblical writer's purpose seems to have been
to communicate background about his people,
rather than to teach specific revealed truths.

16 The Dreamer

One of the "Seven Wonders of the Ancient World," the Great Pyramid was the tomb of Pharaoh Cheops (Khufu). Herodotus says 100,000 men spent 30 years building it. Referring to the superb construction of the pyramids, an Arab expression says: "The world fears time, but time fears the pyramids."

Jacob settled in Canaan and had 12 sons.
Of these sons, Jacob loved Joseph best.
This favoritism led to problems.

NARRATOR *When Joseph's brothers saw that their*
father loved him best of all the sons,
they hated him so much
that they would not even greet him.

Once Joseph had a dream,
which he told to his brothers. . . .

JOSEPH *There we were, binding sheaves in the*
field, when suddenly my sheaf rose to an
upright position, and your sheaves . . .
bowed down to it. . . .

NARRATOR *So the brothers hated Joseph*
all the more. . . .
[One day they plotted his death.]

BROTHERS *Here comes that master dreamer!*
Come on, let us kill him. . . .
We shall then see
what comes of his dreams. . . .

NARRATOR *So when Joseph came up to them . . .*
they took him and threw him
into the cistern, which was empty. . . .
Looking up, they saw
a caravan of Ishmaelites coming. . . .

JUDAH *What is to be gained by killing our*
brother and concealing his blood?
Rather, let us sell him to these

Ishmaelites. . . . After all, he is our
brother, our own flesh.

NARRATOR *His brothers agreed.*

GENESIS 37:4–8, 19–27

When Joseph was taken down to Egypt,
a certain Egyptian . . .
[Pharaoh's chief steward]
bought him. . . .
The LORD blessed the Egyptian's house
for Joseph's sake. . . .

GENESIS 39:1, 5

After a lapse of two years,
Pharaoh had a dream. . . .
Next morning his spirit was agitated.
So he summoned all the magicians
and sages . . . but no one
could interpret his dreams for him. . . .

Pharaoh therefore
had Joseph summoned. . . .

JOSEPH *It is not I, but God*
who will give Pharaoh
the right answer. . . .
God has revealed to Pharaoh what he is
about to do. Seven years of great
abundance are now coming . . .
but these will be followed by seven years
of famine. . . .

NARRATOR *After Joseph left Pharaoh's presence,*
he traveled
throughout the land of Egypt.
During the seven years of plenty . . .

64

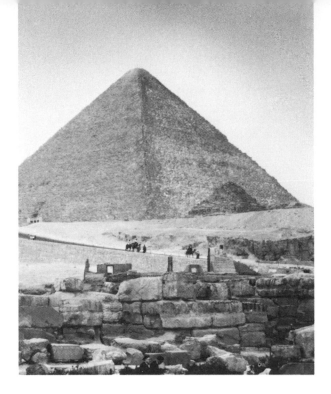

JOSEPH   *Come closer to me. . . .*
I am your brother Joseph,
whom you once sold into Egypt.
But now do not be distressed. . . .
It was really for the sake of saving lives
that God sent me here ahead of you. . . .
So it was really not you
but God who had me come here;
and he has made me a father to
Pharaoh, lord of all his household,
and ruler over the whole land of Egypt.

Hurry back, then, to my father and
tell him: "Thus says your son Joseph:
God has made me lord of all Egypt;
come to me without delay.
You will settle in the region of Goshen."

GENESIS 45:4–10

NARRATOR   *Thus Israel settled in the land of Egypt,*
in the region of Goshen.

GENESIS 47:27

ANCIENT EGYPT

When Joseph arrived in Egypt, we can imagine
that he stared in awe at the great pyramids.
They were already 1,000 years old in his time.

Standing in the shadow of the Pyramid of Cheops,
Joseph possibly studied it in disbelief.
Its base covered 13 acres of land, and its stone peak
pierced the sky 480 feet above the hot sand.
Over two million blocks made up its bulk,
each block weighing about two and one-half tons.

Human slaves, without the aid of machinery,
had shaped these blocks, transported them
from distant quarries, and hoisted them into place.
When Joseph saw the pyramids,
they were still veneered with polished, white stone
that reflected the rising sun like great mirrors.

Called "Joseph barns" by medieval pilgrims,
the pyramids were tombs of Egyptian kings.

Joseph garnered grain in quantities
like the sands of the sea. . . .
When the seven years of famine
set in . . .
Joseph opened all the cities
that had grain
and rationed it to the Egyptians. . . .
In fact, all the world came to Joseph . . .
for famine had gripped
the whole world. . . .

Then Jacob learned
that grain rations were available. . . .

JACOB   *[to sons] Go down to Egypt*
and buy some for us. . . .

NARRATOR   *So ten of Joseph's brothers went down*
to buy an emergency supply
of grain from Egypt. . . .

When Joseph recognized his brothers,
although they did not recognize him,
he was reminded of the dreams
he had about them. . . .

GENESIS 41:1–42:9

Hieroglyphics

The breakthrough in deciphering hieroglyphics
came about by accident.

Some of Napoleon's engineers were digging
near the Rosetta branch of the Nile in 1799.
A worker's shovel struck a huge stone slab.
The face of the slab was covered with writing
in three different languages: hieroglyphics,
demotic (hieroglyphic script), and Greek.

When news of the Rosetta Stone reached France,
a schoolboy named Champollion
was fascinated by the discovery.

Listening wide-eyed to speculations about it,
he resolved to be the one
who would solve the mystery of hieroglyphics.

Learning Greek, Hebrew, Coptic, Syriac,
and Arabic, he undertook, in his twenties,
the task of trying to translate the Rosetta Stone.

Finally, in 1822, after years of tedious work,
Champollion broke the code.
The stone turned out to be a priestly decree
honoring Ptolemy V (196 B.C.).

Champollion died at the early age of 42,
but he left behind him the results of his studies.

Now, whole grammars of hieroglyphics
have been compiled.
With these tools,
libraries of Egyptian writings have come alive.
They shed new light on certain biblical stories.

Carved into the walls of the Pyramid of Unis
are these words:

O king . . .
you have not departed dead;
you have departed living!
You sit upon the throne of Osiris,
with scepter in hand, commanding those who live.

Perhaps the Great Sphinx also amazed Joseph.
This gigantic image, which still fascinates tourists,
was also over 1,000 years old in Joseph's day.

In 1926, archaeologists discovered that its
seven-story human head, jutting from the sand,
was attached to the body of a lion
that covered the length of a football field.
The desert sand had drifted over it and buried it.

Similarly, centuries of desert storms
have dimmed the contours of its headdress.
The cobra, coiled about its forehead—
the symbol of kingship—has all but disappeared.

No doubt Joseph also puzzled over the hieroglyphics
that blanketed the walls of Egyptian temples.
Only recently have scholars learned to read
these "sacred writings."

Legend says that while a prince rested in the shade
of the Sphinx, it spoke to him. It promised
him the throne of Egypt if he would remove
the sand that covered its base.
He did, and went on to become King Thutmose IV.

NEW INSIGHT

Joseph's rise to power in Egypt
was once surrounded with fairy-tale glamor.
How could a Hebrew slave rise so quickly
to a key position in Egyptian government?

We now know from Egyptian records
that around Joseph's time
Egypt fell under the heel of the Hyksos.

These invaders from the north
overran the country with horse-drawn chariots
at a time when these were not yet a part
of the Egyptian arsenal.

This makes Joseph's rise to prominence
more understandable. He rose in a period
of military and political upheaval.

Similarly, other details of the Joseph story
are supported by Egyptian records.

THE ROSETTA STONE
Champollion worked 14 years
on this trilingual inscription
found near Rosetta.
The vital clue came when he identified
Ptolemy's name among
the hieroglyphic characters (top)
and decided that the markings
should be read phonetically,
rather than pictorially
or abstractly.

Beautiful Inscriptions

Chiseled into stone, these hieroglyphic symbols
were concerned with beauty as well as practicality.
The symbols were often brilliantly painted
or coated in gold.

Thriving between 3100 B.C. and A.D. 400,
the writing flowed either horizontally or vertically.
A living creature usually pointed the direction
where one should begin reading.
Some recognizable symbols in the photo are:

sandal strap
(approximating the sound *ankh*),

milk jug (approximating the sound *me*),

bolt (approximating the sound *s*).

A papyrus, dating from 1300 B.C.,
gives detailed instructions for interpreting dreams.
Dream interpretation seems to have been
a highly respected art in Joseph's time.

Egyptian records also tell of massive famines.
One such record contains this communication
from King Zoser to a governor in Elephantine.

*My heart is heavy over the great failure
of the Nile floods for the past seven years.
There is little fruit;
vegetables are in short supply;
there is a scarcity of food in general.*

*Everybody robs his neighbor. . . .
The storehouses have been opened,
but everything in them has been consumed.*

NEW APPEAL

When we think back upon the Joseph story,
two significant points emerge.

First, God did not always act in biblical times
in superspectacular ways.
Rather, he often acted within the framework
of ordinary events and human circumstances.

Second, God did not always act through holy people.
The biblical writer makes this painfully clear.
He does not gloss over Jacob's lie to Isaac,
nor does he excuse the criminal actions
of Joseph's brothers.
He merely reports what happened, without endorsing
the actions or holding them up for imitation.

The biblical figures were everyday people.
But in spite of their defects and weaknesses,
they also had islands of honor and nobility
in their lives.
God used these to advance his work in history.
It is this kind of perspective
that is giving the Bible new appeal and credibility
among modern readers.

This solid gold mask fitted over the head and shoulders
of the mummified 18-year-old king.
The vulture and cobra headdress symbolized royalty;
the beard, divinity.

17

Go Down, Moses

Few pharaohs in Egypt's history rival Rameses II.
His mummified head is still a feature exhibit
in a Cairo museum.
As recent as 1965, Rameses was still grabbing
newspaper headlines.
The newly constructed Aswan Dam had doomed
to a watery grave the 3,000-year-old temple
he built at Abu Simbel on the Nile.

UNESCO engineers came to the rescue.
In a masterpiece of engineering, they dismantled
the temple (with its four six-story statues)
and hoisted it up a 212-foot cliff to dry ground.

It was this same Rameses II
who played such a key role in Israel's history.

Now Joseph and all his brothers
and that whole generation died. . . .
Then a new king, who knew nothing of Joseph,
came to power in Egypt.
He said to his subjects,
"Look how numerous and powerful
the Israelite people are growing,
more so than we ourselves! . . ."

Accordingly,
taskmasters were set over the Israelites
to oppress them with forced labor.
Thus they had to build for Pharaoh
the supply cities of Pithom and Raamses.

EXODUS 1:6–11

"Yes, Wonderful Things!"

Forty years before Rameses II,
the boy-king, Tutankhamen, ruled Egypt.
His royal grave was the only one missed
by tomb robbers of the 12th century.
While tunneling for another tomb,
the thieves carelessly heaped debris over it.
It was finally discovered in 1922
by British archaeologist Howard Carter.

On November 26, Carter peered into the tomb
through a tiny hole. He described what he saw:

As my eyes grew accustomed to the light
details of the room began to emerge slowly
from the mist,
strange animals, statues, and gold. . . .
I was struck dumb with amazement,
and when Lord Carnarvon,
unable to stand the suspense any longer,
inquired anxiously, "Can you see anything?"
it was all I could do to get out the words,
"Yes, wonderful things."

69

HEBREW SLAVERY

Modern archaeologists have unearthed
an ancient stone carving of Rameses II
that confirms the biblical report of city building.
It reads:

*He built the city of Raamses
with Asiatic Semitic slaves.*

In 1927, archaeologists began digging at Tanis.
Today, this Egyptian site has been identified,
almost beyond doubt,
as the ancient city of Raamses.
Visitors to the University Museum
can get an idea how the city was built.
There an ancient Egyptian tomb painting
shows slaves at work in Egyptian brickyards.

The plight of half-naked Hebrew slaves,
working under the hot desert skies,
has been vividly recreated by a modern novelist.

Moses
SHOLEM ASCH

*Their bodies
showed the ribs and backbone starkly.
In the blazing sunlight the black-scorched skin,
wetted by the sweat of anguish and labor,
glistened like copper.*

*Their faces were dumb and careworn,
the lips thin, close-locked, parched. . . .
They did their work in dull silence;
their motion and footsteps maintained
a heavy rhythm under the threat of whips.*

MOSES

Into this situation
stepped the remarkable figure of Moses.
He seems to combine rare extremes in personality.
Perhaps this is why artists find him fascinating.
How do you portray a man who, at times,

was so timid as to fear leading people,
yet, at times, was so bold as to talk back to God?

When Moses was called to lead the people,
he declined: "I am slow of speech . . .
send someone else" (Exodus 4:10–13).
Later, when God grew impatient with him,
Moses snapped:

*"Why are you so displeased with me . . . ?
Was it I who conceived all this people?"*

NUMBERS 11:11-12

BIRTH OF MOSES

Born at a time when Hebrew male babies were
exterminated systematically by Egyptian authorities,
Moses was saved by the ingenuity of his mother
(Exodus 2:1–10).
The story bears a similarity to the legendary birth
of Sargon of Akkad, who lived long before Moses.

Sargon's mother put him in a watertight basket
and set him afloat on the Euphrates River.
He was rescued by a peasant
and became king through the aid of a goddess.

The Greek historian Herodotus reports
similar legends surrounding Near Eastern heroes.
A remarkable escape from death in infancy
seems to have been a folk-history device
to show that a leader was approved by the gods.

Whether the rescue of Moses is factual or symbolic,
the author seeks to authenticate Moses'
divine mission to lead the people.

ADULTHOOD OF MOSES

In his twenties, Moses got into serious trouble.
He struck and killed an Egyptian foreman
for maltreating a Hebrew slave.
Fearful, he fled to Midian,
where he took up employment as a shepherd.

CALL OF MOSES

One day, while grazing his sheep in Midian,
he noticed a nearby bush on fire.
There wasn't anything alarming about it.
Occasionally a dried sagebrush caught fire
in the hot sun, blazed a moment, and died out.
But this time the fire didn't go out.
Moses decided to go over and find out why not.

GOD   *Come no nearer!*
      Remove the sandals from your feet,
      for the place where you stand
      is holy ground.

      I am the God of your father,
      the God of Abraham,
      the God of Isaac,
      the God of Jacob. . . .

      I have witnessed
      the affliction of my people in Egypt. . . .
      I will send you to Pharaoh
      to lead my people, the Israelites,
      out of Egypt.

MOSES *Who am I*
      that I should go to Pharaoh
      and lead the Israelites out of Egypt?

GOD   *I will be with you. . . .*

MOSES *When I go to the Israelites*
      and say to them,
      "The God of your fathers
      has sent me to you,"
      if they ask me, "What is his name?"
      what am I to tell them?

GOD   *I am who am.*
      This is what you shall tell the Israelites:
      I AM sent me to you. . . .
      This is my name forever;
      this is my title for all generations.

          EXODUS 3:4–15

Yahweh

The expression "I am who am"
introduces the Hebrew proper name for God.
Designated by the four letters YHWH,
it is usually translated "LORD" in English Bibles.
The original meaning of YHWH is uncertain,
but a number of scholars suggest the translation,
"I am who am," that is,
"I cannot be named or defined."

Latter-day Jews
never pronounced the sacred name YHWH.
Thus, its original pronunciation became lost.
After some study, medieval scholars decided
to pronounce it Jehovah.

Today, no scholar holds this to be the original
Hebrew pronunciation,
even though some sects still use it.
Modern scholars,
with the newer resources at their disposal,
now believe YHWH was pronounced Yahweh.

Commenting on the burning bush,
one biblical expert makes this observation:

      Understanding the Old Testament
        BERNHARD W. ANDERSON

It should be read
with religious imagination and empathy,
as one would read a piece of poetry;
for it communicates a dimension of meaning
that cannot be cramped
into the limits of precise prose. . . .

Whatever Moses saw with his naked eye
was transformed into a religious "sign"
of the divine presence.
Moses' vision awakened the realization
that he was truly standing on holy ground.

He, indeed, encountered
the "unnameable" and the "undefinable."

71

Story in Stone

Egypt's history began around 3000 B.C.,
when Menes, the first pharaoh,
united its upper and lower "kingdoms."

Around 2600, its "Old Kingdom" period began,
and pharaohs, like Djoser,
ushered in the great age of pyramid building.

Around 2200, a north-south split occurred.
It healed around 2000,
and Egypt began its "Middle Kingdom" period.
This lasted till the Hyksos invasion in 1786.

In 1567 Ahmose I threw out the Hyksos
and launched Egypt's "New Kingdom" period.
During this great era, pharaohs like Rameses II
built monuments that boggle our imaginations.

In 1100 B.C., Egypt's day in the sun ended,
and desert sands buried its ancient glory.

Rameses II,
Egypt's greatest builder.

This temple of Amun
would swallow up St. Patrick's Cathedral in New York.
Taking 2,000 years to build, its columns
are ringed with the boasts of the pharaohs who built it.
The temple is part of a 60-acre complex at Luxor.

Close-up view before engineers began moving the
temple. The stone figure, nestled between the two feet
(center of photo), is about the size of a man.
This gives us an idea of the size of these giant figures.

Carved into the sandstone cliffs on the Nile at Abu Simbel, this temple of Rameses II extended deep into the rock. In 1965, engineers saved it from the waters of the Aswan Dam by cutting it into 30-ton blocks and hoisting it to the dry ground.

View from inside, looking out. Huge columns and walls, blanketed with reliefs and inscriptions, give the temple an atmosphere of awe.

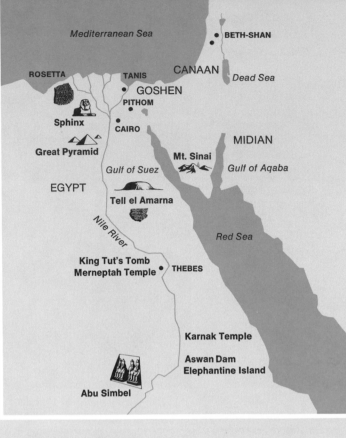

18
The Night That Was Different

Moses returned to Egypt from Midian.
He reported his God-experience to the people
and they believed him.
Then Moses confronted Pharaoh.

MOSES	*Thus says the LORD,* *the God of Israel:* *Let my people go. . . .*
PHARAOH	*Who is the LORD,* *that I should heed his plea* *to let Israel go?* *I do not know the LORD;* *even if I did,* *I would not let Israel go.*

EXODUS 5:1-2

Nine times Moses made his demands.
Nine times Pharaoh shouted, "No!"
After each confrontation, a plague struck Egypt:

the Nile changed to blood,
frogs carpeted the land,
gnats swarmed as thick as dust,
flies buzzed everywhere,
boils infected man and beast,
animals toppled over sick,
hail splintered trees and plants,
locusts devoured what the hail missed,
darkness blanketed the land.

After all of this, Pharaoh still remained obstinate.

FINAL PLAGUE

Then the LORD told Moses,
"One more plague
will I bring upon Pharaoh and upon Egypt.
After that he will let you depart.
In fact, he will not merely let you go;
he will drive you away. . . ."
Moses then said, "Thus says the LORD:
At midnight
I will go forth through Egypt.
Every first-born in this land shall die."

EXODUS 11:1-5

Then God instructed Moses
to prepare the Israelites for the tenth plague.
They must kill a lamb and smear its blood
on the outer door frame of each Israelite house.
Once this is done, they must stay indoors.

For the LORD will go by,
striking down the Egyptians.
Seeing the blood . . .
the LORD will pass over that door.

EXODUS 12:23

Moreover, the Israelites, dressed for departure,
with sandals on their feet and staff in hand,
must eat the lamb.

[God concludes:]
"This day shall be a memorial feast for you,

which all your generations shall celebrate. . . .
When your children ask you,
'What does this rite of yours mean?'
you shall reply,

'This is the Passover sacrifice of the LORD,
who passed over the houses of the Israelites . . . ,
when he struck down the Egyptians,
he spared our houses.'". . .

At midnight
the LORD slew every first-born in the land . . .
and there was loud wailing throughout Egypt,
for there was not a house without its dead. . . .

Pharaoh summoned Moses and Aaron and said,
"Leave my people at once,
you and the Israelites with you! . . .
Take your flocks, too, and your herds,
as you demanded, and begone."

EXODUS 12:14, 26–32

THE PLAGUES REVISITED

Few biblical events
have caused more discussion than the plagues.
The Old Testament does not call them "miracles,"
but "signs" (*'ot* in Hebrew).
Here are two observations concerning them.

Everyday Life in Bible Times
NATIONAL GEOGRAPHIC SOCIETY

Extraordinary as they seem,
these plagues have natural counterparts today.
Silt and microbes
sometimes pollute and redden the Nile in flood.
"The River,"
laments a text ancient in Moses' day, "is blood.
If one drinks of it,
one rejects it as human and thirsts for water."

Floodlands breed gnats and mosquitoes;
even ancients took refuge under netting.

Frogs breed when the river peaks;
hordes hop ashore from freak floods. . . .

As frog swarms die, vermin breed on the carcasses.
Pests such as the screwworm fly
inflame skin of man and beast,
sometimes killing animals.

Though hailstorms rarely hit Egypt,
locusts menace it still.
Some African swarms blanket 2,000 square miles,
stripping the land, fouling the air with excrement,
triggering epidemics as locust bodies rot.
Modern Egypt has tried traps, poisons,
even flamethrowers, but swarms still threaten
devastation about once a decade.
And the khamsin still howls—
the hot desert sandstorm that darkens spring days.

This Karnak carving shows Egyptian slaves carrying a boat. Most ancient countries had slaves. A fourth century B.C. census from Attica (Greece) lists 400,000 slaves, half of the total population.

Interestingly, the Sumerian word for "slave" is *foreigner*, suggesting the source of most slaves. Laws distinguished between native and foreign slaves. Slaves were usually owned by private individuals.

Biblical Eighth Plague Hits Again
DAVID N. NICHOL

London—*Today, more than 3,200 years later,*
this biblical eighth plague . . .
is on the march again. . . .

Restless swarms of locusts
have been extensively reported.
One recently seen in Ethiopia
covered eighty square miles.
A single swarm spotted over Africa's
Somali Republic in 1958 was measured
from the air.
It covered 400 square miles.

With an estimated density of 100,000,000
to 200,000,000 insects to the square mile
this one swarm
represented a minimum of 40 billion locusts. . . .

Though each locust weighs only about two grams,
it eats its own weight every day.
Small as this figure may be, the daily food
requirement for a swarm of 40 billion locusts . . .

amounts to about 90,000 tons.
This would be enough to feed 400,000 people
for a year on the sparse Middle Eastern diet. . . .

A single swarm may travel as far as 3,000 miles,
leaving its wake of destruction,
before it settles to begin a new breeding process.

THE POINT?

What conclusions can we draw from these reports?
Were the plagues natural events or not?
Some say yes. Others say no.

Some hold that only the timing was miraculous.
Others say that the last plague had to be miraculous,
because it bypassed the Hebrew firstborn.

All scholars agree, however,
that speculation about the plagues
risks missing the biblical writer's point:
The plagues were signs
that Yahweh was active in Israel's deliverance.

Freedom Celebration

Today, Jews still celebrate the Passover,
which commemorates their freedom.
It is highlighted by a meal called the seder,
which means "service."
Taking place in the evening,
it begins with the youngest present asking:
"Why does this night differ from all other nights?"

Thus, 3,000 years later,
Yahweh's command to the Israelites
on the eve of the tenth plague is still carried out.
Orthodox Jews still retain the original spirit
of the Passover, or Pesah.
Reform Jews, however, have broadened its meaning.
Here is one statement of the expanded spirit.

The New Haggadah
MORDECAI KAPLAN, EUGENE KOHN,
AND IRA EISENSTEIN, EDITORS

*We have dedicated this festival tonight
to the dream and hope of freedom,
the dream and hope that have filled the hearts of men
from the time our Israelite ancestors
went forth out of Egypt. . . .*

*But the freedom we strive for
means more than broken chains.
It means liberation from all those enslavements
that warp the spirit and blight the mind,
that destroy the soul
even when they leave the flesh alive.
For men can be enslaved in more ways than one.*

*Men can be enslaved to themselves. . . .
When luziness or cowardice keeps them
from doing what they know to be the right,
when ignorance blinds them . . . they are slaves.*

*Men can be enslaved by poverty and inequality.
When the fear of need drives them to dishonesty
and violence, to defending the guilty
and accusing the innocent—they are slaves. . . .*

*Men can be enslaved by intolerance. When Jews
are forced to give up their Jewish way of life,
to abandon their Torah, to neglect
their sacred festivals, to leave off rebuilding
their ancient homeland—they are slaves.*

*Pesah calls upon us to put an end to all slavery!
Pesah cries out in the name of God,
"Let my people go."
Pesah summons us to freedom.*

19

The Exodus

Now, . . . Pharaoh let the people go. . . .
The Lord preceded them,
in the daytime by means of a column of cloud . . .
and at night by means of a column of fire. . . .

When it was reported . . .
that the people had fled, Pharaoh and his servants
changed their minds about them. . . .
The Egyptians, then, pursued them. . . .

Then Moses stretched out his hand over the sea,
and the LORD swept the sea
with a strong east wind throughout the night
and so turned it into dry land.
When the water was thus divided,
the Israelites marched into the sea on dry land,
with the water like a wall to their right and left.

The Egyptians followed in pursuit. . . .
And the LORD so clogged their chariot wheels
that they could hardly drive. . . .

Then the LORD told Moses,
"Stretch out your hand over the sea. . . ."
So Moses stretched out his hand over the sea,
and at dawn the sea flowed back
to its normal depth . . .
[and] covered the chariots and the charioteers
of Pharaoh's whole army. . . .

When Israel saw . . . the great power
that the LORD had shown against the Egyptians,
they feared the LORD and believed in him
and his servant Moses.

EXODUS 13:17, 21; 14:5–9, 21–31

COLUMN OF FIRE

Those who believe that Yahweh used
ordinary events (but in an extraordinary manner)
to deal with Israel
ponder the mention of the columns of fire and clouds.
Could these guiding phenomena have been a volcano
that steered the people
through the desert toward Mount Sinai?

Most scholars, however, have found no evidence
of active volcanoes at this time in the Sinai desert.
They prefer to interpret the columns
as expressions of Israel's experience
of divine guidance during their ventures.

SEA CROSSING

The Bible says 600,000 people crossed the sea.
Most scholars think this figure is intended
in a symbolic sense, not a mathematical sense.
It merely designates a number beyond counting.

The Bible calls the crossing zone *yam suph*.
Early translators interpreted this to mean Red Sea,
but most modern scholars now believe Reed Sea
would be the more accurate description.
This would suggest that the area was a marshland,
typical of lake environs.
The biblical account seems to support this inference
when it says of the Egyptians:
"The LORD so clogged their chariot wheels
that they could hardly drive" (Exodus 14:25).

Whether the onrushing wall of water
was an actual tidelike phenomenon
or a poetic flourish is debated.

WHAT WAS IT LIKE?

What would it be like to relive Israel's flight?
What lay between them and Mount Sinai?
These questions prompted a modern reporter
to retrace the route probably taken by Moses
and the Israelites. His account follows:

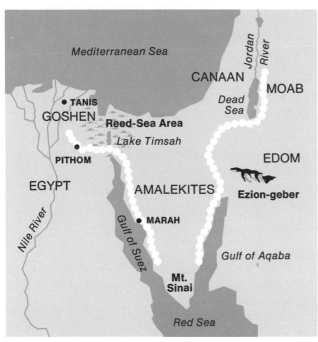

The general route followed by Moses
and the Israelltes to Mount Sinai.
Sometime after the Sinai experience,
they proceeded to Moab,
where they encamped before entering the Promised Land.

To Sinai and the Promised Land
JOHN PUTNAM

Two-thirty A.M.
A knock at the door and a lusty shout,
"Rise . . . we're on our way to Sinai!"
I roll out of a sagging bed . . .
and slip into sweater and slacks.

Doors slam and the murmur of voices builds
as we gather in the dining room
to gulp down bread and eggs.

We pile suitcases and food cartons
atop Suez taxis—old American cars
strengthened for desert work. . . .
We slide through dark, silent streets
to the Suez Canal and cross,

three cars at a time,
on a rattling, wheezing ferry.

Listening
to the parting of ink-black waters at the bow,
I think of those who have journeyed to Sinai
before us: Stone Age hunters,
prisoners bound for Pharaoh's mines . . .
and the children of Israel. . . .

The ferry bumped,
and we stepped ashore on Sinai's fabled sands. . . .
We rolled south along the coastal road. . . .
Our cars left the road
and soon trailed plumes of desert dust.
Here began the Biblical "wilderness of Sin."

On each side rose jagged peaks. . . .
Tumbleweed-like bushes clung to dust.
Dr. Raymond McLain broke the awesome silence:
"As a boy, I pictured the 'wilderness'
as a dark forest, like those I knew in Kentucky.
How different, and even more forceful,
is this wilderness of rock."

Little wonder that here the children of Israel
murmured against Moses, "for ye have brought us
forth into this wilderness, to kill this whole
assembly with hunger" (Exodus 16:3).

Semites knew this land before the Hebrews fled
this way. In these mountains
lay Pharaoh's turquoise mines. . . .
The walls of one mine bear Canaanite characters
carved by Semitic slaves.
These famous proto-Sinaitic inscriptions,
among the oldest writings in our alphabet,
date from the 15th century B.C.
From these crude pictographic symbols—
altered by Phoenicians, Greeks, and Romans—
developed the letters in which this story is written. . . .

Our caravan moved on, past rock-cut cubicles
where Christian hermits once lived
and Bedouin now bury their dead.
We stopped before a stand of willowy tamarisks.

Clouds

A popular "Peanuts" cartoon
shows Charlie Brown, Linus, and Lucy
lying on a hillside studying the sky.
Lucy says: "You can see lots of things in clouds
if you use your imagination. What do you see?"
Linus answers: "Well, those clouds there
look like a map of British Honduras.
And those over there look like Thomas Eakins,
the artist.
And that group there reminds me of the stoning
of Stephen."
Lucy is impressed: "Excellent, Linus!
What do you see, Charlie Brown?"
"Well, I was going to say I saw a ducky
and a horsie, but I changed my mind."

Clouds reminded Hebrews of God's presence
among them. For example, they recalled
God's guidance in their flight from Egypt,
when God preceded them with a cloud.
They also reminded them of God's instructions
to Moses at the foot of Mount Sinai:

*"I am coming to you in a dense cloud,
so that when the people hear me speaking
with you, they may always have faith in you."*

EXODUS 19:9

After the Sinai event, the people built
a portable shrine to house the two stone tablets
containing God's covenant agreement with them
When it was finished, a "cloud covered it"
(Numbers 9:15).

Finally, when Solomon built the temple
in Jerusalem, a cloud descended upon it
(1 Kings 8:10).

Other biblical references to clouds
as signs of God's presence include
Exodus 34:5, Isaiah 19:1, Ezekiel 1:4,
Daniel 7:13, Matthew 17:5, Acts 1:9,
1 Thessalonians 4:17, Revelation 14:14.

*"Manna trees!" shouted Otto.
"In spring insects puncture their bark,
drink the sap, and exude a clear liquid
which solidifies as a sugary globule.
This may well be the flaky substance,
fine 'as hoar frost on the ground,' which sustained
the Hebrews when they faced starvation."*

*Stark mountains rose before us,
only to fall away as we twisted and turned onward.
We rounded a final corner and there . . .
Mount Sinai. . . .*

*We . . . mounted Bedouin saddles
of wood and cloth. . . .*

*Halfway up we dismounted
and climbed rough steps, resting often.
Bare mountains seemed to surge around us
like storm-tossed waves. . . .
At last, we gathered at the small chapel
that marks the top and listened
to a reading of the covenant struck here
by God and His Chosen People:*

*"I am the Lord thy God,
which have brought thee out of the land of Egypt,
out of the house of bondage.
Thou shalt have no other gods before me. . . ."*

*In this awesome setting
the words of each commandment in Exodus 20
rang like hammer blows on an anvil. . . .*

*A few weeks later,
chatting on a hotel terrace by the Sea of Galilee,
I mentioned my trek to an Israeli acquaintance.
His eyes lit up.
He had been there too, briefly, in 1956
when Israeli paratroopers fluttered down on Sinai.
"I'm not a religious man," he mused.
"But there were archeologists with us.
We watched them work,
and we read the Torah, and we studied the land.
And you know, it fit . . . it all fit."*

Desert Days

Striking "signs" accompanied Israel's journey
from Egypt to Mount Sinai.
The psalmist set them to music for all to sing.

The LORD led his people with a cloud by day,
and all night with a glow of fire.
He cleft the rocks in the desert
and gave them water in copious floods. . . .
He rained manna upon them for food . . .
and, like the sand of the sea,
winged fowl fell in the midst of their camp.

PSALM 78:14–15, 24–28

Exodus 17 describes Moses
getting water from a rock by striking it with a rod.
Some people read the episode skeptically,
until British Major C. S. Jarvis reported
seeing water gush from a limestone rock,
when a sergeant of the Sinai Camel Corps
accidentally perforated "the smooth hard crust"
with his shovel.

Similarly,
the "rain of quail" upon the camp of Israel
was once winked at by some sophisticated readers.
Once again, however, history and a knowledge
of the desert shed new light on the episode.

Geographical Twins a World Apart
DAVID S. BOYER

Every year great migrations of quail
wing their way across the Mediterranean
and Red Seas en route between Europe and Africa.
Even today Bedouin of the Sinai peninsula
catch the exhausted birds
after their long flight over water.

A similar incident is recounted
in the histories of the Mormon pioneers.
The last refugees to leave Nauvoo, Illinois,
crossed the Mississippi River in late September
of 1846. Sick and without shelter,
they subsisted for ten days on parched corn.

Then says the History of Brigham Young,
"The Lord sent flocks of quail,
which lit . . . upon the ground within their reach,
which the saints, and even the sick
caught with their hands until they were satisfied."

The quail "in immense quantities had attempted
to cross the river," another Mormon writer added,
"but it being beyond their strength,
had dropped . . . on the bank."

What conclusion should we draw from all this?
Were the desert episodes truly miraculous,
or merely linked to natural causes?

You will find Bible readers on both sides.
One thing—the most important thing—is clear.
As Israelites recalled the chain of striking events
that marked their difficult days in the desert,
they were convinced beyond a shadow of doubt
that the guiding hand of God
was at work in their lives.

This is all that mattered to them.
In the end, it is all that matters to us, as well.

The mountains of the Sinai jut from the desert
floor like great stone altars.
They speak of
protection, danger, challenge, and mystery.

20

The Mountain Encounter

The historian shakes his head.
How did it happen?
How did a band of ex-slaves,
with no organization, no education, no apparent
way to survive, change the tide of history?
For this is exactly what Moses and the Hebrews did.

The historian shakes his head:
"How do you explain such a phenomenon?"

The biblical writer's own explanation is simple.
At the foot of a mountain in the Sinai desert,
the Israelite community encountered Yahweh.
That experience utterly transformed them.

Here's a modern journalist's firsthand report
of a visit
to the famous spot where it all happened.

Which Mountain Did Moses Climb?

GORDON GASKILL

I've seen many deserts,
but none like the gaunt tortured wasteland
sliding away under the wings of our small plane.
Somewhere down there, around 1250 B.C.,
Moses and his people made the most famous
Long March in all history. . . .
On the shore of the Gulf of Suez,
we piled into a jeep and set off. . . .

At last, 5,000 feet above sea level,
we wound up in a narrow chasm-like valley
and stopped by the walls of an ancient monastery,
St. Catherine's.
I know of no other spot
that so justifies the phrase "out of this world." . . .
Close by the southern wall of St. Catherine's,
the mountain rears up so steeply that it keeps the
monastery in shadow part of the day.
The climb to the top takes two or three hours. . . .

At the very top is a small flat area. . . .
Here, it is said, Moses lived 40 days and nights
communing with God. . . .
A Muslim mosque and tiny Christian chapel
mark the spot. The view in all directions
is stupendous: over great gulfs and deserts,
and rearing peaks of granite
that cast ever-longer purple shadows
as the sun sinks over Africa.

Next morning,
we arose so early the sky was still black.
Soon the bell of the monastery began pealing out
its morning call as it has for centuries,
33 strokes, one for each year of Jesus' life.

Around us,
people of three great faiths were waking up, too.
Christian pilgrims began making coffee.

A party of Jewish hikers
began crawling from sleeping bags,
to climb to the summit

while the morning was still fresh and cool.
Our Muslim driver began touching his head
to the ground in the first Muslim prayer of the day,
bowing toward holy Mecca. . . .

As we drove away,
the valleys and desert were still in shadow,
but the sun was rising fast out of Arabia,
and I saw its first rays strike the top
of Mount Moses to bathe it in flaming gold. . . .

Was it up there that it really happened?
Or was it on the peak . . . farther north?
Or was it one of the many other peaks
other scholars have suggested? . . .
No matter how plausibly professors argue,
the Mount Moses now fading away behind us
would remain, for most people,
the place it really happened.

BIBLICAL STORY

Here is the biblical story of what happened
at Mount Sinai.

NARRATOR *In the third month after their departure*
from the land of Egypt . . .
the Israelites
came to the desert of Sinai. . . .
While Israel was encamped here
in front of the mountain,
Moses went up the mountain to God.

GOD *Tell the Israelites:*
You have seen for yourselves . . .
how I bore you up on eagle wings
and brought you here to myself.
Therefore, if you hearken to my voice
and keep my covenant,
you shall be my special possession,
dearer to me than all other people. . . .
You shall be to me a kingdom of priests,
a holy nation. . . .

NARRATOR   *Moses went and summoned
the elders of the people.
He set before them all that the LORD
had ordered him to tell them. . . .*

PEOPLE   *Everything the LORD has said,
we will do. . . .*

NARRATOR   *On the morning of the third day
there were peals of thunder . . .
and a heavy cloud over the mountain,
and a very loud trumpet blast,
so that all the people in the camp
trembled. . . .
When the LORD came down to the top
of Mount Sinai, he summoned Moses
to the top of the mountain. . . .
Then God
delivered all these commandments:*

GOD   *I, the LORD, am your God,
who brought you out of Egypt,
that place of slavery.*

*You shall not have other gods
besides me.
You shall not carve idols. . . .*

*You shall not take the name
of the LORD, your God, in vain. . . .*

*Remember
to keep holy the sabbath. . . .*

*Honor your father
and your mother. . . .*

You shall not kill.

You shall not commit adultery.

You shall not steal.

*You shall not bear false witness
against your neighbor. . . .*

*You shall not covet your neighbor's
wife . . .
nor anything else that belongs to him.*
EXODUS 19:1–20; 20:1-17

NARRATOR   *Moses then wrote down
all the words of the LORD and,
rising early the next day,
he erected at the foot of the mountain
an altar and twelve pillars
for the twelve tribes of Israel.
Then, having sent certain young men
of the Israelites
to . . . sacrifice young bulls . . .
Moses took half of the blood . . .
and sprinkled it on the people. . . .*

MOSES   *This is the blood of the covenant
which the LORD has made with you
in accordance with all these words. . . .*

NARRATOR   *The glory of the LORD
settled upon Mount Sinai.*
EXODUS 24:4–8, 16

84

IDENTITY AND DESTINY

This dramatic covenant experience
transformed the Israelites
from a band of ex-slaves into a chosen people.
It gave them an identity and a destiny.
Here's how one modern Jew expresses it.

Jewish Existence and Survival
WILL HERBERG

Israel is not a "natural" nation;
it is, indeed, not a nation at all
like the nations of the world.
It is a supernatural community, called into being
by God to serve his eternal purposes in history.

It is a community
created by God's special act of covenant,
first with Abraham . . .
and then, supremely, with Israel collectively
at Sinai. . . .
Apart from the covenant, Israel is as nothing
and Jewish existence a mere delusion.
The covenant is at the very heart of the Jewish
self-understanding of its own reality.

Israel experienced God at a specific point in time
and at a particular place on the globe.
This gives the religion of Israel its uniqueness.

Apart from Christianity and Islam,
which both owe their origin, in part, to Israel,
no other religion came about as did Israel's.
Other religions sprang from nature;
Israel's sprang from history.

Consistent with the conception of her origin,
Israel saw Yahweh's law not as something negative.
Rather, Israel saw it as something deeply positive.
The commandments were concrete signs

Modern Jews
celebrate the fall festival of Simchat Torah
(Rejoicing in the law).
The faces reflect the psalmist's words:
"How I love your law, O LORD! . . ." (Psalm 119:97)

of God's personal love for his people.
Only in this light can modern readers appreciate
the psalmist when he prays:

How I love your law, O LORD!
It is my meditation all the day. . . .
I keep your decrees and love them deeply.
PSALM 119:97, 167

Israel saw God's law as freeing them
"from" their own ignorance and passion
and freeing them
"for" a life of love and service.

Israel's law is spelled out in the Book of
Deuteronomy with remarkable detail and clarity.
In Moses' own words,
it is not mysterious and remote.

It is not up in the sky, that you should say,
"Who will go up in the sky to get it for us
and tell us of it, that we may carry it out?"

Nor is it across the sea, that you should say,
"Who will cross the sea to get it for us
and tell us of it, that we may carry it out?"

No, it is something very near to you,
already in your mouths and in your hearts.
DEUTERONOMY 30:12–14

Israel's law is totally uncompromising toward evil.
The law cannot tolerate it.
This is mirrored in numerous laws,
such as the following:

If an unjust witness takes the stand against a man . . .
and if after a thorough investigation
the judges find that the witness is a false witness
and has accused his kinsman falsely,
you shall do to him
as he planned to do to his kinsman.
Thus shall you purge the evil from your midst.
DEUTERONOMY 19:16–19

But Israel's laws also showed
deep sensitivity and humanity.

85

After a priest had admonished Israelite soldiers
to trust in Yahweh, an officer was instructed
to make this announcement before battle:

Is there anyone who is afraid and weakhearted?
Let him return home,
lest he make his fellows fainthearted as himself.

DEUTERONOMY 20:8

On several occasions,
the Bible reports that large numbers of soldiers
stepped from the ranks and did return home.

Showing similar sensitivity to human nature,
we find this law:

When a man is newly wed,
he need not go out on a military expedition,
nor shall any public duty be imposed on him.
He shall be exempt for one year for the sake of
his family, to bring joy to the wife he has married.

DEUTERONOMY 24:5

Finally, we find laws such as the following:

You shall not violate the rights of the alien
or of the orphan,
nor take the clothing of a widow as a pledge.

DEUTERONOMY 24:17

When you knock down the fruit of your olive trees,
you shall not go over the branches a second time;
let what remains
be for the alien, the orphan, and the widow.

DEUTERONOMY 24:20

COVENANT FORMAT

The external format of the Sinai covenant
(like God's covenant with Abraham)
took a pattern familiar to ancient peoples.
It closely paralleled pacts made between
powerful kings and lesser kings in Mesopotamia.

In these pacts (suzerainty treaties),
the greater king (suzerain) pledged certain favors
to lesser kings (vassals) who, in turn,

pledged special allegiance to the greater king.
Likewise, the blood ceremony,
by which Moses sealed the covenant,
was not an unfamiliar practice in ancient times.
A fourth-century B.C. historian has preserved
a description of the "blood ceremony"
used by Scythians.

Histories, IV
HERODOTUS

When Scythians
swear an oath or make a solemn compact,
they fill a large earthenware bowl with wine
and drop into it a little of the blood
of the two parties to the oath. . . .

Then they dip into the bowl a sword . . .
and speak a number of prayers;
lastly, the two contracting parties
and their chief followers
drink a mixture of wine and blood.

Ancient blood rites such as this
help us to understand
the symbolic action of Moses at Mount Sinai.
When Moses sprinkled half the blood on the altar
(symbol of God) and half on the people,
he was showing that a real life bond now existed
between God and Israel.

FINAL NOTE

Some students of the Bible are surprised to learn
that some religious groups
number the Ten Commandments differently.
For example, Jews regard the words
"I am the LORD your God" as the first commandment.
Most Christians treat this statement
as an introduction to the sentence that follows,
"You shall not have other gods besides me."

Jews treat the sentence
"You shall not have other gods besides me"
as the first part of the second commandment

This Jewish elder plays a *shofar* at the conclusion of Yom Kippur. Made from a hollow ram's horn, it is shaped by plunging it into boiling water. Often the horn was engraved and a mouthpiece attached. The shofar gives off a piercing, nonmusical sound.

Life and Worship

The covenant experience
introduced a new life-style into Israel.
The Ten Commandments
provided the guidelines for it.
Likewise, Israel's covenant experience
introduced a new worship style among its people.
We find it described in the Book of Leviticus.
This book derived its name from the tribe of Levi.
The Levites were set apart by Moses
to serve as the priestly ministers of the people.

Indicative of Israel's new worship style
is the Day of Atonement, Yom Kippur.
This day was set aside annually to seek forgiveness
from God for the sins of the past year.
It was the only day of the year
when Aaron (or the reigning high priest)
entered the Holy of Holics, the inner sanctuary
that housed the Ark, containing the two tablets
upon which the covenant terms were inscribed.

Standing alone, behind the sanctuary curtain,
the high priest sprinkled blood
to atone for the sins of the entire community.
After this ceremony, an unusual rite followed.

When he has completed the atonement rite . . .
Aaron shall bring forward the live goat.
Laying both hands on its head,
he shall confess over it all the sinful faults . . .
of the Israelites, and so put them on the goat's head.
He shall then
have it led into the desert by an attendant. . . .
The man who has led away the goat . . .
shall wash his garments and bathe his body in water;
only then may he enter the camp.

LEVITICUS 16:20–26

which includes, for them, the words
"You shall not carve idols."

In a similar way, other variations arise.
The important thing, however,
is not the numbering of the commandments,
but the commandments themselves.

Although this rite was externally dramatic,
the important thing was not the rite,
but the internal spirit that accompanied it.
A spirit of internal repentance and restitution
was essential.

21
On Eagle's Wings

An Arab saying reads:

When Allah finished making the desert
he had two lumps of clay left.
With one he made the camel;
with the other he made the palm tree.

Without the camel and the palm tree,
humans could not survive the desert.
Even with them, the desert tends to exclude people.
One of the most hostile features of the desert
is the unpredictable sandstorm.
It blows up suddenly and, just as suddenly,
vanishes into nowhere. One Sahara sandstorm
wiped out a caravan of 2,000 men and 1,800 camels.

On other occasions,
the desert is visited by rare rainstorms.
These storms leave in their wake
a lovely array of instant flowers
that spring up, bloom, and die overnight.

For all its delicate beauty, however,
the desert is a forbidding place for people.
More than any other land surface,
it jostles human pride.
It speaks to people of their human limitations.

INTO THE DESERT

Moses and the people stayed at Mount Sinai
for about a year.
Then they broke camp and set out into the desert,
in search of the land Yahweh promised them.

The desert into which the Hebrew caravans went
was made up of three regions:
stretches of sand, where nothing grew;
expanses of rock, with an occasional spring;
and patches of semiarid land, with just enough
growth to nourish sheep and goats.

This vast wilderness of sand and rock
became the stage for the 40-year-long drama
of Israelite history that now began.
The fourth book of the Bible, the Book of Numbers,
narrates it with disarming candor and honesty.

Once the Israelites penetrated the desert,
discouragement set in.
The honeymoon days of Mount Sinai quickly faded.
Any desert traveler who has experienced
the blazing heat of the Sinai can understand the
Israelite reaction. The sun beats down torridly,
and the oven-hot winds of the khamsin
take their toll on even the hardiest nomad.

This does not excuse the Israelite reaction,
but it does help us appreciate why the people
began to hanker for the green fields of the Nile delta.

"Spread out your tent cloths . . . lengthen your ropes
and make firm your stakes" (Isaiah 54:2).
Hebrews probably lived in tents like this one,
which belongs to a modern Bedouin
of the Negeb Desert.

Soon, discouragement gave way to outright protest
and dissatisfaction.

Would that we had meat for food!
We remember the fish we used to eat without cost
in Egypt, and the cucumbers, the melons . . .
and the garlic.
But now we are famished;
we see nothing before us but this manna.

NUMBERS 11:4–6

The situation went from bad to worse,
and the people singled out Moses as their target.

Why have you brought the LORD's community
into this desert
where we and our livestock are dying?
Why did you lead us out of Egypt,
only to bring us to this wretched place
which has neither grain nor figs nor vines . . . ?
Here there is not even water to drink!

NUMBERS 20:4–5

Soon, threats of rebellion were hurled at Moses.
A band of rebels confronted him to his face.

Enough from you! . . .
Are you not satisfied . . .
to make us perish in the desert,
that you must now lord it over us?
Far from bringing us to a land
flowing with milk and honey,
or giving us fields and vineyards for our inheritance,
will you also gouge out our eyes?
No, we will not go.

NUMBERS 16:3, 13–14

Moses stood his ground.
Shortly after the confrontation,
the dissenters met with a violent death.

Rebellion was not the only problem Moses faced.
He and his people had to contend with threats
from without as well.

Foreign kings, on occasion,
refused the Israelites passage through their lands.

An oasis blooms out of rock and sand
near modern Jericho.

END OF AN ERA

Eventually, the end arrived.
After 40 years of wandering,
the Israelites emerged from the desert.
They found themselves
standing on the high plateaus of Moab.
Stretching out before them and below them
lay a luxurious valley as far as the eye could see.
It was the Promised Land.

Moses gave orders to pitch camp.
Then he called the people together for instructions
before entering the land.
The Book of Deuteronomy records the gist and spirit
of his series of instructions.
Moses explained how Israel's desert experience
was a means of testing their loyalty to Yahweh.

Remember how for forty years now the LORD . . .
has directed all your journeying in the desert,

89

The Biblical Way of Life

The image of a mother eagle
teaching her young ones to fly
was vividly described recently by a modern observer.

The Biblical Way of Life
BARNABAS AHERN

*I shall never forget the day
that I stood on the barren plain at Petra
with its walls of blood-red rock.
Glancing up,
I saw a large bird soar out from a mountain crag.
Something dropped from its back
like a pellet of lead.
In a moment the pellet unfolded,
and I saw a little bird stretching its wings to fly.*

*Before long, however, the uprush of wind
proved too strong and the little bird,
once more a stone in the sky, began to drop.
In an instant the mother bird swooped down
and caught it on her back
to bear it aloft for a second trial.*

*This time
the young bird sustained itself longer in flight;
but once more it crumpled before the wind
and began to drop.
But the ever-present mother saved it again
for a third testing.
As before, the pellet dropped, the wings opened,
but this time the young bird flew off.*

*so as to test you by affliction
and find out whether or not it was your intention
to keep his commandments.*

*He therefore let you be afflicted with hunger,
and then fed you with manna,
a food unknown to you and your fathers,
in order to show you
that not by bread alone does man live,
but by every word that comes forth
from the mouth of the LORD.*

DEUTERONOMY 8:2–3

*Then Moses recited the words of this song
from beginning to end,
for the whole assembly of Israel to hear:*

*Give ear, O heavens, while I speak. . . .
For I will sing the LORD's renown. . . .
Is he not your father who created you?
Has he not made you and established you?*

*Think back on the days of old. . . .
Ask your elders and they will tell you. . . .
The LORD found them in a wilderness,
a wasteland of howling desert.
He shielded them and cared for them,
guarding them as the apple of his eye.*

*As an eagle incites its nestlings forth
by hovering over its brood,
so he spread his wings to receive them
and bore them up on his pinions.*

DEUTERONOMY 31:30; 32:1–11

DESERT EXPERIENCE

Like Moses' own desert experience,
Israel's desert experience
made the people aware of God in a new way.
The desert served as a schoolroom,
where they learned their infidelity and weakness
and God's fidelity and power.

90

Yahweh had revealed himself to be
a God of loving-kindness,
not a selfish tyrant or a blind force in nature.
Yahweh made a covenant and kept it,
even when Israel failed to do so.
Like an eagle, he rescued the people
when they faltered and failed.

DEATH OF MOSES

The Book of Deuteronomy ends
with Moses' death.

So there, in the land of Moab,
Moses, the servant of the LORD, died . . .
and he was buried in the ravine
opposite Beth-peor in the land of Moab,
but to this day no one knows
the place of his burial. . . .

For thirty days the Israelites wept for Moses
in the plains of Moab,
till they had completed the period of grief.

DEUTERONOMY 34:5–8

It is, indeed, an irony of history
that great leaders who fight valiantly for a cause
often die without enjoying the results of it.
Moses was no exception.

CONCLUSION

The death of Moses
is the concluding entry in the Jewish Torah,
the first five books of the Bible.
These books are Genesis, Exodus, Leviticus,
Numbers, and Deuteronomy.
Sometimes called the Book of Moses,
the Torah is the foundation
upon which the rest of the Old Testament is built.

Modern Desert Experience

Inspired by Israel's experience,
many people today still "go out to the desert"
to try to deepen their awareness of God.
In most cases, it amounts to little more
than a temporary "retreat" from life.
Nevertheless,
it serves the same purpose as the desert of old.

Carl Sandburg expressed the value of the desert
when he said:

A man must get away now and then
to experience loneliness.
Only those who learn how to live with loneliness
can come to know themselves and life.

I go out there and walk and look at the trees
and sky.
I listen to the sounds of loneliness.
I sit on a rock or a stump and say to myself,
"Who are you, Sandburg?
Where have you been,
and where are you going?"

John the Baptist began his career in the desert
(Matthew 3:1).
Jesus entered the desert before his ministry
(Matthew 4:1).
Jesus returned to the desert to pray
(Matthew 14:13, 23).
Jesus led his followers into the desert to teach them
(Matthew 15:33).

22
Library of Books

What the Jews Believe
PHILIP S. BERNSTEIN

When the synagogue of which this writer is now
minister burned down, an Irish policeman
dashed to the ark and seized the Torah.
He handed it to the rabbi
who was rushing up to the building.
"Here," he said, "I have saved your crucifix."
Well, the Jews have no crucifix,
but the policeman had the right idea:
the scrolls are the most sacred symbol of Judaism.

As we have seen, the five scrolls of the Torah
developed piecemeal over many centuries.
For a long time, they were passed on orally.
Around campfires, flickering under desert skies,
Hebrew bards recited the Torah narratives.
There are reports of Jewish bards
who could recite the entire Torah by heart.

Eventually, scribes recorded these narratives.
They wrote to the same impulse
that moved Isaiah the prophet.

Now come, write it on a tablet . . .
that it may be in future days an eternal witness.
                                      ISAIAH 30:8

The Torah, like the Old Testament in general,
evolved not as a single scroll or book,
but as a library of literature
put together by many writers over many centuries.

This explains why the Torah sometimes
contains an idea or comment that developed
long after the historical period with which it deals.
Here some explanation is needed.

FIRST-PERSON HISTORY

Modern people think of history
in the third person.
Israelites thought of it in the first person.
For example, for the Israelites
the Exodus was not something that happened
to *them.*
Rather, it happens to *us.*
We are all there in the person of our ancestors.
Thus, *we* too are freed by it.

Israelites regarded the past as alive.
For each bore within himself the results of the past.
Therefore, he returned "in memory" to the past,
relived it, and made it his own.
Thus, the biblical writer did not hesitate
to add the experiences of later Israelites
to the original story.

All of this annoys the modern historian,
who wishes the biblical writer
would have described the biblical event
precisely the way it happened.

But the biblical writer
had a totally different purpose in mind.
He wanted to do much more than inform readers
about what happened centuries ago.
He wanted his readers to relive the events
and to experience their deeper meaning personally.

Thus, a Black slave singing "Go Down, Moses"
probably had a better grasp
of the deeper meaning of the Exodus event
that the biblical writer sought to communicate
than a biblical scholar sitting at his desk
trying to do a "literary X ray" of the text
to study it objectively.

Ancient Stories

Another "library of literature"
that was passed on orally for centuries
is *Grimm's Fairy Tales*.
It includes such famous literary creations as
Snow White, Cinderella, and Sleeping Beauty.

The Grimm brothers lived in Germany
when such tales were popular among peasants.

Happily Ever After . . .
GEORGE KENT

The stories
were part of a great oral tradition
in existence long before men knew how to write.
Some had been collected and published,
but many others had never been written down,
and only a few aged peasants here and there
remembered them.

When they died, the tales,
some of them dating back thousands of years,
would die with them.

To avoid this situation, the Grimm brothers
tracked down old peasants who knew the stories.
One excellent source was a tailor's wife.

Not only did she tell her stories well, but she
told them each time in exactly the same words.
If she went too fast and was asked to repeat,
she would tell them slowly, without change.

Eventually, the brothers collected 86 stories.
Then, in 1812, a few days after Christmas,
the first of 20,000 editions of the *Fairy Tales*
came off the presses. It was an immediate hit.

Thus it happened that the tales passed
from the oral to the written medium,
much as the Torah did in early biblical times.

DEAD SEA SCROLLS

People ask,
"Do we have the original biblical manuscripts?"
The answer is no.

Remarkably, the oldest copies we have
were discovered between 1947 and 1956.
One of the experts involved with the discoveries
from the start tells how it happened.

The Qumran Story
ROLAND DE VAUX

During the summer of 1947, a young Bedouin . . .
was tending his goats on the shore of the Dead Sea.
One of the goats disappeared.
Trekking up a mountainside in search of it,
Muhammad saw a hole in the spongy, rocky surface.
He threw a stone and heard something break.
Afraid, he ran away.

The next day
Muhammad returned with his cousin. . . .
Climbing through the hole and dropping to the
floor of the cave, they first groped in darkness;
but as their eyes grew accustomed,
they made out some jars with lids against the wall.
They opened one; it was empty.
They opened another one; it too was empty.
They opened still another
and from this one they took some hides that were
rolled up and inscribed and wrapped in linen.
The linen smelled so badly,
that they left it behind and took only the scrolls.

These young men were making
the first discovery of the Dead Sea Scrolls;
it was the beginning of a great adventure.

The discovery turned out to be the start
of the biggest biblical bonanza of all time.

Soon, other caves were found and searched.
Eventually, 11 caves yielded over 600 scrolls
and thousands of fragments from scrolls.
About one-third of these were biblical writings.

The scrolls were apparently hidden in the caves
by Essenes (Jewish "monks"),
who transported them from their Qumran library
when Roman armies invaded the area in A.D. 70.

The scrolls are important for two reasons.
First, they are nearly 1,000 years older
than the oldest manuscripts we previously had.
This brings us amazingly closer
to the original documents.

Second, the nonbiblical scrolls
not only fill a gap of missing Jewish history
between 200 B.C. and A.D. 50,
but also provide important new background data
to help clarify biblical writings from this period.

DATING THE SCROLLS

A fascinating chapter in the Dead Sea Scroll story
was trying to find out how old they were.
Here's how one newspaper reported the event.

Geiger Counters Prove Age of Biblical Scrolls
CATHOLIC UNIVERSE BULLETIN

New York—(NC)—*Pope Pius XII's statement
that "true science" discovers God
in an ever-increasing degree
has been graphically illustrated here.*

*Geiger counters have been used
by nuclear scientists to verify the age
of ancient Hebrew scrolls of the Book of Isaiah. . . .*

Popular Science *monthly, published here,
told the story. . . .*

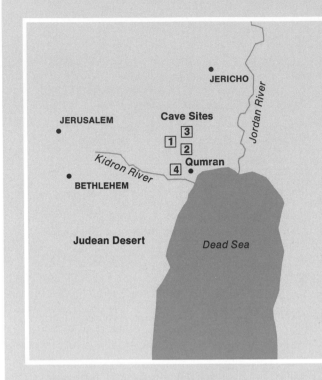

CAVE 1
Found in 1947, this cave yielded a large number of scrolls
(three in their original containers).
Among the discoveries was the Isaiah Scroll.

CAVE 2
Discovered in February 1952 by a Bedouin,
this cave contained a number of important fragments
from the lost Hebrew text of the Book of Sirach.

CAVE 3
Discovered in March 1952,
this cave yielded two badly oxidized copper scrolls.
The scrolls were written in Hebrew and listed sites
where treasures were supposedly buried in Palestine.

CAVE 4
This cave was searched
by archaeologists in September 1952.
Fragments of over 400 manuscripts were found.
Also found were manuscripts concerning
the beliefs and practices of the Qumran community.

Seven other caves were found.
The last cave was found in 1956.
It ranks with caves 1 and 4 as major discoveries.
From it came the famous "Temple Scroll,"
containing 66 columns of religious rules,
festive sacrifice descriptions,
and laws for the king and his army.

Two of the jars from Cave 1.
They served as containers for some of the scrolls.
Ancients frequently used jars like these
to protect important documents.

Hanging by ropes, work crews searched 200 caves
in the Dead Sea area. Eleven caves yielded
treasures of scrolls, coins, and pottery.
Cave 4 (front center section of this cloverleaf)
housed the richest find: over 400 different manuscripts.

Portion of a biblical scroll
found at Qumran.
Stitch marks on the right side
show where the first leaf
of the scroll was sewn
to a prior leaf.
Stitching was done with thread
made from animal gut.
Hebrew writing on the scroll
reads from right to left.

DEAD SEA SCROLLS

Too brittle to be unrolled, these oxidized copper scrolls
were found in Cave 3. They were coated with plastic,
cut with a tiny electric saw,
and pieced together for reading.

Scholars sifted and strained the dirt of cave floors
for precious scroll fragments.
They were then cleaned and pieced together
like a jigsaw puzzle.
This fragment
is inscribed in Hebrew
and dates from
the first century A.D.

*Some language scholars said the scrolls were
written in the Middle Ages. But the Geiger counters
dated them back to the time of Christ,
as archeologists had asserted.*

*Willard F. Libby, University of Chicago radio
chemist, burned fragments of the linen wrappings
around the scrolls to pure carbon.
Then, he measured their radioactivity.*

*He concluded that the flax from which the linen
had been made was alive and breathing 1,917 years
ago. . . . Libby noted, however, that there must be
allowance for error of a century or two either way.*

Popular Science *commented:*

*"When the atom bomb first mushroomed
its message of death and destruction into the sky . . .
there were many who speculated
on the future uses of atomic energy.
But few if any put Bible study on their list.*

*"Now . . .
we find the seeming miracle has come to pass.
Science is revealed as the handmaid of religion. . . .
Cosmic rays that bombarded the earth when Christ
was born have left behind a coded message
for nuclear physicists to decipher.*

*"It was strangely fitting that nuclear scientists,
turning from war to peacetime research,
should undertake the task of determining the age
of an ancient transcript of the Book of Isaiah,
usually considered
the greatest of the Old Testament prophets.*

*"For it was Isaiah who, 25 centuries ago,
envisioned a time when the weapons of war
would be reconverted forever into the tools of peace:*

*"'They shall beat their swords into plowshares,
and their spears into pruning-hooks;
nation shall not lift up sword against nation,
neither shall they learn war any more.'"*

BIBLICAL SCROLLS

Ancient scrolls were usually made of papyrus,
a paperlike product made from marsh reeds
that grew along the Nile in Egypt.
Sheets the size of typing paper
were glued or sewed together
in rolled-up lengths of about 30 feet.

Scribes wrote on the scrolls
in six- or seven-inch columns
that read from right to left.
Writing was done with a reed,
whose point was shredded to form a tiny brush.

In time, animal hide was substituted for papyrus.
This led to a more durable, leather material,
called parchment. By the fourth century after Christ,
parchment replaced both papyrus and animal hide.
This continued until the tenth century,
when paper became the common writing material.
The difficulty and awkwardness of rolling scrolls
led to the first book (codex) around A.D. 200.

When writing on scrolls,
biblical writers did not divide their writings
into chapters and verses—as we now find in the Bible.
Credit for dividing books into chapters
goes to thirteenth-century scholars.
Sixteenth-century scholars took the final step
and numbered the verses for easy reference.

In Jesus' time,
strict precautions surrounded the copying of scrolls.
Duplicates were made for each synagogue
by scribes who followed the strictest instructions.

Looking like green bamboo with tassles on top,
papyrus grew along the banks of the Nile.
The infant Moses was found among papyrus reeds
(Exodus 2:3-5).
Egyptians used the stalks not only for writing materials,
but also for fabrics, rope, blankets, and even boats.
Stalks grew to heights of 20-25 feet.

The Jewish Jesus
ROBERT ARON

*It is the duty of the scribe to prepare himself
by silent meditation for that holy task.
He must have before him a copy of the Pentateuch
[Torah] which has been corrected and verified.*

*The scribe must refer to it continuously
and never write a word from his own memory
or without first pronouncing it aloud.*

*Special care must be taken
in writing the divine names. Before each of these
the scribe must pronounce the formula:
"I intend to write the Holy Name."
If he forgets one single time,
the scroll is unfit to be read in public.
It must be entirely rewritten.*

MINIATURE SCROLLS

The Book of Deuteronomy says of the Torah:

*Take to heart these words. . . .
Bind them at your wrist as a sign*

and let them be as a pendant on your forehead.
Write them on the doorposts
of your houses and on your gates.

DEUTERONOMY 6:6–9

Orthodox Jewish males over 13 years
still wear *tefillin,* or *phylacteries,* at weekday prayer.
These miniature leather boxes contain tiny scrolls
of four biblical passages: Exodus 13:1–10, 13:11–16,
Deuteronomy 6:4–9, 11:13–20.

One box is attached to the left arm (near the heart),
as a sign
that the wearer subjugates his heart to God.

The other is attached to the forehead,
as a sign that he subjugates his mind to God.

Matthew 23:5 reports that Jesus had strong words
for some Pharisees who made a show of these boxes:
"All their works are performed to be seen.
They widen their phylacteries and wear huge tassels."

Many Jews attach a small box, called a *mezuzah,*
to the right doorposts of their houses.
This box contains the Shema and other verses
from Deuteronomy 11:13–20.
It proclaims that the house is Jewish,
and it reminds them that the house
is the temple of God, not too unlike the temple.

The Shema is the first lesson in faith
that the small Jewish child learns.
It is also the last prayer
heard from the lips of a dying Jew.
Recited twice daily by devout Jews, it reads:

Hear, O Israel!
The LORD is our God, the LORD alone!
Therefore, you shall love the LORD, your God,
with all your heart,
and with all your soul,
and with all your strength.

DEUTERONOMY 6:4–5

Biblical Translations

The word *Bible*
comes from the Greek, meaning "book."
The word *testament* comes from the Greek,
meaning "last will and testament" or "covenant."

Thus, for believers, the expression *Old Testament*
refers to God's original covenant with Israel,
mediated by Moses.
The expression *New Testament* refers to God's
final covenant with all people, mediated by Christ.

The Old Testament was translated from Hebrew
into Greek by Jewish scholars around 200 B.C.
It was badly needed, because many Jews living
in Greek-speaking nations no longer knew Hebrew.

The translation was called the *Septuagint* (seventy)
after the number of Alexandrian (Egyptian) Jewish
scholars reputedly involved in the task.

The Septuagint contains a number of writings
that modern Jews omit from their canon
of biblical writings:

Judith	Sirach
Tobit	Baruch
1 and 2 Maccabees	Esther (longer version)
Wisdom	Daniel 3:24–90;13–14

Modern Jews follow ancient Palestinian Jews who,
unlike their Greek-speaking brothers in Alexandria,
gave lesser weight to writings in Greek.
Catholics follow the Septuagint version;
most Protestants do not.

Jerome made the first official Latin translation
of the Bible around A.D. 400.
It was called the *Vulgate* (common use) version.
The first complete English translation
was made in the 14th century.

Time Chart

1200 BC	Joshua invades Canaan
	Judges rule Israel
1175	Philistines enter Canaan
1020	Samuel anoints Saul
1000	David becomes king
960	Solomon succeeds David
922	Solomon dies
	North-South split

Mediterranean Sea

MEGIDDO

SHECHEM

CANAANITES

BETHEL

AI

GIBEON

PHILISTINES

(JERUSALEM)

LACHISH

PEOPLEHOOD NATIONHOOD

Books

Joshua	1 Chronicles
Judges	2 Chronicles 1–10
Ruth	Psalms
1 Samuel	Proverbs
2 Samuel	Song of Songs
1 Kings 1–11	

Over 300 inscribed clay tablets (like these)
were unearthed at Amarna in Egypt.
Called the *Tell el Amarna Letters,*
some were letters from Canaanite city-states
asking Pharaoh Akhenaton to help repel
marauding bands of *Habiru.*
The Pharaoh had his own problems and could not comply.
The letters testify that the situation in Canaan
was deteriorating in the years prior to Israel's actual
invasion of it.

23
Stage of History

"Moses is dead!"
When the reality of these words began to sink in,
some Israelites had second thoughts
about entering the promised land of Canaan.

Their fears were ill-founded, however.
Excavated records testify
to the growing weakness of Canaanite city-states
about this time.

PROMISE FULFILLED

Joshua took command of the Israelites.
Appointed by Moses before he died, Joshua fired
the desert-hardened Hebrews with his own faith.

When preparations were complete,
horns sounded everywhere.
As the great wave of Israelites thundered downhill
to cross the Jordan,
the entire valley echoed with shouts.
Yahweh's ancient promise was being fulfilled.

TO ABRAHAM
Look about you . . . ;
all the land that you see
I will give to you
and your descendants forever.
GENESIS 13:14–15

TO ISAAC
I will give all these lands,
in fulfillment of the oath
that I swore
to your father Abraham.
GENESIS 26:3

TO JACOB
I, the LORD, am the God
of your forefather Abraham
and the God of Isaac;
the land on which you are lying
I will give to you
and your descendants.
GENESIS 28:13

TO ISRAELITES
I will take you as my own . . .
and bring you into the land
which I swore to give
to Abraham, Isaac and Jacob.
EXODUS 6:7–8

TWIN EVENTS

The first Israelites to ford the Jordan
were the priests carrying the Ark of the Covenant.

No sooner had the priestly bearers of the ark
waded into the waters . . .
than the waters flowing from upstream halted . . .
while those flowing downstream . . .
disappeared entirely.
JOSHUA 3:15–16

The entire mass of Israelites
crossed over without accident or loss of life.
The shouts of the people mounted;
Yahweh was with them, as he had been
when they crossed the Reed (Red) Sea.

The stoppage of the Jordan River,
matching the stoppage of the Reed Sea,
points up the connection between the two events.
They were opposite sides of the same coin.
The Reed Sea crossing
marked Israel's *exit* from a land of slavery;
the Jordan crossing
marked Israel's *entry* into a land of freedom.

The stoppage of the Jordan River
has been much discussed. Some ask:
"Could the event have been connected
with an earthquake that blocked the Jordan?"
The question is not out of line
because the Jordan lies along an earth fault,
which has caused many earthquakes in history.

The most recent major earthquake
occurred in 1927, killing over 500 people.
A landslide from this earthquake
blocked the Jordan for 24 hours.
Similar earthquakes occurred in 1906 and 1924.

Besides records of modern earthquakes,
the prophets Amos and Zechariah
refer to them also in their writings.

And the valley
of the LORD's mountain shall be filled up . . .
as it was filled up by the earthquake
in the days of King Uzziah of Judah.

ZECHARIAH 14:5

Some experts think an earthquake
lies behind the story of the sudden destruction
of Sodom and Gomorrah.

The LORD rained down sulphurous fire
upon Sodom and Gomorrah. . . .
As Abraham
looked down toward Sodom and Gomorrah . . .
he saw dense smoke over the land
rising like fumes from a furnace.

GENESIS 19:24–28

Coal and petroleum deposits, still found in this area,
could have ignited and produced this description.

Once again, God's action in Israel's history
could have occurred within the context
of ordinary events and circumstances.
Only the "timing" needs to have been extraordinary.

CELEBRATION

When the Israelites were safe on the other side,
they pitched camp at a site called Gilgal.
To celebrate the event, Joshua took the 12 rocks
from the river, on which the priests stood.
Erecting a monument, he said to the people:

In the future,
when the children among you ask their fathers
what these stones mean,
you shall inform them,
"Israel crossed the Jordan here on dry ground."

For the LORD, your God, dried up the waters . . .
as the LORD, your God, had done at the Red Sea . . .
in order that all the peoples of the earth
may learn that the hand of the LORD is mighty,
and that you may fear the LORD, your God, forever.

JOSHUA 4:21–24

In later years, the Hebrew psalmist composed
this song to commemorate the crossings:

The sea beheld and fled;
Jordan turned back.
The mountains skipped like rams,
the hills like the lambs of the flock.

Why is it, O sea, that you flee?
O Jordan, that you turn back?
You mountains, that you skip like rams?
You hills, like the lambs of the flock?

PSALM 114:3–6

Once settled at Gilgal, the people gathered
to celebrate the feast of the Passover (Joshua 5:10–12).

The Jordan, Palestine's largest river,
coils over 200 water miles in length.
Its average width is about 90 feet;
its depth rarely exceeds 10 feet.

Palestine runs from above the Sea of Galilee
to below the Dead Sea (about 150 miles in length).
It is bound on the west by the Mediterranean Sea
and on the east by the hill country and desert.
The western hills rise 2,500 feet above sea level;
the eastern hills soar to nearly 3,000 feet.
The valley itself goes from 700 feet below sea level
in Galilee to about 1,300 feet below sea level
in the Dead Sea area.

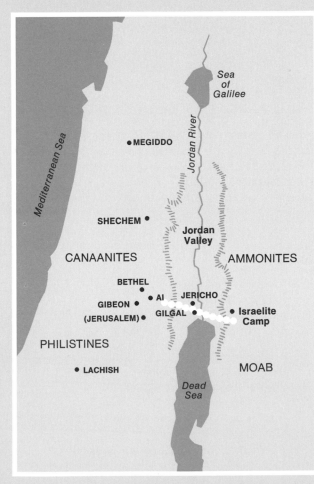

The Land

The land itself was a spectacular site.
To eyes used to the sandy dunes of the Sinai desert,
it must have seemed like a land "flowing with
milk and honey" (Deuteronomy 26:9).

About the size of Vermont,
the land lies in the same latitude as Georgia.
The heart of the land
is a ten-mile-wide valley, running north and south.
The floor of the valley slopes southward,
dropping to about 1,300 feet below sea level.

Walling in both sides of the valley are barren hills.
Looking like piles of unfinished creation,
the hills accentuate its depth.

Though the Sea of Galilee looks peaceful here,
six-foot waves crash along the shoreline
when winds swoop down from the surrounding hills.
Archaeological evidence suggests
the sea was once entirely circled by dwellings.

From these Mediterranean waters,
ancient fishermen caught sea creatures
and extracted their famous purple dyes from them.
Now snorkel divers explore the same waters
along Israel's "Sunshine Coast."

Salt-encrusted driftwood sparkles in the sun.
Lying 1,300 feet below sea level,
and 1,200 feet deep in spots,
the Dead Sea has no outlet.
Arabs claim that in ancient times
no bird could survive flight
across the acrid-smelling waters.

Over the western ridge of hills
sprawls the Mediterranean Sea,
with its exciting cliffs and elegant white beaches.

At the north end of the valley is the Sea of Galilee,
a fisherman's paradise even to this day.
Sixty-five airline miles south is the Dead Sea.
The two seas are linked by the Jordan River.
To an airplane pilot, the river looks like a giant
snake coiling downhill through dark green foliage.

The Dead Sea is the lowest body of water on earth;
its salt content is six times that of the ocean.
Not even the poorest swimmer can sink in it.
An ancient tale
is still told about the water's buoyancy.

The Bible as History
WERNER KELLER

During the siege of Jerusalem in A.D. 70,
it is said that the Roman army commander Titus
sentenced certain slaves to death. . . .
He had them bound together by chains
and thrown into the sea
at the foot of the mountains of Moab.
But the condemned men did not drown.
No matter how often they were thrown into the sea
they always drifted back to the shore like corks.
This inexplicable occurrence
made such a deep impression upon Titus
that he pardoned the unfortunate offenders.

24

The Walls Came Tumbling Down

O God . . .
not with their own sword did they conquer the land,
nor did their own arm make them victorious,
but it was your arm and your right hand. . . .
Through your name
we trampled down our adversaries.

PSALM 44:1–6

Yahweh is the real hero of the Book of Joshua.
He guided his people to victory
and gave them the land.

ANCIENT GRAVEYARDS

When all the kings of the Amorites and Canaanites
heard that the LORD had dried up
the waters of the Jordan before the Israelites . . .
they were disheartened
and lost courage at Israel's approach.

JOSHUA 5:1

Joshua's first target was Jericho.
Next he stormed the cities of Ai and Gibeon.
They fell before his armies.
The battles are reported in the Book of Joshua.

Though listed in some Bibles as a "historical" book,
Joshua is not historical
in our modern sense of the word.

First of all, like the Torah, the Book of Joshua
deals with an early period in Israel's history.
Many of its battle legends
were handed down orally for generations.
Only later were they committed to writing.

Second, the battle accounts were simplified,
and the time-lapse between them telescoped.
This is a characteristic of oral communication.
But there was also a deeper reason.
The editor wanted to make sure
that the point of the book was not lost:
Yahweh, not Joshua's armies, was responsible
for the takeover of the Promised Land.

To stress this point, the Hebrew psalmist
composed this song to eulogize the event:

Archaeologists have excavated
many of the sites recorded in the Book of Joshua.
The location of such sites is rather easy to spot.
They normally assume the appearance of a lone hill
standing in an otherwise flat area.

Called "tells," these hills house the remains
of a long-destroyed city.
Wind, rain, and the centuries have camouflaged
the sites with a "skin" of earth and grass,
giving them a hill-like appearance.

The systematic excavation of tells began in 1890.
Instead of digging haphazardly into tells
for buried treasures, archaeologists
sliced into them, as one cuts into a cake.
This method revealed at one glance
all the strata that made up the mound or tell.
Other methods were to cut steps into the tell
or to sink pits into various points of it.

To understand how the layers of a tell developed,
we must recall that when an ancient city
was destroyed by fire, war, or famine,
the wreckage was not carted away.
New settlers merely leveled the old city,
often made of adobe huts, and built on the debris.
Often the walls of the destroyed city
were merely built higher for the new city.
Thus, the walls contained the tell as it grew.

Some tells have 10 or 12 strata,
meaning that 10 or 12 cities are stacked there
in pancake fashion. The University of Chicago
uncovered 20 strata in the 13-acre tell
at Megiddo (1 Kings 9:15).
The site has witnessed so many historic battles
that the author of the Book of Revelation
made it the symbolic site for the final battle
on earth between the forces of good and evil.
The book refers to the site as Armageddon,
that is, *har* (Mount) Megiddo (Revelation 16:16).

BROKEN POTTERY

The first thing archaeologists look for in a tell
is pieces of broken pottery.
Called the "alphabet of archaeology,"
pottery does not decay, takes many shapes,
and contains many decorations. It breaks easily.
Since ancient housewives wanted to keep up with
the times, they bought pottery of newer designs
when old pottery broke.

There were also improvements
in methods of firing clay as time went on.

All of this is studied by archaeologists.
Thus, when a piece of pottery is found in a tell,
archaeologists can date it
with remarkable accuracy.
The shape, style, design, and firing method
place it in a definite period of history.

Pottery was also used as a kind of writing tablet.
This was a practical way of using broken pottery
in a day when writing materials were scarce.
An inscribed piece of pottery
is especially valuable to archaeologists.

PUZZLES

The Book of Joshua says
that Joshua captured the city of Lachish (10:32).

Describing his excavations at this site in 1965,
one archaeologist gives this report:

The World of David and Solomon
G. ERNEST WRIGHT

I found great piles of smashed pottery
that we could readily date
to the time of Joshua. . . .
Other tells fill out a picture
of a series of city-state capitals destroyed,
strongly supporting the account of the campaigns
in Joshua 10.

But archaeologists have also run into problems.
For example, the Bible reports:

Joshua destroyed Ai by fire, reducing it to
an everlasting mound of ruins, as it remains today.
JOSHUA 8:28

How could this be? Excavations indicate
that Ai was abandoned long before Joshua's time.
In fact, the Hebrew word *Ai* means "ruin."
G. Ernest Wright offers this explanation:

Our dig at Bethel, only two miles away,
yielded a vital clue.
Stripping away the swaths of rubble,
we worked our way past 1200 B.C.
Suddenly, we encountered signs of a raging fire—
piles of charcoal debris, some five feet deep,
in the remains of well-built homes.
Undoubtedly, Hebrew scribes
had accurately recorded the burning, but tradition
shifted the incident to the "ruin" nearby.

A second archaeological problem is Jericho.
The Book of Joshua reports Yahweh as saying:

I have delivered Jericho and its king
into your power.
Have all the soldiers circle the city,
marching once around it.
Do this for six days, with seven priests
carrying ram's horns ahead of the ark.
On the seventh day march around the city

seven times, and have the priests blow the horns.
When they give a long blast on the ram's horns
and you hear that signal,
all the people shall shout aloud.
The walls of the city will collapse,
and they will be able to make a frontal attack.

JOSHUA 6:2–5

So it happened. Archaeological excavations
show that the walls of Jericho did collapse
at one period in their long history.
But the collapsed walls
date from a period other than Joshua's.
Perhaps they are the wreckage of an earthquake.

The Jericho problem is compounded by the fact
that archaeologists can find no evidence of life
in Jericho dating from Joshua's period.
Commenting on its absence, G. Ernest Wright says:
"Perhaps the centuries
have eroded all signs of Joshua's victory."

This would not be surprising,
for the site at Jericho dates from about 5000 B.C.
It is the oldest city on earth.
Archaeologists estimate
that, prior to Joshua's attack on the city,
its walls had been repaired or rebuilt 16 times.

THE BAN

They observed the ban by putting to the sword
all living creatures in the city: men and women,
young and old, as well as oxen, sheep and asses.

JOSHUA 6:21

The military practice of the ban *(herem)*
was common among ancient peoples.
Although this practice shocks us,
we should recall the saturation bombings
and the mass executions of Jews in World War II.
These modern atrocities do not justify
the ancient ban, but they do sober our outrage.

108

Digging Up Yesterday

What would it be like
to spend a summer in Israel as a volunteer,
helping archaeologists excavate a tell?
Here's a report of a typical day,
which begins before sunrise.

From a Volunteer's Viewpoint . . .
CHARLOTTE D. LOFGREEN

The music,
coming over a loudspeaker at maximum volume,
is a mixture of Israeli and John Philip Sousa . . .
as you trudge in the dark
to rows of sinks to brush your teeth.
Nourishment is bread and milk or coffee. . . .
The work groups
slowly place one foot in front of the other,
up the hill until their area is reached.
A bucket, trowel, pick,
and sundry equipment is placed in your hand.
An area inspector advises you on filling buckets,
hauling buckets, and emptying buckets. . . .

Buckets of pottery may be found in a single day;
a new wall, bones, charred logs, cult objects,
and home utensils are the most common finds.
Everything must be photographed. . . .
It is exciting to discover a missing piece
in the puzzle of man's history.
A small ostracon (a piece of pottery with writing
on it) may give an important message. . . .

The afternoon brings a welcome rest or study time.
Since this tell
has been designated as an educational dig,
half of the camp is taking classes. . . .

By late afternoon,
most volunteers are ready to wash pottery
and learn the secrets it can reveal.
Piece by piece, each find is catalogued. . . .
The student feels satisfied
when at last, he can identify the correct age,
type, burnishing, and culture of his piece.

Tell site at Beer-Sheva.

Volunteers from many nations
work in their area squares,
surrounded by well-trimmed catwalks.

An inscription on the rim of a stone bowl.
The inscription is in Old Hebrew script.

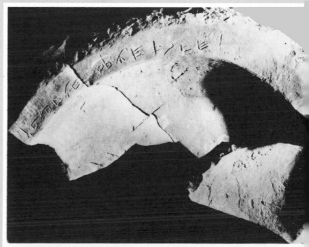

More to the point, however,
is an appreciation
of Israel's incomplete understanding of God
in this early stage of her history.
This understanding was a highly primitive one;
it would take centuries of revelation
under the prophets to develop and mature.

For the present,
Israel thought of Yahweh as a nationalistic God.
As other nations had special "protector-gods,"
so Israel had Yahweh.
And any enemy of Israel
was automatically an enemy of Yahweh.

Moreover, at this point in her history,
Israel had no idea of an afterlife.
This revelation would come much later.
Therefore, Israel assumed
that Yahweh executed judgment
upon wicked people (enemies) in *this* life.
Thus, to chastise an enemy
was to act as the instrument of Yahweh's justice—
a noble occupation.

The portrait of Yahweh in the Book of Judges
was a highly primitive rendering.
Yahweh was a God of battles and victories.
He ordered wars,
took Israel's side, and destroyed Israel's enemies.

Only with the passage of time
would this portrait be filled out in full color
and refined drastically by the prophets.

25
Charismatic Leaders

The Book of Joshua ends on a deeply religious note.
Joshua assembles the people
to renew the covenant with Yahweh.

Thus says the LORD . . .
"I brought your father Abraham
from the region beyond the River. . . .
I made his descendants numerous,
and gave him Isaac.
To Isaac I gave Jacob and Esau.
To Esau I assigned the mountain region of Seir . . .
while Jacob and his children
went down to Egypt.

"Then I sent Moses and Aaron. . . .
After you witnessed what I did to Egypt,
and dwelt a long time in the desert,
I brought you into the land. . . .
Now, therefore, fear the LORD
and serve him completely and sincerely. . . ."

So Joshua made a covenant with the people . . .
at Shechem,
which he recorded in the book of the law of God. . . .
Then Joshua dismissed the people,
each to his own heritage.

After these events,
Joshua, son of Nun, servant of the LORD, died.

JOSHUA 24:2–29

What happens when a leader dies
and there is no one to take his place?

This problem faced Israel after Joshua's death.
It came into sharp focus when Israelites of Joshua's
generation died and a new generation arose.

Abandoning the LORD, the God of their fathers . . .
they followed other gods. . . .

The anger of the LORD flared up . . .
and he delivered them over to plunderers
who despoiled them. . . .

The LORD raised up judges to deliver them. . . .
But when the judge died,
they would relapse and do worse.

JUDGES 2:12–19

BACKTRACK

Whereas the Book of Joshua
shows Israel totally committed to Yahweh,
the Book of Judges paints a different picture.
Israel is depicted as constantly backtracking
on her commitment.

The book is a back-and-forth replay
of the same fourfold theme:
sin, punishment, repentance, and forgiveness.
Like a drama in four acts, the same play repeats
itself over and over during the Era of the Judges.

Act I   Israel sins
Act II   Yahweh punishes
Act III   Israel repents
Act IV   Yahweh forgives

Typical of this cycle is the story
of Israel's struggle against the Ammonites.

Act I

The Israelites again offended the LORD, serving
[other] gods. . . .

Act II

The Lord became angry with Israel
and allowed them to fall into the power of . . .

the Ammonites. For eighteen years
they afflicted and oppressed the Israelites. . . .

Act III

The Israelites said to the LORD,
"We have sinned. Do to us whatever you please.
Only save us this day."
And they cast out the foreign gods. . . .

Act IV

Some time later,
the Ammonites warred on Israel. . . .
The elders of Gilead . . .
said to Jephthah, "Be our commander
that we may be able to fight the Ammonites." . . .

The spirit of the LORD came upon Jephthah. . . .
Thus were the Ammonites brought into subjection
by the Israelites.

JUDGES 10:6–16; 11:4–6, 29–33

The impression the Book of Judges conveys is this:
Israel prospers or suffers in direct proportion
to her loyalty to Yahweh and his covenant.

JUDGES

Jephthah's leadership role against the Ammonites
introduces us
to the role of the "judges" in Israelite history.
It also illustrates
how these leaders rose to power in Israel.

Israelite judges were not black-robed men
who sat in courtrooms and decided legal cases.
Rather, they were military champions
who surfaced at critical periods
to defend Israel against her enemies.
We might compare them to Joan of Arc
in French history.
She appeared with the right kind of leadership
at the right moment in history.

Because judges were believed to be endowed
by God with special gifts of wisdom and courage,

111

scholars refer to them
as charismatic or "gifted" leaders.

The judges were not always holy people.
On the contrary, they were products of their time.
Yahweh acted through them,
in spite of their personal shortcomings.
Such a person was Samson.

Belonging to the tribe of Dan in the north,
he is said to have owed his legendary strength
to a vow never to cut his hair.
A mistress, Delilah,
entered his life, coaxed the secret from him,
and betrayed him to the Philistines.
Imprisoned, blinded, and ridiculed, Samson later
avenged himself when his hair grew back.

NARRATOR *The lords of the Philistines assembled
to offer a great sacrifice
to their god Dagon
and to make merry. . . .*

LORDS *Call Samson that he may amuse us.*

NARRATOR *So they called Samson from prison,
and he played the buffoon before them.
. . . Then they stationed him
between the columns. . . .*

SAMSON *O LORD GOD, remember me!
Strengthen me. . . .*

NARRATOR *Samson grasped
the two middle columns
on which the temple rested
and braced himself against them,
one at his right, the other at his left.*

SAMSON *Let me die with the Philistines!*

NARRATOR *He pushed hard, and the temple fell
upon the lords and all the people in it.*
JUDGES 16:23–30

Once again the fourfold theme
of the Book of Judges is dramatized:
sin, punishment, repentance, and forgiveness.

BOOK OF RUTH

Rounding out the 200-year Era of the Judges
is the Book of Ruth.
This brief book opens in the midst of a great famine
that struck Israel.

The book's heroine, Naomi,
sets out with her husband and two sons to Moab.
There her husband dies.
Her two sons marry Moabite women (non-Jews).
Soon, tragedy strikes; both sons die.

Naomi decides to return home.
Ruth, wife of one of her dead sons,
decides to go with Naomi. She says:

*Wherever you go I will go,
wherever you lodge I will lodge,
your people shall be my people,
and your God my God.
Wherever you die I will die,
and there be buried.*
RUTH 1:16–17

The two women arrive back at harvest time.
While gathering grain in a field,
Ruth meets Boaz, the wealthy owner of the field.
When Boaz learns that he is a relative
of Ruth's dead husband, he decides to marry her.
Thus, he honors the ancient custom
that a kinsman is responsible for a widow's care.
In time, Ruth bears him a son.

*They called the boy Obed.
He was the father of Jesse,
the father of David.*
RUTH 4:17

Though written at a later period of Jewish history,
the Book of Ruth
follows the Book of Judges in the Bible.
It acts as a *bridge book* between
the Era of the Judges and the Era of the Kings.
It does this by having its setting

in the last days of the Era of the Judges
and by presenting the genealogy
that leads to David, Israel's greatest king.

In addition, the book challenges
overnationalistic Jews to widen their vision
about God's concern for non-Jewish peoples.
It does this by presenting Ruth, a non-Jew,
as a direct ancestor of David.

New Testament writers used
the line of descendancy in the Book of Ruth
to indicate Jesus' descendancy from David.

*A family record of Jesus Christ, son of David. . . .
Boaz was the father of Obed, whose mother
was Ruth. Obed was the father of Jesse,
Jesse the father of King David.*

MATTHEW 1:1-6

Ruth is presented as the direct ancestor of David,
portrayed here by Michelangelo.

Brink
of Disaster

Israel was like a ship without a rudder
when the Era of the Judges ended.
The Book of Judges says:
"In those days there was no king in Israel;
everyone did what he thought best" (21:25).
Into this leadership vacuum stepped Samuel.

Although the details of Samuel's life
are wrapped in obscurity,
his role in history is as bright as the noonday sun.
For this reason alone, he deserves to have
two books of the Bible bear his name.

Some scholars label Samuel
the last judge and the first prophet (1 Samuel 3:20).
But Samuel does not fit the description
of either a judge or a prophet
in the strict biblical sense.
Perhaps the best way to describe him
is to call him a *bridge person* between
the Era of the Judges and the Era of the Kings.
For he is the one who announces
and anoints Saul as Israel's first king.

DOUBLE THREAT

When Samuel stepped into the spotlight,
Israel was in serious danger
both from within and from without.

The danger from within was caused by
a drift of the people away from the covenant.
Worse yet, it was aggravated by a growing tendency
by some Jews to blend into their worship of Yahweh
certain features of the Canaanite worship of Baal.

Bowl with typical Philistine decoration.

This gave rise to further danger and disunity.
During the Era of the Judges,
the 12 tribes of Israel divided themselves
into territorial states.
The terrain of Palestine,
carved up by ravines and mountainous areas,
made communication between tribes difficult.
The only real source of unity, therefore,
was their common worship of Yahweh,
symbolized by a central sanctuary at Shiloh,
where the Ark of the Covenant was housed.
When worship distortions set in,
their real source of tribal unity began to crumble.

As if this was not enough,
external threats to Israel began to develop.
Canaanite strongholds still pockmarked Palestine.
Now they grew more bold and began to harass
the tribes.
An even worse threat was the Philistines,
who now occupied a large part
of the coastal region along the Mediterranean Sea.

Today, archaeologists can easily trace
Philistine growth and expansion
by the unique design of their pottery.
It bore a striking resemblance
to the geometric markings found on pottery
in the Aegean sector of the Mediterranean.
The Philistines probably came from this area.

But the Philistines were artists in another way.
They began to mine and process iron ore
south of Palestine (1 Samuel 13:19–22).
This new material gave them a definite superiority
in fighting weapons, namely, spears and swords.
Israel's armies found themselves
on the losing end of an arms race.

Finally, a major military showdown
shaped up between Israel and the Philistines.
The bloody battle took place near modern Tel Aviv.
When the dust of battle cleared,
tradition says 30,000 Israelites lay dead.

More tragic yet was the destruction of Shiloh,
Israel's religious capital.
The Ark of the Covenant was kidnapped
and paraded off in triumph by the Philistines.

The people cried out in horror and disbelief:
"Gone is the glory from Israel,
because the ark of God had been captured"
(1 Samuel 4:22).

For seven nightmarish months,
the Ark remained in enemy hands.
Finally it was recovered.
Samuel used the occasion to warn the people.

*If you wish with your whole heart
to return to the LORD . . . worship him alone.
Then he will deliver you
from the power of the Philistines.*

1 SAMUEL 7:3

The people answered:
"We have sinned against the LORD" (1 Samuel 7:6).

To reverse the downhill skid in Israel,
Samuel reluctantly decided
that the nation must have a king.
He realized the dangers of human kingship,
but it seemed to be Yahweh's will.
The man selected was a military hero, Saul.

Then, from a flask . . .
Samuel poured oil on Saul's head . . .
"The LORD anoints you
commander over his heritage.
You are to govern the LORD's people Israel,
and to save them
from the grasp of their enemies roundabout. . . ."

After taking over the kingship of Israel,
Saul waged war
on all their surrounding enemies. . . .
Wherever he turned,
he was successful and fought bravely.

1 SAMUEL 10:1; 14:47–48

But success has a way of turning a man's head.
Soon Saul began to follow his own mind;
he grew insensitive to the spirit of Yahweh.

Then the LORD spoke to Samuel:
"I regret having made Saul king,
for he has turned from me
and has not kept my command."

1 SAMUEL 15:10–11

Thus Saul became one of the great tragic figures
of Old Testament history.

As the star of Saul dipped below the horizon,
the star of another young man began to rise.

27
Man of Destiny

In Palestine brooks,
you can still spot water-smooth stones,
like the fabled disk David used against Goliath.
Alert tourists quickly pocket them
and bring them home as souvenir paperweights.
Fingering one of these flat stones helps to bridge
the 3,000-year gap that separates David from us.

As a youth, David was a shepherd.
While his flocks munched grass on the hillside,
David practiced the sheepherders' time-honored
defense against unwelcome intruders: the slingshot.

Little did he realize that this skill would catapult
him into the limelight of Israelite history.
The moment came when Philistine armies
invaded Israel and set up camp for an assault.
A sporting Philistine warrior of monstrous size
issued a pre-battle challenge to duel any Israelite.

Fingering one of these stones helps to bridge
the 3,000-year gap that separates David from us.

115

Young David, not an Israelite warrior at the time,
figured the odds
and surprised everyone by calling the challenge.

The slow-moving Goliath was no match
for the agile youth and his deadly sling.
David's shepherding days were over
and his career as a warrior was launched.

With natural battle instincts, and a flashing
personality to match, the young warrior
soon captured the imagination of everyone.
Even Saul was eclipsed in the public eye by David.
The First Book of Samuel reports:

At the approach of Saul and David . . .
women played and sang:

"Saul has slain his thousands,
and David his ten thousands."

Saul was very angry and resentful
of the song, for he thought:
"They give David ten thousands,
but only thousands to me. . . ."

And from that day on,
Saul was jealous of David.

1 SAMUEL 18:6–9

MANHUNT

Saul's jealousy mounted until, one day,
David was forced to flee for fear of his life.
A manhunt for David followed.

NARRATOR   *Men from Ziph came to Saul . . .*
reporting [where] David was hiding. . . .
So Saul went off down to the desert . . .
to search for David. . . .
Saul camped beside the road. . . .
David, who was living in the desert,
saw that Saul
had come into the desert after him. . . .

DAVID   *Who will go down into the camp with me*
to Saul?

ABISHAI   *I will.*

NARRATOR   *So David and Abishai went among*
Saul's soldiers by night and found Saul
lying asleep within the barricade,
with his spear thrust into the ground
at his head. . . .

ABISHAI   *God has delivered your enemy*
into your grasp. . . .
Let me nail him to the ground
with one thrust of the spear;
I will not need a second thrust!

DAVID   *Do not harm him, for who can*
lay hands on the LORD's anointed
and remain unpunished?
As the LORD lives, it must be the
LORD himself who will strike him,
whether the time comes for him to die,
or he goes out and perishes in battle.
But the LORD forbid
that I touch his anointed!
Now take the spear which is at his head
and the water jug,
and let us be on our way.

NARRATOR   *So David took the spear and water jug*
from their place at Saul's head,
and they got away without anyone's
seeing or knowing or awakening.
All remained asleep. . . .

[Then David crossed a ravine,
opposite Saul's camp.
Shouting at the top of his voice,
he woke the entire camp
and taunted them.]

DAVID   *Go, look:*
where are the king's spear
and the water jug that was at his head?

1 SAMUEL 26:1–12, 16

116

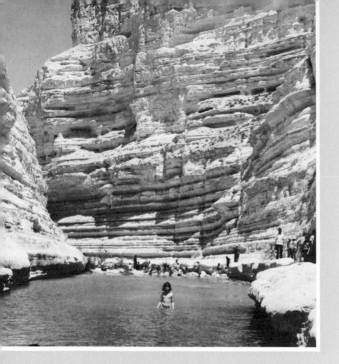

Was It Here?

David taunted Saul
across a ravine like this canyon at Ein Avdat.
Some think this is the actual spot of the taunt.

The water shown here is from a spring.
It is one of the few major water sources
of the Negeb Desert.

Water was *sold* on Jerusalem street corners.
Water was even more precious outside of towns.
Thus the Israelites assure the Edomites:

*"If we or our livestock drink any of your water,
we will pay for it."*

NUMBERS 20:19

Living water—water from a spring or stream—
was preferred to still water from pools.
Sheep, however, preferred still water.
This explains the psalmist's words:

*The Lord is my shepherd. . . .
Beside restful waters he leads me.*

PSALM 23:1-2

Against this backdrop, it is easy to see
how water became a popular biblical symbol
for life and salvation (John 4:10–11; 7:37–39).

FRIENDSHIP

In spite of Saul's jealousy of David,
a deep friendship developed between Saul's son,
Jonathan, and David.

*And Jonathan entered into a bond with David,
because he loved him as himself.*

1 SAMUEL 18:3

When Jonathan was killed in battle,
David wept over his fallen body.

*I grieve for you, Jonathan my brother!
Most dear have you been to me;
more precious have I held love for you
than love for women.*

2 SAMUEL 1:26

SAUL'S DEATH

Saul's resentment of David ended
only with Saul's death in battle.
The death of Saul came at Mount Gilboa.
Seeing his three sons killed before his eyes,
Saul fell, grief-stricken, on his own sword.

After Saul's death,
the men of Judah anointed David king.

*When the Philistines heard
that David had been anointed king of Israel,
they all took the field in search of him.*

2 SAMUEL 5:17

A dramatic battle followed,
and David routed the Philistines.
He crushed the power of the "sea people" forever.

Dominating Jerusalem
is the octagonal Dome of the Rock,
a mosque built by Arabs
in the seventh century A.D.
It was nearly destroyed by fire in 1448,
started by children who had climbed
inside the dome with candles
to hunt for pigeon eggs.
The dome
was heavily damaged by mortar fire
in the 1948 Arab-Israeli War.
Beneath the dome
lies a 40-by-60-foot rock,
said to be the site where Abraham
led Isaac to be sacrificed.
David chose this spot for the temple.

ERA OF DAVID

Under the magic of David's leadership,
Israel began her "years of lightning."
With remarkable insight, David made Jerusalem
the center of government and worship.
Today, it still ranks
among the great symbol cities of all time.

A modern novelist has recaptured
the love Israelites had for Jerusalem.
He describes an old woman's pilgrimage to the city.

The Source
JAMES A. MICHENER

Like many Hebrews of her generation
she longed for Jerusalem
as bees long for spring to open the flowers
or as lions trapped in the valley hunger for the hills.

It was the golden city, the site of the temple,
the focus of worship, the target of longing. . . .

It was a distance of more than ninety miles
over difficult and wearing terrain,
to be finished in the hot time of autumn,
so that the journey occupied eight days.
Mother and son left the zigzag gate at dawn,
a tall pair dressed in the cheapest clothes,
shod in heavy sandals and carrying staves.
On their backs they carried a little food,
in their purses a few pieces of silver. . . .

Leading his gaunt mother,
who had no idea as to where the city lay,
Rimmon started south through the olive grove. . . .

[Other Israelites were also headed for Jerusalem.]
Those who could afford to do so
led animals for sacrifice at the temple altars,
and one could hear
the lowing of cattle and the cry of sheep.

Jewish pilgrims leave prayers
penciled on paper
in the cracks of the Western (Wailing) Wall.
"O LORD of hosts, hear my prayer"
(Psalm 84:9).

Off to the side of the Dome of the Rock,
and at a lower level, is the Western (Wailing) Wall.
The stones encased in it are all that remains
of the Jerusalem temple destroyed by the Romans in A.D. 70.
Jews come from all over the world to worship here.

Others carried chickens intended for their own
consumption and some women had white doves
captured in cages made of reeds:
these were for the temple.
A few farmers rode donkeys, but most came on foot
to worship at the central shrine of the Hebrews,
to see with their own eyes
the everlasting glory of Jerusalem. . . .

[Once in Jerusalem] many fell to their knees,
to think that they had lived to see this city,
but Gomer noticed that Rimmon stood apart,
staring at the extraordinary walls. . . .
Watching her son absorb the wonder of Jerusalem
she tried to guess
what divine need had brought him to this spot,
but she knew not. . . .

In the morning they rose early
and left the mount of olives, returning inside the city,
where they worshiped at the temple,

Gomer standing outside with the women
while her son went into the sacred place
to gaze at the holy of holies,
to which only a few priests were admitted.
Later he joined his mother to observe
the animal sacrifices during which perfect bulls
were led lowing to the altar,
and here as the solemn rite
was concluded, with incense penetrating the brain,
Rimmon caught an understanding
of man's eternal submission to Yahweh;
and as the sacrificial fires twisted upward
the significance of his faith was burned into his
consciousness.
This city he would remember forever,
and on the sixth day Gomer heard him whispering,

"O Jerusalem,
if I forget you let my eyes be blinded,
let my right hand lose its cunning."

119

GREAT HOUR

After Jerusalem was set up as the nation's capital,
David ordered
the Ark of the Covenant to be brought to the city.

Amid shouts of joy and great festivity,
the Ark was solemnly escorted to Jerusalem
by the picked men of Israel (2 Samuel 6:1–15).
As the men approached the city gates,
the excitement of the people broke into singing.

Lift up, O gates, your lintels . . .
that the king of glory may come in!
Who is this king of glory? . . .

Lift up, O gates, your lintels . . .
that the king of glory may come in!
Who is this king of glory?
The LORD of hosts; he is the king of glory.

PSALM 24:7–10

Once inside the city,
the Ark was placed in the tent built for it.
David himself made offerings before the Lord.
When he finished, he blessed the people,
and they left for their homes (2 Samuel 6:12–19).

The psalmist commemorated the event in song.

And of Zion they shall say:
"One and all were born in her;
And he who has established her
is the Most High LORD."
They shall note, when the peoples are enrolled:
"This man was born there."
And all shall sing, in their festive dance:
"My home is within you."

PSALM 87:5–7

FROM DAVID'S LINE

Life in Jerusalem settled down to normal.
Then one day David was strolling through his palace
with Nathan the prophet.
Suddenly, he stopped and turned to Nathan.

DAVID — *Here I am living in a house of cedar,*
while the ark of God dwells in a tent!

NATHAN — *Go, do whatever you have in mind,*
for the LORD is with you.

NARRATOR — *But that night*
the LORD spoke to Nathan.

GOD — *Go, tell my servant David,*
"Thus says the LORD . . .

This stone portrayal
of the portable shrine,
which carried the Ark of the Covenant
from place to place,
was found in excavations
at Capernaum.
It dates from about Jesus' time.

*I will raise up your heir. . . . It is he
who shall build a house for my name.
And I will make his royal throne
firm forever. I will be a father to him,
and he shall be a son to me. . . .
Your house and your kingdom
shall endure forever. . . ."*

NARRATOR *Nathan reported all these words
and this entire vision to David.
Then King David
went in and sat before the LORD.*

DAVID *Who am I, Lord GOD . . .
that you have brought me
to this point? . . .*

*Great are you, Lord GOD!
There is none like you
and there is no God but you. . . .*

*You have established for yourself
your people Israel as yours forever,
and you, LORD, have become their God.*

*And now, LORD God,
confirm for all time the prophecy
you have made.*

2 SAMUEL 7:2–25

This prophecy of a messiah ("anointed one")
from the kingly line of David
became the cornerstone of Israel's faith.
The psalmist set it to music.

*"I have found David, my servant;
with my holy oil I have anointed him. . . .
He shall say of me, 'You are my father. . . .'
And I will make him the first-born,
highest of the kings of the earth. . . .*

*"His posterity shall continue forever,
and his throne shall be like the sun before me;
like the moon, which remains forever—
a faithful witness in the sky."*

PSALM 89:21–38

Medieval cathedral at Amiens, France.

Bible in Stone

Like David,
medieval Christians showed a special concern
for God's house.

For the many Christians
who could not own a personal Bible,
or who could not read,
the cathedral was a "Bible in stone."

On a Sunday afternoon,
you could walk around the cathedral
and "read" the fascinating stories
of the Old and New Testaments
in the life-sized statues of the cathedral's walls
and the beautifully colored stained glass
of the cathedral's windows.

121

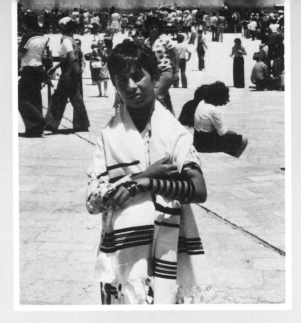

This boy has just completed
his Bar Mitzvah ("Son of the Law").
This ceremony takes place when a boy
reaches his 13th birthday.

Modern Judaism

It is customary to think of modern Judaism
as being made up of three main groups:
Reform, Conservative, Orthodox.

A rabbi comments on the relationships
among these groups.

Judaism
STUART E. ROSENBERG

*All three groups hold more in common
than their divisions seem to indicate.
All stress belief in the unity of God
and proclaim their joint desire to bear witness,
as Jews, to the word of God,
as given to their ancestors at Sinai.
All are in agreement with most of the traditional
theological concepts, although each grouping gives
these their own shadings and interpretation. . . .
Modern Judaism, to be sure, like all of Gaul,
is divided into three parts.
Essentially, however, it is the noun "Judaism"
that is more important to all three groups
than the new-found adjectives, "Reform,"
"Orthodox," or "Conservative."*

Concerning "messianism," Rabbi Rosenberg says:

*Orthodox Jews still pray
for the coming of the Messiah, and believe
that the redemption of the world awaits his advent. . . .
All regard him as God's messenger,
endowed with the power and authority
to cleanse the world of its evil.
While Orthodox Jews believe in a personal Messiah,
it is a man, not a God-man, they mean.
He will serve as the "anointed one,"
the king of Israel, and will lead his people
as the "light of the nations."*

*The Messiah, they believe, will not come
until Israel is restored to its place
as the Messiah-people in the land of Israel,
where their moral example may serve
to remind the world of the teachings of the Lord. . . .*

*Conservative and Reform Jews, by and large,
do not accept the idea of a personal Messiah. . . .
Rather, they say, Judaism was essentially
concerned with the quality of human life that would
be experienced in "The Days of the Messiah."
Thus, they see Jewish messianism
as the provider of a distinctive Jewish theology:
it helps to project mankind forward to a Golden Age
yet to come. . . .*

*The age to come, "The Days of the Messiah,"
need not necessarily be regarded as being
outside history, but may even be possible
within the time of man. . . .
Jewish theology is inevitably earthbound
and leads to the conclusion that in the long run,
and in this world, God is going to be the winner,
because man, whom he created in his image,
can learn to repent of his evil ways and do good.
This life can be transformed when man
does God's will and welcomes him
into the events of history.*

This prophecy of a future messiah
gave new focus to the covenant.
At Sinai the covenant was set up in a general way
between Yahweh and the people.
Now it is linked specifically with the Davidic kings,
who represent the kingdom
and are responsible for its welfare.

Clay Feet

NEW TESTAMENT INTERPRETATION

New Testament writers
saw God's promise of a future messiah
from David's house fulfilled in Jesus. Luke writes:

NARRATOR   *In the sixth month,*
           the angel Gabriel was sent from God
           to a town of Galilee named Nazareth,
           to a virgin betrothed to a man named
           Joseph, of the house of David.
           The virgin's name was Mary.

ANGEL   *Rejoice, O highly favored daughter!*
           The LORD is with you.
           Blessed are you among women.

NARRATOR   *Mary was deeply troubled by his words,*
           and wondered what his greeting meant.

ANGEL   *Do not fear, Mary.*
           You have found favor with God.
           You shall conceive and bear a son
           and give him the name Jesus.
           Great will be his dignity
           and he will be called
           Son of the Most High.
           The Lord God will give him
           the throne of David his father.
           He will rule over the house of Jacob
           forever
           and his reign will be without end.
                              LUKE 1:26-33

Napoleon once said:

I have so inspired men
that they would die for me . . .
the lightning of my eye, my voice,
a word from me,
then the sacred fire was kindled in their hearts.
I do, indeed, possess the secret
of this magical power that lifts the soul.

David, too, possessed a strange, magical power
that could lift the souls of men.
Here's how one modern writer describes it.

_____
Kingly Glory and Ordeal
ROBERT WALLACE

David's ability
to inspire love and loyalty was remarkable;
no other biblical figure,
until the appearance of Christ, approaches it.
During one battle in which he was severely pressed,
David expressed a longing
for a drink of cool water from a well in Bethlehem,
apparently several miles distant.
Without hesitation three of his men
broke through the enemy lines to gratify the whim.

On another occasion,
David and his soldiers had to flee for their safety.
A foreigner (Ittai), who had just joined David,
wanted to go with them.

DAVID   *Why should you also go with us? . . .*
         You are a foreigner. . . .
         You came only yesterday, and shall I
         have you wander about with us today,
         wherever I have to go? . . .

ITTAI   *As the LORD lives . . .*
         your servant shall be
         wherever my lord the king may be,
         whether for death or for life.
                                        2 SAMUEL 15:19–21

Another insight into David's character
is found in the Second Book of Samuel.
David, Abishai, and several of David's officers
were passing a certain place.

NARRATOR   *As David was approaching . . .*
           a man named Shimei . . .
           was coming out of the place,
           cursing as he came.
           He threw stones at David. . . .

SHIMEI   *Away, away,*
           you murderous and wicked man! . . .

ABISHAI   *Why should this dead dog*
           curse my lord the king?
           Let me go over . . . and lop off his head.

DAVID   *What business is it*
           of mine or of yours . . .
           that he curses? Suppose the LORD
           has told him to curse David;
           who then will dare to say,
           "Why are you doing this?". . .
           Let him alone and let him curse. . . .
           Perhaps the LORD will look upon my
           affliction and make it up to me. . . .

NARRATOR   *David and his men*
           continued on the road,
           while Shimei kept abreast of them
           on the hillside, all the while cursing
           and throwing stones and dirt as he went.
                                        2 SAMUEL 16:5–13

NOT ALL SAINT

But there was another side to David.
For some reason, many people don't expect
the heroes of the Bible to have clay feet.
The Bible erases this false notion quickly—
often violently.

Unmatched as a warrior and king, David was like
every other man when it came to human weakness.
His court historian
leaves us a brutally honest report of the sin
that planted tragedy in David's personal life.

NARRATOR   *One evening*
           David rose from his siesta
           and strolled about
           on the roof of the palace.
           From the roof
           he saw a woman bathing,
           who was very beautiful.
           David . . . was told,
           "She is Bathsheba . . .
           wife of Uriah [a soldier on duty]. . . ."

           Then David sent messengers
           and took her. . . .
           He had relations with her. . . .
           She then returned to her house.

           But the woman had conceived,
           and sent the information to David,
           "I am with child."

           [When a plot to cover up the act fails,
           David sent a letter to Joab,
           Uriah's commanding officer.]

           "Place Uriah up front,
           where the fighting is fierce.
           Then pull back and leave him
           to be struck down dead."

           [Joab obeyed David's order.]

When the wife of Uriah
heard that her husband had died,
she mourned her lord.
But once the mourning was over,
David sent for her
and brought her into his house.
She became his wife
and bore him a son.

2 SAMUEL 11:2–27

CONFRONTATION

Then followed a dramatic encounter
between Nathan, the prophet, and King David.

NATHAN *Judge this case for me!*
In a certain town there were two men,
one rich, the other poor.
The rich man had flocks and herds
in great numbers.
But the poor man had nothing at all
except one little ewe lamb. . . .
He nourished her, and she grew up
with him and his children.
She shared the little food he had. . . .
Now, the rich man received a visitor,
but he would not
take from his own flocks and herds
to prepare a meal for the wayfarer. . . .
Instead
he took the poor man's ewe lamb
and made a meal of it for his visitor.

DAVID *As the LORD lives,*
the man who has done this
merits death! . . .

NATHAN *You are the man! . . .*
Why have you spurned the LORD
and done evil in his sight? . . .

DAVID *I have sinned against the LORD.*

NARRATOR *Then Nathan returned to his house.*

2 SAMUEL 12:1–15

Sheep

A man's wealth, in biblical times,
was often measured by the size of his flocks.

Sheep furnished milk, cheese, and butter.
The ordinary Israelite ate mutton
only on major feasts and at major celebrations.

Sheep also furnished wool for clothing.
Here we should note that not all sheep were white.
Some were brown and some were black.

The care of sheep was demanding.
They had to be protected against wild beasts
and theft (Amos 3:12, John 10:10).
Sometimes the shepherd had to protect his flocks
with his naked hands (1 Samuel 17:34–35).

Finally, the sheep had to be protected
against the weather itself.
Commenting on the natural elements,
Laban says to Jacob in Genesis 31:40:

How often
the scorching heat ravaged me by day,
and the frost by night, while sleep fled my eyes!

Against this backdrop, we can see why
the shepherd became a popular biblical symbol.

125

TRAGEDY

Tragedy now descended upon David.
The son born of Bathsheba died.
Next, Absalom, David's son by a prior wife,
revolted against his father.
Although David instructed his commander, Joab,
to deal mercifully with Absalom, Joab slew him.
Moved deeply by these events, David repented.

Have mercy on me, O God, in your goodness;
in the greatness of your compassion . . .
wash me, and I shall be whiter than snow. . . .

A clean heart create for me, O God,
and a steadfast spirit renew within me. . . .
Give me back the joy of your salvation,
and a willing spirit sustain in me. . . .

My sacrifice, O God, is a contrite spirit;
a heart contrite and humbled, O God,
you will not spurn.

PSALM 51:1–19

DEATH OF DAVID

Finally, death came for David.
As it neared, David's eldest son, Adonijah,
sought to proclaim himself the new king.
The prophet Nathan undercut the move.
He informed Bathsheba, who prevailed upon David
to designate their second son, Solomon, as king.
David, then, gave Solomon these instructions:

I am going the way of all mankind.
Take courage and be a man.
Keep the mandate of the LORD, your God,
following his ways . . .
that you may succeed in whatever you do,
wherever you turn.

1 KINGS 2:2–3

Then runners carried the news to all Israel:
"David is dead! Solomon is king!"

29
Israel's
Soul Book

It began as a four-day climb up Mount Hood.
About 9,000 feet up, a blinding blizzard struck.
Sixteen-year-old Gary Schneider and two friends
tunnelled into a snowbank to wait out the storm.

For eleven days the storm continued to rage.
The boys' sleeping bags grew wet and lumpy;
their food supply dwindled to a meager ration
of two spoonfuls of pancake batter daily.
Their sole comfort was the Bible.

Ordeal on Mt. Hood
PHILIP YANCEY

They read aloud, taking turns, eight hours a day.
It was an eerie scene—three bodies propped up
on their elbows inside a five-foot square,
the Bible lit
by a spooky, reflected light from the tunnel.
Psalms seemed to fit best—
David wrote many of them
while trapped in situations not unlike theirs—
hungry, lonely, sometimes even in a cave. . . .
"Wait on the Lord," he said. "Trust him."
It was hard.

Finally, on the 16th day, the weather cleared,
and the three boys crawled from their snow cave.
Weakened badly by their ordeal,
they could take only a few steps at a time.
Later in the day, rescuers caught sight of them.
Their ordeal was over.

126

THE BOOK OF PSALMS

David is often credited
with writing the Book of Psalms.
Actually, he probably wrote only a handful of them.

Ancient peoples frequently credited authorship
to a great person who began or gave support
to an important literary project.
Started in David's time, the Book of Psalms
was not completed until about 400 B.C.
Thus, over 600 years elapsed before all 150 psalms
were collected together in the form they now have.

The arrangement in the Book of Psalms
is not the order in which they were written.
Nor are the psalms arranged
with any special theme or idea in mind.
Later editors did divide them into five booklets,
probably in imitation of the Torah.
The Book of Psalms played a key role
in the life and worship of the Israelites.

It is first of all a prayerbook.
It puts into prayer form
the history, beliefs, and feelings of the Israelites.

Thus, more than any other book of the Bible,
it allows us to glimpse the "soul" of the Israelite.
We see how he talks to God
in times of deep doubt, depression, and joy.

Second, the Book of Psalms is a song book.
The Israelites were an emotional people;
they expressed their total being in prayer.
"To sing is to pray twice," they believed.
Moreover, they knew that singing has a way
of touching the deepest part of people
and shaping their spirit as nothing else can.

"Give me the making of the songs of a nation,"
said one revolutionary,
"and I care not who makes its laws."
The Israelites would have agreed.

Children learned the lyrics and melodies
of the psalms just as children of slaves
in southern cotton fields
learned the Negro spirituals from their elders.

Perhaps even more than the books of the law,
the Book of Psalms helped to shape the spirit
of the common people of Israel.

To catch the spirit in which the psalms were sung,
let us imagine two settings.

The first is under the open skies at night.
Gathered around several campfires are Israelites,
relaxing after a day's work.
Suddenly, a colorfully dressed man rises.
A musical instrument is slung over his shoulder.
He strums it a few times and the crowd hushes.
Then, he strums it again and begins to sing.

This blind harpist from Karnak
dates back to Hebrew slave days in Egypt.
Equipped with eight strings and sound box below,
the harp was played with both hands.
Singers used the harp to accompany many of their psalms.

Hearken, my people. . . .
What our fathers have declared to us,
we will not hide from their sons . . .
that they too may rise and declare to their sons. . . .

God did wondrous things, in the land of Egypt. . . .
He cleft the sea and brought our fathers through,
and he made the waters stand as in a mound.
He led them with a cloud by day,
and all night with a glow of fire. . . .

For when God struck the rock,
waters gushed forth, and streams overflowed. . . .
He rained manna upon our fathers for food. . . .
And he rained meat upon them like dust. . . .

And he brought them to his holy land . . .
and settled the tribes of Israel in their tents.

But they tempted and rebelled
against God the Most High,
and kept not his decrees. . . .

He abandoned his people. . . .
Their priests fell by the sword,
and their widows sang no dirges.

Then the Lord awoke, as wakes from sleep
a champion overcome with wine;
and he put his foes to flight. . . .
And he chose David, his servant,
and took him from the sheepfolds. . . .
And he tended our fathers with a sincere heart,
and with skillful hands he guided them.

PSALM 78:1–28, 54–72

These Tel Aviv dancers remind us
that psalms were not merely sung, but performed.

Children learned the psalms from their elders
and sang them at play and at worship.

"We will not hide from our sons . . .
the glorious deeds of the LORD."

Psalm 78:4

Sea of Galilee in the background.

Psalms as Poetry

A poetic dimension found in some psalms,
but lost in translation, was acrostic construction.
Each successive line began
with one of the 22 letters of the Hebrew alphabet.
Here's an attempt to duplicate the idea
in translating the opening lines of Psalm 112.

A happy man is one who reveres the LORD,
believing and loving what the LORD commands.
Children of strength will flow from him;
descendants of his will all be blessed.
Enjoyment and prosperity will visit his house.

Another poetic dimension of many psalms
is their rhyme scheme.
Unlike English poets,
the Hebrew poet did not utilize sound rhyme,
but thought rhyme.
This means he relates two lines,
either by repeating, opposing, or completing
the thought of one line in a second line.

Repetition:

My heart quakes within me;
the terror of death has fallen upon me.

PSALM 55:5

Man is like a breath;
his days, like a passing shadow.

PSALM 144:4

Opposition:

The wicked man borrows and does not repay;
the just man is kindly and gives.

PSALM 37:21

At nightfall, weeping enters in,
but with the dawn, rejoicing.

PSALM 30:6

Completion:

Unless the LORD guard the city,
in vain does the guard keep vigil.

PSALM 127:1

It is better to take refuge in the LORD
than to trust in princes.

PSALM 118:9

Sometimes the psalmist relates several lines.
Here are two examples.

Softer than butter is his speech,
but war is in his heart;
his words are smoother than oil,
but they are drawn swords.

PSALM 55:22

Because my heart was embittered
and my soul was pierced,
I was stupid and understood not;
I was like a brute beast in your presence.

PSALM 73:21–22

In conclusion,
because the psalms are poetic pieces,
they do not yield their treasures readily.
They resist the hurried observer
and open themselves only to the prayerful reader.

These musicians, unearthed at Nineveh, date from the seventh century B.C. Cymbals and lyres similar to these were used in performing the psalms.

Praise him with sounding cymbals,
praise him with clanging cymbals.

Let everything that has breath
praise the LORD!

Alleluia.

PSALM 150

Other psalms were designed as a back-and-forth chant between the leader of song and the people. Drums and trumpets enhanced the dialogue.

LEADER   *Give thanks to the LORD, for he is good,*
PEOPLE   *For his mercy endures forever. . . .*

LEADER   *Who made the great lights,*
PEOPLE   *For his mercy endures forever. . . .*

LEADER   *Who led his people through the wilderness,*
PEOPLE   *For his mercy endures forever. . . .*

LEADER   *And freed us from our foes,*
PEOPLE   *For his mercy endures forever.*

PSALM 136:1, 7, 16, 24

THEMES

Many attempts have been made to group psalms according to themes. One possible grouping is praise psalms, wisdom psalms, royal psalms, thanksgiving psalms, lament psalms.

PRAISE PSALMS

The psalms often begin with the word *Alleluia*, which means "Praise Yahweh!"

As in Psalm 150, the opening line was probably intoned by a soloist.
Then the people or the choir joined in.

O LORD, my God, you are great indeed! . . .
You have spread out the heavens like a tent-cloth;
you have constructed your palace upon the waters.
You make the clouds your chariot;
you travel on the wings of the wind. . . .

TEMPLE WORSHIP

A second setting in which the psalms were sung was in the temple on holidays and on the Sabbath. At these times
the psalms were not merely sung, but performed.

Psalm 150 gives us an insight into how elaborate these performances were.
We can read the psalm in 20 seconds.
Actually, it probably took closer to 20 minutes— or even two hours—to perform.

Apparently written as a grand finale to worship, it was intended to be sung, played, and danced.
Thus it involved a leader of song, a chorus, musicians, dancers, and the entire congregation.
The leader of song coordinated the whole, signaling when each group was to come in.

Alleluia.

Praise the LORD in his sanctuary,
praise him in the firmament of his strength.
Praise him for his mighty deeds,
praise him for his sovereign majesty.
Praise him with the blast of the trumpet,
praise him with lyre and harp,
praise him with timbrel and dance,
praise him with strings and pipe.

You water the mountains from your palace. . . .
You raise grass for the cattle,
and vegetation for men's use,
producing bread from the earth,
and wine to gladden men's hearts. . . .

You made the moon to mark the seasons;
the sun knows the hour of its setting.
You bring darkness, and it is night;
then all the beasts of the forest roam about . . .
and seek their food from God. . . .

How manifold are your works, O LORD!
In wisdom you have wrought them all.

PSALM 104:1-24

WISDOM PSALMS

These psalms deal chiefly with human conduct
and how it affects a person's happiness.
They frequently begin with "Happy the man."
Wisdom psalms usually draw comparisons between
the wise and the foolish, the just and the unjust.

Happy the man
who follows not . . . sinners . . .
but delights in the law of the LORD. . . .
He is like a tree planted near running water . . .
whose leaves never fade.

Not so the wicked, not so;
they are like chaff
which the wind drives away.
Therefore in judgment
the wicked shall not stand. . . .

The LORD watches over the way of the just,
but the way of the wicked vanishes.

PSALM 1:1-6

ROYAL PSALMS

Royal psalms concern the king.
Beginning with Yahweh's promise to David,
the king became more than a political figure.
He became a religious symbol as well.
Each new king was seen as a step toward

the "king of kings," the promised Messiah,
who would come from David's line.

Consequently, psalms were composed
to celebrate the coronation of each new king.
Psalm 101 sounds like the king's oath of office.

I will walk in the integrity of my heart . . .
I will not set before my eyes any base thing. . . .
He who walks in the way of integrity
shall be in my service. . . .
He who speaks falsehood
shall not stand before my eyes.

PSALM 101:2-7

The introduction to Psalm 20 reads like a toast
to a new king at his coronation banquet.

The LORD answer you in time of distress;
the name of the God of Jacob defend you!
May he send you help from the sanctuary. . . .
May he grant you what is in your heart
and fulfill your every plan.

PSALM 20:1-5

Psalm 72 reads like the people's prayer to God
for the new king.

O God,
with your judgment endow the king. . . .
May he endure as long as the sun. . . .
May his name be blessed forever.

PSALM 72:1, 5, 17

THANKSGIVING PSALMS

These psalms are expressions of gratitude to Yahweh
for some benefit or blessing.

O LORD, my God,
I cried out to you and you healed me. . . .

You changed my mourning into dancing;
you took off my sackcloth and clothed me
with gladness. . . .

O LORD, my God,
forever will I give you thanks.

PSALM 30:3, 12-13

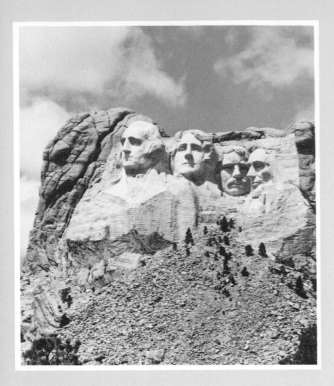

The Psalmist Was Right

Unless the LORD build the house,
they labor in vain who build it.
Unless the LORD guard the city,
in vain does the guard keep vigil.

PSALM 127:1

The Psalms: Hymnbook of Humanity
JAMES DANIEL

In 1787 the Constitutional Convention
meeting at Philadelphia was near failure
because the 13 former colonies could not agree
on a form of effective national government.
When the deadlock appeared too great
for human power to break,
81-year-old Benjamin Franklin rose to his feet.
All his life, he said, he had been convinced
that the Psalms were right in saying,
"Except the Lord build the house,
they labor in vain to build it."
He moved that the delegates begin
the next day's meeting with a prayer
offered by a Philadelphia clergyman.
The motion carried. . . .
Congress still observes Franklin's precedent.

LAMENT PSALMS

Lament psalms are perhaps the most difficult
for modern people to understand.
In these "songs of woe,"
the poet pours out his heart to Yahweh,
often in extreme and contradictory language.

The psalmist's purpose
is not to give a literal description of his afflictions.
This is why these psalms are often more poetic.

O LORD, hear my prayer. . . .
Withered and dried up like grass is my heart;
I forget to eat my bread. . . .
I have become like an owl among the ruins.
I am sleepless, and I moan;
I am like a sparrow alone on the housetop. . . .

My days are like a lengthening shadow,
and I wither like grass.

PSALM 102:1-12

Lament psalms often deal with defeat
at the hands of an enemy
or injury at the hands of a wicked man.
In some of these psalms,
the violence voiced by the psalmist shocks us.
God is addressed as a bloodthirsty avenger.

O God,
smash their teeth in their mouths. . . .
Let them vanish like water. . . .
Let them dissolve like a melting snail.

PSALM 58:7-9

Again:

O daughter of Babylon, you destroyer,
happy the man who shall repay you
the evil you have done us!
Happy the man who shall seize and smash
your little ones against the rock!

PSALM 137:8-9

What can be said of these violent "prayers"?

The answer is not simple.
We must remember, however,
that the psalms were composed at a time
when Israel had no clear idea of life after death.
Reward and punishment in an afterlife
did not emerge fully until the second century B.C.,
and only then in vague terms.

Thus, the psalmist assumed
that God would punish the wicked
and reward the good in *this* life.
Seen in this light,
the psalmist's prayer for vengeance
was really a prayer for justice.

We must remember, too,
that Israel's first ideas of God were primitive.
Only with the passage of time and more revelation,
especially through the prophets,
did these ideas of God develop and mature.

Although the Book of Psalms was edited
after Israel's concept of God had passed beyond
the primitive expressions of earlier psalms,
the editor included them anyway.
There is an honesty here that is appealing.

The inclusion of these psalms
gives us a yardstick
to measure how Israel's idea of God
matured over the years.

There is a final feature about the lament psalms.
They almost always end with an act of faith.
Even though the psalmist cannot understand
why God allows wicked people to go unpunished,
he never doubts God.

But my trust is in you, O LORD;
I say, "You are my God."

PSALM 31:15

Song of Songs

Closely related to the Book of Psalms
is the tiny biblical book called the Song of Songs.
This book is short enough to be printed
on the front page of any daily newspaper.

Although the Song of Songs, which is a love poem,
is attributed to David's son Solomon,
it was set down in writing long after his death.
This need not rule out the possibility
that it derives its inspiration from Solomon.
Here is a sample of its poetic text.

Arise, my beloved, my beautiful one, and come!
For see,
the winter is past, the rains are over and gone.
The flowers appear on the earth . . .
and the song of the dove is heard in our land.
The fig tree puts forth its figs,
and the vines, in bloom, give forth fragrance.
Arise, my beloved, my beautiful one, and come! . . .
My lover belongs to me and I to him.

SONG OF SONGS 2:10-16

The Song of Songs reads like a love song,
because it is a love song.
Some experts think that it was used
as part of the Israelite marriage ceremony.
The bride and groom saw their love as a covenant
with each other, similar to the covenant between
Yahweh and Israel.

Thus the poem has two levels of meaning.
On the surface it describes the love of two people.
At a deeper level, however, it symbolizes the love
between Yahweh and Israel.

133

Psalms and Life

The Israelites prayed the psalms
not just to have obstacles removed,
but also to receive strength to carry on.
They prayed not just to have doubts erased,
but also for courage to keep walking in the dark.

Today, people still derive
similar strength and courage from the psalms.

Sea Psalm

During World War II, Eddie Rickenbacker
and a crew of seven crashed into the Pacific.
All supplies were lost in the crash,
except for four small oranges.
After eight days it rained,
and the men were able to collect water to drink.
On another occasion,
a seagull landed on Rickenbacker's head.
He caught it for food which the men shared.

After 21 days, rescue came.
Seven of the eight men were still alive.
One of the things that kept them going was a prayer
session each day.

One of the most popular prayers they used
was the following psalm.

LORD, *you have examined me*
and you know me.
You know everything I do; from far away
you understand all my thoughts.

You see me, whether I am working or resting;
you know all my actions.
Even before I speak,
you already know what I will say.

You are all around me on every side;
you protect me with your power.
Your knowledge of me is too deep;
it is beyond my understanding.

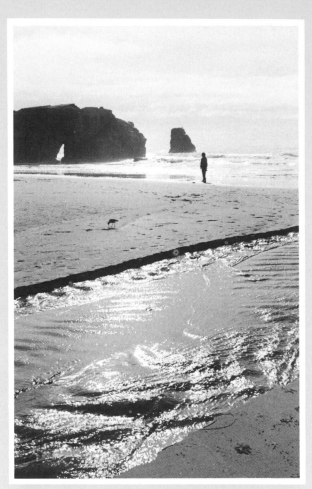

"Where could I get away from your presence?"
Psalm 139:7

Where could I go to escape from you?
Where could I get away from your presence?

If I went up to heaven, you would be there;
if I lay down in the world of the dead,
you would be there.
If I flew away beyond the east
or lived in the farthest place in the west,
you would be there to lead me,
you would be there to help me. . . .

I praise you because you are to be feared;
all you do is strange and wonderful. . . .
O God, how difficult I find your thoughts;
how many of them there are!

PSALM 139:1–17
Today's English Version

Prison Psalm

American Vietnam prisoners found similar strength in the psalms.

Salvation
GEORGE W. CORNELL

Almost all of them say that faith
and the power of prayer sustained them. . . .
Chaplain Aronis details this conversation
with one of the returning PWs:

"Without God,
I would not have been able to survive,"
the ex-PW said.

"In other words, God really helped you?"

"No, not merely helped.
I mean it when I say I could not have made it
without God pulling me through." . . .

PWs told of setting up worship services. . . .
"The most frequently used verses of Scripture,"
he said, "was the 23rd Psalm."

The LORD is my shepherd; I shall not want.
In verdant pastures he gives me repose;
beside restful waters he leads me;
he refreshes my soul.

He guides me in right paths for his name's sake.
Even though I walk in the dark valley
I fear no evil; for you are at my side
with your rod and your staff that give me courage.

You spread the table before me
in the sight of my foes;
you anoint my head with oil; my cup overflows.

Only goodness and kindness follow me
all the days of my life;
and I shall dwell in the house of the LORD
for years to come.

PSALM 23

Passion Psalms

Jesus made frequent use of the psalms.
After the Last Supper,
he and his disciples prayed Psalms 115–119.

The LORD is with me; I fear not;
what can man do against me?
The LORD is with me to help me,
and I shall look down upon my foes. . . .
This is the day the LORD has made;
let us be glad and rejoice in it.

PSALM 118:6–7, 24

While hanging on the cross,
Jesus prayed Psalm 22.

My God, my God,
why have you forsaken me? . . .
I am a worm, not a man. . . .
All who see me scoff at me; they mock me . . . :

"He relied on the LORD; let him deliver him,
let him rescue him, if he loves him.". . .

I am like water poured out;
all my bones are racked.
My heart has become like wax
melting away within my bosom.
My throat is dried up like baked clay,
my tongue cleaves to my jaws;
to the dust of death
you have brought me down. . . .

They have pierced my hands and my feet;
I can count all my bones.
They look on and gloat over me;
they divide my garments among them,
and for my vesture they cast lots.

PSALM 22:2–19

Finally when death arrived,
Jesus prayed Psalm 31.

Into your hands I commend my spirit.

PSALM 31:6

30
The King
Who Failed

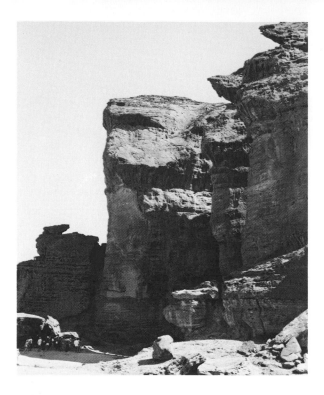

Solomon's Mines Found in Arabia
UNITED PRESS INTERNATIONAL

WASHINGTON (UPI)—*Geologists believe
King Solomon's lost gold mines have been found.*

*The U.S. Geological Survey
says it has discovered the fabled Ophir . . .
in Saudi Arabia. . . .*

*Dr. Robert Luce, a USGS geologist
who was a member of the study team of American
and Saudi geologists, said . . .*

*"Our investigations have now confirmed
that the old mine could have been as rich as
described in Biblical accounts and, indeed,
is a logical candidate to be the lost Ophir. . . .
We believe the legendary King Solomon's lost mines
are no longer lost."*

*The Bible reports that King Solomon . . .
and King Hiram brought 31 tons of gold
to Jerusalem from Ophir.
Although four books of the Bible mention Ophir,
its location is never pinpointed.*

This newspaper report recalls the prosperity
that surrounded the reign of Solomon.
Solomon had a kind of Midas touch.
If David united Israel, Solomon made it a power.

Clever in politics and shrewd in finance,
Solomon entered the arena of international trade.
Money poured in, and the economy ballooned.

With the increased income,
Solomon stockpiled Israel's arsenal,
purchasing an army of war horses and chariots.

*Solomon collected chariots and drivers;
he had one thousand four hundred chariots
and twelve thousand drivers. . . .
Solomon's horses were imported from Cilicia. . . .
A chariot imported from Egypt
cost six hundred shekels.*

1 KINGS 10:26–29

Archaeological digs at Megiddo, Hazor, and Gezer
bear further evidence
of Solomon's national defense program.

WISDOM

But Solomon's real fame lay in his reputed wisdom.
It is this side of Solomon's portrait
that the First Book of Kings paints most vividly.

Standing guard over the centuries, these copper-bearing rocks jut from the desert hills near Ezion-geber. In the vicinity are copper mines worked by Solomon's laborers and new mines being worked by modern Israelis.

Just as David launched
the "psalm" literature of the Bible,
so Solomon launched its "wisdom" literature.

When Solomon was crowned king, around 960 B.C.,
he prayed to Yahweh for wisdom.

"O LORD, my God,
you have made me, your servant, king
to succeed my father David;
but I am a mere youth,
not knowing at all how to act. . . .
Give your servant, therefore,
an understanding heart
to judge your people
and to distinguish right from wrong. . . ."

So God said to him:
"Because you have asked for this—
not for a long life for yourself,
nor for riches . . .
I do as you requested."

1 KINGS 3:7–12

Describing Solomon's wisdom, the Bible says:

God gave Solomon wisdom . . .
as vast as the sand on the seashore. . . .
He was wiser than all other men . . .
and his fame spread. . . .
Men came to hear Solomon's wisdom
from all nations.

1 KINGS 5:9–14

To dramatize Solomon's wisdom,
the biblical writer relates this narrative:

NARRATOR *Two harlots came to the king*
and stood before him.

1ST WOMAN *By your leave, my lord,*
this woman and I
live in the same house,
and I gave birth in the house
while she was present.

On the third day after I gave birth,
this woman also gave birth. . . .
This woman's son died
during the night. . . .

Later that night
she got up and took my son. . . .
I rose in the morning to nurse my
child, and I found him dead.
But when I examined him
in the morning light, I saw
it was not the son whom I had borne.

2ND WOMAN *It is not so! . . .*

NARRATOR *Thus they argued before the king. . . .*

SOLOMON *Get me a sword.*

[A sword is brought in.]

Cut the living child in two,
and give half to one woman
and half to the other.

1ST WOMAN *Please, my lord,*
give her the living child—
please do not kill it! . . .

SOLOMON *Give the first one the living child!*
By no means kill it,
for she is the mother.

1 KINGS 3:16–27

THE TEMPLE

Solomon's final achievement
was to fulfill his father's dream and build a temple
for Yahweh.

The temple was built of stone dressed at the quarry,
so that no hammer, axe, or iron tool
was to be heard in the temple during construction.

1 KINGS 6:7

Jewish rabbis said that metal was not used
because it was the symbol of war.
The temple, on the contrary, was a symbol of peace.

137

The temple took over seven years to complete.

Its walls were lined
from floor to ceiling beams with cedar paneling. . . .
In the innermost part of the temple
was located the sanctuary
to house the ark of the LORD's covenant. . . .
Solomon overlaid the interior of the temple
with pure gold. . . .
The walls on all sides . . . had carved figures.
1 KINGS 6:15–29

When the temple was finished,

the priests brought the ark of the covenant . . .
to its place beneath the wings of the cherubim
in the sanctuary, the holy of holies. . . .

There was nothing in the ark but the two stone tablets
which Moses had put there at Horeb [Mount Sinai],
when the LORD made a covenant
with the Israelites.
1 KINGS 8:6–9

When the moment came to dedicate the temple,

Solomon stood before the altar . . .
stretching forth his hands toward heaven, he said,

"LORD, God of Israel,
there is no God like you. . . .
If the heavens and the highest heavens
cannot contain you,
how much less this temple which I have built!"
1 KINGS 8:22–27

Jews regarded the temple as the palace of Yahweh.
To enter it was to appear before Yahweh's face.

DECLINE OF A KING

Solomon's career ended in tragedy.
Prosperity and fame took their toll.
The king's court gradually took on the pageantry
and glitter of a typical oriental court.
Solomon also adopted the oriental custom
of taking many wives—even foreign ones.

When Solomon was old
his wives had turned his heart to strange gods,
and his heart
was not entirely with the LORD, his God,
as the heart of his father David had been. . . .

So the LORD said to Solomon:
"Since this is what you want,
and you have not kept my covenant . . .
I will deprive you of the kingdom
and give it to your servant. . . .
I will leave your son one tribe
for the sake of my servant David
and of Jerusalem, which I have chosen."
1 KINGS 11:4, 11–13

Wearing a prayer shawl
and a phylactery about his forehead and arm,
this youth carries the Torah following a prayer service
before Jerusalem's Western Wall.

New Temple

In New Testament times,
Jesus showed deep regard for the temple.
He was presented in the temple (Luke 2:22).
He expelled merchants from it (John 2:16).
He taught in it daily (Matthew 26:55).
Yet Jesus placed himself above the temple.
Matthew 12:6 has Jesus say:

"I assure you,
there is something greater than the temple here."

John 2:19–21 adds:

"Destroy this temple . . .
and in three days I will raise it up.". . .
He was talking about the temple of his body.

A dramatic incident occurred in the temple
at the moment of Jesus' death.

Suddenly the curtain of the sanctuary
was torn in two from top to bottom.

MATTHEW 27:51

From that point on,
the temple declined rapidly in Jewish history.
Then dawned the fateful day.
True to Jesus' prophecy,
Roman armies destroyed the temple in A.D. 70.
Today, all that remains of it is the Western Wall,
which once supported the temple terrace.

New Testament writers called Jesus' followers
the new temple. Paul wrote:

You form a building which rises on the foundation
of the apostles and prophets,
with Christ Jesus himself as the capstone.

Through him the whole structure is fitted together
and takes shape as a holy temple in the Lord;
in him you are being built into this temple,
to become a dwelling place for God in the Spirit.

EPHESIANS 2:20–22

Again:

Are you not aware that you are the temple of God,
and that the Spirit of God dwells in you?

1 CORINTHIANS 3:16

Peter wrote:

Come to him, a living stone, rejected by men
but approved, nonetheless, and precious in God's eyes.
You too are living stones,
built as an edifice of spirit, into a holy priesthood,
offering spiritual sacrifices
acceptable to God through Jesus Christ.

1 PETER 2:4–5

Finally, Jesus said:

"Where two or three are gathered in my name,
there am I in their midst."

MATTHEW 18:20

139

31
Wisdom of Israel

RUSSIA   *Pray to God
but continue to row to the shore.*

CHINA   *Fool me once, shame on you;
fool me twice, shame on me.*

ITALY   *The same fire that burns the straw
purifies the gold.*

GREECE   *When the fox cannot reach the grapes,
he says they are sour.*

JAPAN   *At the first glass, we drink the wine;
at the second, wine drinks the wine;
at the third, the wine drinks us.*

SPAIN   *Who loses the right moment, loses all.*

IRELAND   *Long sleep makes a bare back.*

Every nation has its proverbs.
Cervantes called a proverb
"a short sentence based on long experience."
Lord Russell called it
"the wisdom of many and the wit of one."

Many of Israel's wisdom sayings are recorded
in the Book of Proverbs,
one of the Wisdom Books of the Bible.
Solomon's name is often linked to this book.
This is not because he wrote it,
but because he was the ideal of Israelite wisdom.

*God gave Solomon wisdom . . .
as vast as the sand on the seashore.*

1 KINGS 5:9

SEVEN BOOKS

Many Christian Bibles include the following
as Wisdom Books:

Job   Song of Songs
Psalms   Wisdom
Proverbs   Sirach
Ecclesiastes

Here we should note that Jews and Christians divide
the Old Testament books into different categories.
Roughly, the two divisions match up this way:

Jews	*Christians*
Torah (Law)	Torah (Law)
Writings	Writings (Wisdom Books)
Prophets (Latter &	Prophets (Latter prophets)
Former)	History (Former prophets)

THREE AREAS

Judaism, like other religions,
may be viewed in terms of creed, cult, and code:

creed	what members believe,
cult	how members worship,
code	how members live out their belief
in everyday life.

In ancient Israel,

priests	dealt mostly with creed and cult,
scribes	with code and style,
prophets	with all three—rebuking errant
members and encouraging the weak.

Thus, priests were linked mainly to the *law*,
scribes with the *writings* or wisdom literature,
prophets with the *prophetic* literature.

Chinese commune workers near modern Canton.

Chinese Wisdom

About the same time that Israelite scribes
were compiling the Book of Proverbs,
a wise person named Confucius
was using the same method to teach in China.
For nearly a century and a half,
his sayings were passed on orally by his disciples.
Around 350 B.C., they were compiled in the
Analects of Confucius. Some examples are:

*To see the right
and not do it is want of courage.* (2:24)

*A scholar who loves comfort
is not worthy of the name.* (14:3)

*When a man of forty is hated,
it will be so to the end.* (17:26)

A heart set on love will do no wrong. (4:4)

The fault is to cling to a fault. (15:29)

SCRIBES

Scribes still operate today
in countries where illiteracy is high.

Before the invention of printing,
scribes also copied all books.
Historical records explain how a nobleman in Italy
employed 45 scribes for two years to copy
200 books for his private library.

Scribes were first used in Israel because even kings
and generals could not read or write.
Thus, a kind of secretary was needed for them.
Because the scribe's job
put him in touch with a wide range of knowledge,

he became highly informed in many matters.
Referring to the scribe, the Book of Sirach says:

*He treasures the discourses of famous men . . . ;
he studies obscure parables. . . .
He is in attendance on the great,
and has entrance to the ruler.
He travels among the peoples of foreign lands
to learn what is good and evil among men.*

SIRACH 39:2–5

Around 500 B.C.,
scribes began to collect and write down
what they learned about good and evil.
Thus, the Book of Proverbs was born.

BIBLICAL WISDOM

The Book of Proverbs states its purpose
in a brief foreword.
It is to help everyone, especially the young,
learn what is right, just, and honest.

The book's 31 chapters consist of short,
easy-to-remember sayings about everything
from how to win friends and influence people
to reasons for staying sober.

The sayings are not all original with Israel.
Many were collected from foreign sources.
Hebrew scribes, then, adapted them
to fit Israel's faith and practical needs.

For example, one section of the Book of Proverbs
deals with instructions for young men
studying to be courtiers.
When Israel switched her government
from rule by judges to rule by kings,
a program was needed
to train young men to work around the king.

As a guide for this program,
Israel borrowed ideas from the Egyptians.
Here are some directives adapted from a program
of the Egyptian, Amen-em-ope.

When you sit down to dine with a ruler,
keep in mind who is before you.

PROVERBS 23:1

Rescue those who are being dragged to death,
and from those tottering to execution withdraw not.
If you say, "I know not this man!"
does not he who tests hearts perceive it?

PROVERBS 24:11–12

MEDITATION TRIGGERS

Other proverbs are designed to prod the Israelite
into meditating on the ordinary things of life.
Among these are the so-called numerical proverbs,
popular among Arabs.

Three things are too wonderful for me,
yes, four I cannot understand:
the way of an eagle in the air,
the way of a serpent upon a rock,
the way of a ship on the high seas,
and the way of a man with a maiden.

PROVERBS 30:18–19

Again:

Under three things the earth trembles,
yes, under four it cannot bear up:
under a slave when he becomes king,
and a fool when he is glutted with food;
under an odious woman when she is wed,
and a maidservant
when she displaces her mistress.

PROVERBS 30:21–23

142

What is Meditation?

Some people ask:
"Are meditation and prayer the same thing?"

Although we sometimes treat them as such,
technically, they are different.
An example may help.
A young person described this experience:

It was my junior year in high school.
I was listening to some music.
I wasn't thinking about a thing.
I was just enjoying the sound.

Suddenly, I found myself
wondering about something I once read:
"Music is love in search of a word."

I liked the expression,
even though I never fully understood its meaning.
I still don't know if I do.

Anyway, it occurred to me
that praying to God was like that at times.
I sometimes feel that I want to pray to God,
but I can't seem to find the words to do it.
That's kind of like "love in search of a word."

Then something strange happened to me.
All of a sudden I was just filled with words;
and I began to express myself to God
as never before in my life.
I talked to him from the depths of my heart—
about my problems, my doubts, even my dreams.
For the first time, I think, I really prayed.

The young person's experience
is a perfect illustration of what prayer is.
It illustrates, also, three forms prayer can take:
contemplation, meditation, conversation.

The first part of the experience
was *enjoying* something (listening to music).
This corresponds to *contemplation*.

The second part was *exploring* an idea
("Music is love in search of a word").
This corresponds to *meditation*.

The third part was *expressing* one's self
("I began to express myself to God").
This corresponds to *conversation*.

Prayer can involve each of these three forms.
Moreover, the three forms frequently occur together,
like three sides of the same triangle.

Contemplation is *enjoying* the presence of God.
Meditation is *exploring* something about God.
Conversation is *expressing* oneself to God.

Sometimes, however, as the young person noted,
prayer doesn't seem to fit any of these categories.
It is simply "love in search of a word."
"When it comes to prayer," said John Bunyan,
"it is better to have a heart without words
than words without a heart."

MEMORY PATTERNS

A number of proverbs follow a set form.
No doubt this facilitated memorizing them.
The form usually takes one of three patterns.
The first is *contrast*.

A tranquil mind gives life to the body,
but jealousy rots the bones.

PROVERBS 14:30

A mild answer calms wrath,
but a harsh word stirs up anger.

PROVERBS 15:1

A second poetic pattern is *completion*.
Some point is made in the first half of a verse
and completed in the second half.

The start of strife is like the opening of a dam;
therefore, check a quarrel before it begins!

PROVERBS 17:14

He who has compassion on the poor
lends to the LORD,
and he will repay him for his good deed.

PROVERBS 19:17

A final poetic pattern
is that of the *simile* or *metaphor*.

The man who is slack in his work
is own brother to the man who is destructive.

PROVERBS 18:9

Like the man who seizes a passing dog by the ears
is he who meddles in a quarrel not his own.

PROVERBS 26:17

SIMPLE PROSE

Not all the instructions in the Book of Proverbs
are put in these poetic patterns.
Some are merely expressed in vivid prose.
An example
is this caution against excessive drinking:

Who have wounds for nothing?
Who have black eyes?
Those who linger long over wine. . . .

Look not on the wine when it is red,
when it sparkles in the glass.
It goes down smoothly;
but in the end it bites like a serpent. . . .
Your eyes behold strange sights,
and your heart utters disordered thoughts;
you are like one
now lying in the depths of the sea,
now sprawled at the top of the mast.

PROVERBS 23:29–34

YOU WONDER

As you read these proverbs, you may wonder:
How do they relate to the rest of the Bible?
The answer lies in Israel's concept of religion.
Life and religion were inseparable.
Consequently, the biblical writer is concerned
about every phase of human existence.

Nevertheless, the editor of the Book of Proverbs
does attempt a specific connection between God
and the quest for knowledge.

The fear of the LORD
is the beginning of knowledge.

PROVERBS 1:7

In other words, without an appreciation of God,
people cannot begin to appreciate God's creation.

LATER CONNECTION

New Testament writers found another connection.
Chapter 8 of the Book of Proverbs
speaks of wisdom as a person.

"When he established the heavens I was there . . .
when he fixed fast the foundations of the earth . . .
then was I beside him as his craftsman."

PROVERBS 8:27–30

Compare this to John's description of Jesus.

He was present to God in the beginning.
Through him all things came into being,
and apart from him nothing came to be.

JOHN 1:2-3

Paul linked Jesus and wisdom explicitly.
He called Jesus the wisdom of God
(1 Corinthians 1:24).

Thus, New Testament writers portrayed Jesus

as the personification of the wisdom
that the ancient wisemen sought.

"I am the light of the world.
No follower of mine shall ever walk in darkness;
no, he shall possess the light of life."

JOHN 8:12

"If you live according to my teaching . . .
then you will know the truth,
and the truth will set you free."

JOHN 8:32

Early American Wisdom

Poor Richard's Almanac is a fine example
of early American *wisdom* literature.
A study of it helps us understand better
Israel's Book of Proverbs.
Benjamin Franklin, the *Almanac*'s author, wrote:

I consider it a proper vehicle for conveying
instructions among the common people,
who bought scarcely any other books;
I therefore filled all the little spaces that occurred
between the remarkable days of the calendar
with proverbial sentences.

These proverbs were the "Sayings of Poor Richard."
Franklin collected them from all nations.
In this respect, his self-taught knowledge
of German, French, Italian, Latin, and Spanish
came in handy.

Franklin did not merely translate the proverbs,
but also simplified them for the common people.
An example is this saying:

Fresh fish and new-come guests smell,
but that after they are three days old.

Franklin shortened it to read:
Fish and visitors stink in three days.

After 25 years of publishing the *Almanac,*
Franklin put out an anniversary edition in 1757.
The preface describes a country auction,
where people are complaining of high taxes.
Franklin has a wise man address the people.
He tells them
that the taxes they lay upon themselves
are far heavier than those
imposed by the government.

We are taxed twice as much by our idleness,
three times as much by our pride,
and four times as much by our folly.

Throughout the wise man's speech
occurs a host of proverbs that had appeared
in earlier editions of the *Almanac.*

He who is good at making excuses
is seldom good for anything else.

If a man could have half his wishes,
he would double his trouble.

A plowman on his knees
is higher than a gentleman on his legs.

145

MACEDONIA

Black Sea

PHRYGIA

Mt. Ararat

MESOPOTAMIA

Mediterranean Sea

JERUSALEM

Red
Sea

EGYPT

Time Chart

Jeroboam	Rehoboam	922 BC		
	Others	915		
Others		901		
		883	Ashurnasirpal II	
Omri		876		
Ahab	Jehoshaphat	870		
		859	Shalmaneser III	
Ahab's sons	Others	850		
Jehu		842		
		824	Others	
Others		815		
Jeroboam II		786		
	Uzziah	783		
Others		745	Tiglath-pileser III	
	Others	742		
Hosea		732		
		727	Shalmaneser V	
North falls		722	Sargon II	
	Hezekiah	715		
		705	Sennacherib	
	Others	687		
		680	Esarhaddon	
		669	Others	
	Josiah	640		
		612	Assyria falls	Nabopolassara
	Others	609		
		605		Nebuchadnezzar
	Jehoiachim	598		
	First attack	597		
	Zedekiah			
	South falls	586		

NATIONHOOD
EXILE

Books

1 Kings 11–22	Hosea
2 Kings	Amos
2 Chronicles 10–31	Micah
Isaiah 1–40	Nahum
Jeremiah	Habakkuk
Lamentations	Zephaniah
Baruch	

32

From Brothers to Rivals

Some years ago, a report was filed on Indians of South Dakota's Pine Ridge reservation.

Grim Poverty Stalks the Land of Red Cloud
JAMES FITZGERALD

Government studies show that the life expectancy
for the American Indian is 43 years,
while that of the white man is 67 years.
Of the 10,000 Indians on the Pine Ridge reservation,
800 families have no home of their own.
88 percent live in slum conditions.
Some of these people must live in tents and
abandoned automobile bodies even in midwinter.
Half of the reservation's population is unemployed,
largely because they must live 30 miles or more
from the nearest public transportation. . . .

Half of the people on the reservation are under 21.
Yet there are no public movie theaters,
drive-ins, bowling alleys. . . .
Only about one home in ten has electricity.
And of the 500 telephones on the reservation,
most are in government offices or at trading posts.

All of the government offices
and the 58 bed government hospital are located
on the far southwestern corner of the reservation.
Indians having business or needing medical help
must, in most cases, travel 90 to 100 miles. . . .
Nine out of ten lack proper dental care.
75 percent of them have no safe water supply.

VIOLENCE

In the light of situations like this,
it was not surprising that some Indians
responded with violence to dramatize their plight.
Concerning this kind of violence,
historian Arnold Toynbee said:

Human beings are committing acts of violence
because they feel that they are being treated
not as persons but as things . . .
and in many cases
they have found by infuriating experience
that recourse to violence is the only means
by which they can extort attention
to legitimate claims and genuine grievance.

Ignoring legitimate claims and genuine grievance
stirred up violence in Israel
at the death of Solomon.

During the latter half of his reign,
Solomon taxed the twelve tribes heavily in money
and manpower for national building projects.
There was always the whispered suspicion
that he favored the two southern tribes,
Benjamin and Judah.

When Solomon died and his son Rehoboam took
the throne, the suspicion broke into the open.
The angry northern tribes sent a delegation
to the new king and demanded reform.

NARRATOR *King Rehoboam consulted the elders*
who had been in his father's service
while he was alive. . . .

KING *What answer do you advise me*
to give this people?

ELDERS *If today you will be the servant*
of this people and submit to them,
giving them a favorable answer,
they will be your servants forever.

NARRATOR	*But he ignored the advice the elders had given him, and consulted the young men who had grown up with him and were in his service.*
KING	*What answer do you advise me to give this people . . . ?*
ADVISORS	*This is what you must say . . . : "Whereas my father put a heavy yoke on you, I will make it heavier. My father beat you with whips, but I will beat you with scorpions."*

1 KINGS 12:6–11

The king followed the advice of the young men.
The ten northern tribes reacted swiftly.
Uniting under a leader named Jeroboam,
they broke with the southern tribes.

David's work of unifying Israel
went pouring down the drain of history.
In 922 B.C. the kingdom split into two nations:
the South, Judah; and the North, Israel.

LIFE IN THE NORTH

The leaders of the North
set up religious centers at Bethel and Dan,
in opposition to Jerusalem.
These new centers not only crippled religious unity,
but also set the stage for idolatry later.

A crisis arose after Jeroboam's death.
As yet the North had no clear line of kingship,
and so the throne fell
to whoever was strong enough to seize it.

Not until the reign of Omri
did a definite line of kingship develop.
Thus, the 25 years
between Jeroboam's death and the rise of Omri
were checkered with plots and assassinations.

Omri finally stabilized the political situation.

First, he established Samaria as the North's capital.
Next, he arranged for his son, Ahab,
to marry a Phoenician princess named Jezebel.
Thus Phoenicia and the North became allies.

With his government stabilized, Omri expanded
his kingdom by subduing Mesha, king of Moab.
Omri's brilliant career ended with his death.

When Ahab mounted the throne, problems began.
Jezebel badgered him into allowing her
to bring altars and priests of Baal to Samaria.
Religious unity, already weakened by keeping
the people from Jerusalem, began to crumble.
Soon Baalism began to make inroads in the North.

CULT OF BAAL

Baalism has been clarified in recent years.
At modern Ras Shamra (site of ancient Ugarit
on the northern Mediterranean coast),
archaeologists found tablets relating to the cult.

Baal was one of many gods
worshiped by Israel's neighboring nations.
Following the rhythm of the changing seasons,
he died and revived each year.
His lovemaking with his female partner
revived all fertility of womb and field.
Baal worshipers imitated their God.

Since most Israelites
were uneducated herdspeople and farmers,
the cult of Baal held a fascinating appeal—
especially when Yahweh seemed to turn a deaf ear
to their prayers in time of famine.
After all, wasn't Yahweh a "desert" God?
Did he know about crops and flocks?
Perhaps they should turn to Baal for help in these.

It was this situation that caused the prophets
Elijah and Elisha to rise up during Ahab's reign.
With their appearance,
the Era of the Prophets dawned in Israel.

149

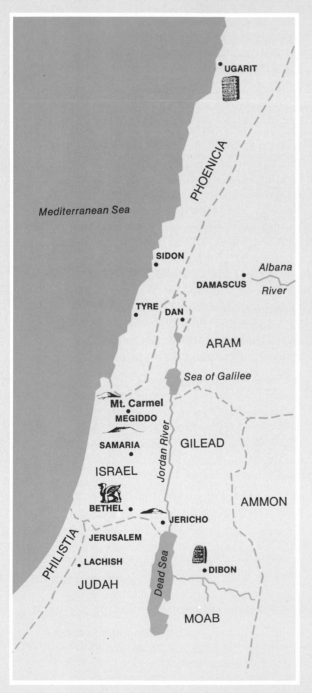

UGARIT
Inscribed tablets were found here (now Ras Shamra)
and supply invaluable data about Baalism.
The tablets are written in a Canaanite dialect
somewhat similar to pre-Mosaic Hebrew.

MEGIDDO
Excavations at this location clarify biblical accounts
relating to the era of Solomon
and the North-South split of Israel in 922 B.C.

SAMARIA
The palace begun by Omri and completed by Ahab
was unearthed
by a team of Anglo-American archaeologists.
Beautiful ivory carvings confirmed biblical reports
about this "ivory palace" (1 Kings 22:39).

DIBON
The Moabite Stone, found here,
tells of King Mesha's revolt against Israel.
The stone is now housed in the Louvre in Paris.

33

Two
Who Said "No"

No tourist who has read his guidebook carefully
can enter the port of Haifa
without thinking of Elijah, the prophet.
From the starboard side of incoming ships,
you get a striking view of Mount Carmel.

At that site, nearly 25 centuries ago,
Elijah made a dramatic stand against Baalism.
Before a standing-room-only crowd,
he took on 450 prophets of Baal all by himself.
The First Book of Kings describes the contest.

ELIJAH   *I am the only surviving prophet*
of the LORD,
and there are four hundred and fifty
prophets of Baal.
Give us two young bulls.
Let them choose one . . .
and place it on the wood,
but start no fire.
I shall prepare the other
and place it on the wood,
but shall start no fire.
You shall call on your gods,
and I shall call on the LORD.
The God who answers with fire is God.

PEOPLE   *Agreed! . . .*

NARRATOR   *Taking the young bull*
that was turned over to them, they . . .
called on Baal from morning

to noon, saying, "Answer us, Baal!"
But there was no sound,
and no one answering.
And they hopped around the altar. . . .

ELIJAH   *Call louder, for he is a god*
and may be meditating,
or may have retired,
or may be on a journey.
Perhaps he is asleep
and must be awakened.

NARRATOR   *They called out louder*
and slashed themselves with swords
and spears, as was their custom,
until blood gushed over them.
Noon passed
and they remained in a prophetic state
until the time for offering sacrifice.
But there was not a sound;
no one answered,
and no one was listening.

Then Elijah . . .
built an altar in honor of the LORD. . . .
When he had arranged the wood,
he cut up the young bull
and laid it on the wood. . . .

ELIJAH   *Answer me, LORD! . . .*

NARRATOR   *The LORD's fire came down*
and consumed the holocaust. . . .
Seeing this,
all the people fell prostrate . . .

PEOPLE   *The LORD is God!*
The LORD is God!

1 KINGS 18:22–39

This story,
like others about Elijah,
was passed on orally for centuries.
Based on actual circumstances,
it was probably simplified to make its point:
the power of faith in Israel's prophets.

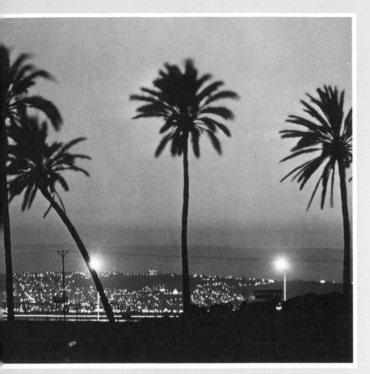

"Elijah climbed to the top of [Mount] Carmel. . . .
'Look out to sea,' he directed his servant."
1 Kings 18:42–43

of Anne Frank *where the young Dutch Jew
affirmed her conviction that "in spite of everything,
I still believe that people are really good at heart."*

*"At our family seder Monday night,"
Rabbi Bronstein said,
"my own daughter read that passage
and the room became as silent as it could be."*

*The North Shore spiritual leader quickly added . . .
that the new seder rite
is not a memorial but a "redemptive experience,
a celebration of our deliverance. . . ."*

*He continued,
"Because the future may well be the greatest period
of Jewish spirituality, we have given prominence
to the tradition of the 'fifth cup.'"*

*The "fifth cup" is the ceremonial glass of wine
placed on the table for the prophet Elijah who,
it is believed, will usher in the messianic age.*

The Fifth Cup

Elijah is described as departing life
in a fiery chariot, amid a whirlwind (2 Kings 2:11).
Symbolic or not,
the description gave rise to Jewish belief
that Elijah would return some day.

Orthodox Jews still place an empty chair for Elijah
at each seder meal.
Reform Jews put new stress on the "cup of Elijah"
in their revised seder rite.

New Seder Celebration
ROY LARSON

*In an interview . . .
Rabbi Bronstein said a new seder rite
has long been overdue. . . .*

*In a collection of supplementary resources . . .
is the well-known passage from* The Diary

Already Come

Some New Testament Jews
thought Jesus was Elijah returned (Matthew 16:14).
Others thought John the Baptist was (John 1:21).
Jesus, however, said:

*"I assure you, though,
that Elijah has already come,
but they did not recognize him. . . ."
The disciples then realized
that he had been speaking to them
about John the Baptizer.*

MATTHEW 17:12–13

*God himself will go before him,
in the spirit and power of Elijah,
to turn the hearts of fathers to their children
and the rebellious to the wisdom of the just,
and to prepare for the Lord a people well-disposed.*

LUKE 1:17

ELISHA

After Elijah departed,
his prophetic charisma passed to Elisha, his disciple.
Elisha continued the fight against Baalism.

Elisha was also recalled in New Testament times.
Jesus referred to this incident (Luke 4:27).

NARRATOR   *Naaman, the army commander*
of the king of Aram,
was highly esteemed and respected
by his master. . . .
But valiant as he was,
the man was a leper.

Now the Arameans had captured
from the land of Israel in a raid
a little girl, who became the servant
of Naaman's wife.

GIRL   *If only my master would present himself*
to the prophet in Samaria,
he would cure him of his leprosy.

NARRATOR   *Naaman went and told his lord*
just what the slave girl
from the land of Israel had said.

KING   *Go. I will send along a letter*
to the king of Israel.

NARRATOR   *So Naaman set out. . . .*
To the king of Israel
he brought the letter, which read:
"With this letter I am sending
my servant Naaman to you,
that you may cure him of his leprosy."

When he read the letter,
the king of Israel tore his garments. . . .

KING   *Am I a god*
with power over life and death . . . ?
You can see he is only looking for
a quarrel with me! . . .

ELISHA   *Why have you torn your garments?*
Let him come to me and find out
that there is a prophet in Israel.

NARRATOR   *Naaman came. . . .*
The prophet sent him the message:
"Go and wash seven times in the Jordan
. . . and you will be clean."

NAAMAN   *[angry] I thought*
that he would surely come out
and . . . invoke the LORD *his God,*
and would move his hand over the spot,
and thus cure the leprosy.
Are not the rivers of Damascus . . .
better than all the waters of Israel?
Could I not wash in them
and be cleansed? . . .

SERVANTS   *If the prophet had told you*
to do something extraordinary,
would you not have done it?
All the more now,
since he said to you,
"Wash and be clean,"
should you do as he said.

NARRATOR   *So Naaman went down*
and plunged into the Jordan seven times
at the word of the man of God.
His flesh became again
like the flesh of a little child,
and he was clean.

2 KINGS 5:1–14

In the months that followed,
Elisha's reputation as a miracle worker soared.
In fact, some scholars believe
that many of the miracle stories about him
took on legendary proportions.

Regardless of how you interpret them, however,
the point the stories make remains unmistakable:
Elisha was a spiritual giant
whose religious and political importance
extended even beyond the borders of Israel.

This seventh-century B.C. relief
bears out the Assyrian king's boast:
"The heads of their warriors I cut off
and formed into a pillar over against their city."
Assyrians were masters of psychological warfare,
sending paid agents ahead to frighten people with tales
of the advancing army's size, strength, and brutality.

JEHU

Jehu inherited problems
not only from within, but also from without.
One of these was the nation of Assyria,
which began to bully tiny nations in the Near East
about the time of the North-South split.

Excavated records provide a grim insight
into Assyrian battle tactics.
One inscription tells how the Assyrian king
(Ashurnasirpal II) treated defeated peoples.

Their young men and their maidens,
I burned in fire.

A second boast by the same king reads:

The heads of their warriors I cut off
and formed into a pillar over against their city.

An excavated stone carving
shows Assyrian soldiers doing precisely this.

A companion carving shows enemy soldiers
stripped and impaled on spikelike poles
outside the city walls.

Somehow Jehu and his immediate successors
survived the Assyrian menace.
But the day was not far off
when their luck would run out.

AHAB'S SUCCESSORS

When Ahab died, problems arose.
King Mesha of Moab revolted against Israel.
Moabite opposition to Israel is reported
not only in the Bible (2 Kings 3:1–5), but also
on the Moabite Stone found at Dibon. It reads:

As for Omri, king of Israel . . .
I [Mesha] have defeated him and his house.

Ahab's two sons followed their father to the throne,
but they were irresponsible kings.
Finally, Elisha put an end to the House of Omri.
He had Jehu, a military leader, anointed king.

Behind wicker shields, archers shoot past
the bodies of prisoners impaled outside the city walls.
A battering ram is ready
to punch through the city wall or tunnel under it.

Found in Nimrud, an Assyrian palace site,
this black limestone pillar contains five panels of pictures.
Intended to be read horizontally around the four sides,
each panel is captioned above. The second panel
from the top depicts Jehu (842–815 B.C.) paying tribute to
Shalmaneser. The obelisk is now in the British Museum.

Buried Story

Back in the middle 1800s,
when archaeology was still in its infancy days,
an adventuresome young Englishman,
Austen Layard,
got excited about the treasures of the Near East
by reading the *Arabian Nights*.

He left England and journeyed to the Near East.
There he organized Arab work crews
and began digging into the desert sands
for lost treasures.

NIMRUD (CALAH)

Here diggers unearthed the Assyrian palace
of Ashurnasirpal II. A contemporary of Ahab,
he was succeeded by Shalmaneser III,
to whom Jehu paid tribute (see page 155).
Also found were wall panels carved in stone.
Some depict Assyrian battle practices;
one depicts Tiglath-pileser III, king of Assyria.

This remarkable relief found at Nimrud
shows the Assyrian king, Tiglath-pileser III, being driven
in his state chariot. An attendant holds an umbrella
to shield him from the hot desert sun.

One day
his searches paid off beyond his dreams.
The shovel of one of his workmen
struck something solid in the sand.

When the tons of sand around it were removed,
the object turned out to be a six-foot,
four-sided, black obelisk,
which once belonged to Shalmaneser III.

One of the obelisk panels
contained a captioned carving of Jehu,
kneeling in humble tribute
before the mighty Assyrian monarch.
The caption read:

Jehu, son of Omri.
I received from him silver, gold, and javelins.

156

34

More Voices of Protest

A UN study says
that 75 percent of the world's population
under the age of 15
lives in third-world countries.

It also says that every 30 seconds
100 more children are born in these countries.
Twenty of these children will die in childhood.
Of the 80 children who survive,
60 will never get any modern medical care
in their childhood years.

In his book *The Great Ascent,*
Robert Heilbroner probes what it means
to live in a third-world country. He asks:
What would we have to do to an American family
to reduce it to the level of a third-world family?
His answer is startling.

We would have to begin by emptying
the living room and bedrooms of all furnishings.
We may leave a few moth-eaten blankets
and some threadbare clothes for the family.
A pair of beaten-up shoes may be left
for the father, but for no one else.

Next, we would move to the kitchen.
Again, everything must go.
Some matches, a sack of flour, some salt,
and a little sugar may stay on a wooden shelf.
So may a few onions and dried beans.
A few potatoes—already in the garbage—
may be retrieved for tonight's meal.

Now, we take away the house itself.
The family may move into the garage—
providing it is not too good.
If it is, the family moves into the tool shed.
It is crowded, but it is not uncommon
for some third-world families
to live in a space the size of a large bed.

But now the real work begins.
We must remove all other houses on the street.
We must also rip up the streets and sidewalks.
Similarly, all forms of communication
and public service are discontinued—
all newspapers, magazines, radios
(except one for the entire community).
There is a two-room school three miles away.
There is also a makeshift medical station
staffed by an unskilled attendant ten miles away.

Finally, all money goes.
Each family may keep about five dollars
to guard against the kind of tragedy
reported in the *New York Times,*
where a third-world peasant went blind
because he did not have the small fee
he thought he needed for entry into a hospital.

Meanwhile, the father must work
for as little as $100 a year.
If he rents land to grow some small crops,
a third of his produce goes to the owner.
Food is a constant problem.
Some third-world children have been known to eat
the undigested oats picked out of horse droppings.

Our job is now complete.

POVERTY AND SPLENDOR

During the reign of Jeroboam II,
Israel enjoyed an era of prosperity.
But amid the glitter of Israel's great society
lay the telltale signs of decay.
Baalism was still bubbling up here and there.
There was also a wide gap between rich and poor.

Archaeological digs at Samaria
testify to the lopsided luxury that once existed there.
Excavators found palaces and hovels side by side.
They also discovered luxurious ivory carvings,
confirming biblical reports of "ivory apartments"
(Amos 3:15; 6:4).

CRIES OF PROTEST

Into this sick society
entered the first writing prophets, Amos and Hosea.
They are called "writing" prophets
because their words were collected together
and recorded in separate books of the Bible.

Included among these men are four major prophets
(long writings) and twelve minor prophets (short
writings). The major prophets are:

Isaiah   Ezekiel
Jeremiah   Daniel

The minor prophets include:

Hosea   Jonah   Zephaniah
Joel   Micah   Haggai
Amos   Nahum   Zechariah
Obadiah   Habakkuk   Malachi

Also included among the Prophetic Books
are two other works (associated with Jeremiah):
the Book of Lamentations and the Book of Baruch.

For the most part,
prophets and kings walk along together in the Bible.
Where you find one, you usually find the other.

The reason for this is that part of the prophet's job
was to advise and correct the king.
This dual function stands out clearly
in the case of King David and Nathan.

Nathan was both
a "foreteller" (he foretold to David God's promise)
and a "forthteller" (he condemned David's crime
against Uriah).

This double ivory comb (ca. 1200 B.C.),
dug up at Megiddo,
is not unlike ivory carvings found at Samaria.

PANDORA'S BOX

The event
that provoked the writing prophets into action
was not just exploitation of the poor.
Rather, it was a flood of evil
that now began to engulf both kingdoms.

Disunity between the two kingdoms
opened the lid of a giant Pandora's box.
From it poured out every kind of abuse:
idolatry, adultery, oppression of the poor,
and religious formalism.

Religious formalism was especially widespread.
Failing to serve Yahweh in their daily lives,
the people eased their consciences
by multiplying altars, sacrifices, and rituals.
Religion became a shell—all show and no soul.

158

Giants of Faith

The Prophets
EMIL G. KRAELING

Without the prophets
there would have been no apostles and martyrs;
Jesus of Nazareth
would have remained at his carpenter's bench,
unheard of and unsung;
there would have been no Judaism;
Mohammed
would have stayed an unknown camel driver.

This is another way of saying
that the prophets kept faith alive in Israel
when it flickered and almost went out.

The prophets disturbed the comfortable,
and comforted the disturbed.

35
God of Concern

Ezekiel Today
EAMONN O'DOHERTY

A recent cartoon shows
a bearded fanatic in sackcloth and sandals
carrying a placard . . .
"Repent, for the end is at hand!"
Behind him the sky is criss-crossed
by rockets and war planes. . . .

In the caption,
a bystander remarks to his companion:
"Have you noticed?
No one's laughing at him any more!"

The cartoon reflects . . .
what many people think of Old Testament prophets.
They feel that the prophets,
if they were alive today,
would be bearded fanatics
with no message for our times . . .
warning that the end is at hand.

AMOS

The prophets were not out of it.
They were very much with it.
They knew what was going on and they spoke out
against it. Such a man was Amos.

Born at Tekoa, near Bethlehem,
Amos was not a northerner, but a southerner.

159

Nor does he seem to have been especially prepared
for his prophetic mission.
On the contrary, he himself said:

I was no prophet . . .
I was a shepherd and a dresser of sycamores.
The LORD took me from following the flock,
and said to me,
Go, prophesy to my people Israel.

AMOS 7:14–15

Amos turned over his flocks and sycamores
to hired hands and left the ravines and hills
of Judah for the North.
After a 30-mile journey, he came to Bethel,
one of the religious centers
that Jeroboam had set up in the North.

This dust-covered farmer must have made
a strange impression on the crowds
milling about the temple grounds.
But his words probably seemed
even more quaint to the city dwellers.
Written portions of his prophetic message
are checkered with colorful rural images:

a prey in the mouth of a lion (Amos 3:4);
a bird caught in a snare (Amos 3:5);
a mangled sheep being carried home
by a weeping shepherd to prove to its owner
that it had been killed, not stolen (Amos 3:12);
a fig tree stripped bare by locusts (Amos 4:9).

But Amos' images in no way obscured his message.
Pointing his finger at the complacent rich,
he scorched their ears saying:

Thus says the LORD . . .
"They sell the just man for silver,
and the poor man for a pair of sandals.
They trample the heads of the weak
into the dust of the earth."

AMOS 2:6–7

If social injustice was bad in the North,
religious worship was even worse.

Ignoring Yahweh's covenant in the marketplace,
the people tried to bribe Yahweh in the temple.
Amos condemned this religious formalism.

Thus says the LORD. . . .
"I spurn your feasts,
I take no pleasure in your solemnities;
your cereal offerings I will not accept. . . .
Away with your noisy songs! . . .

"But if you would offer me holocausts,
then let justice surge like water,
and goodness like an unfailing stream."

AMOS 5:16, 21–24

DAY OF DARKNESS

Referring to the "Day of the Lord,"
which people looked forward to
as a day of triumph for Israel over her enemies,
Amos said:

Woe to those who yearn for the day of the LORD!
What will this day of the LORD mean for you?
Darkness and not light!

AMOS 5:18

On the day when I punish Israel for his crimes,
I will visit also the altars of Bethel.
The horns of the altar shall be broken off
and fall to the ground.

AMOS 3:14

PREDICTABLE RESPONSE

The reaction to Amos' words was swift and expected.

Amaziah, the priest of Bethel,
sent word to Jeroboam, the king of Israel:
"Amos has conspired against you here within Israel;
the country cannot endure all his words.
For this is what Amos says:
'Jeroboam shall die by the sword
and Israel shall surely be exiled from its land.'"

To Amos, Amaziah said:
"Off with you, visionary, flee to the land of Judah!
There earn your bread by prophesying,
but never again prophesy in Bethel;
for it is the king's sanctuary and a royal temple."

AMOS 7:10–13

So Amos departed from Bethel.

POINT OF AMOS

The Bible doesn't say how Amos ended his days.
Presumably, he shook the dust from his feet
and returned to his farm in Tekoa.

Amos has been called the prophet of social justice.
This is a valid observation, but we would miss
the key point about Amos if we stopped here.

Amos didn't reveal any new, revolutionary doctrine;
he merely refocused attention on the commandments.
Israel had forgotten
that while three concerned their relationship to God,
seven concerned their relationship to each other.

HOSEA

Coming after Amos was Hosea.
He, too, was appalled by the evil in Israel
and spoke out against it fearlessly.
His words, however,
had a more compassionate ring
than did the words of Amos.
Perhaps this was because of the tragedy
in his own personal life.

Actually, little is known of Hosea,
except that he seems to have married an adultress.
He loved her deeply in spite of her infidelity.

Conditioned by this painful experience,
Hosea tried to draw Israel back to the covenant
by love rather than by threat.
He compared Yahweh's love for Israel
to that of a loyal husband for his disloyal wife.

God of Amos

The God of Amos was a God of concern.
He scorned those who burned incense one day a week
and exploited the poor on the other six days.
Yahweh's concern embraced all people,
especially the poor and the weak.
And he expected those who worshiped him
to share his concern.

In New Testament times,
Jesus fleshed out Amos' image of God.
Speaking to legalistic Pharisees, he said:

"Woe to you lawyers also!
You lay impossible burdens on men
but will not lift a finger to lighten them."

LUKE 11:46

"I was hungry and you gave me no food,
I was thirsty and you gave me no drink . . .
naked and you gave me no clothing. . . .
As often as you neglected to do it to one of these
least ones, you neglected to do it to me."

MATTHEW 25:42–45

Basil, a fourth-century Christian bishop,
told wealthy Christians:

The bread that you store up
belongs to the hungry;
the cloak that lies in your chest
belongs to the naked;
the gold that you have hidden in the ground
belongs to the poor.

If she runs after her lovers . . .
she shall not find them.
Then she shall say,
"I will go back to my first husband,
for it was better with me then than now."

HOSEA 2:9

Hosea compared Yahweh to a loving father.

When Israel was a child I loved him,
out of Egypt I called my son.
The more I called them,
the farther they went from me. . . .
They did not know that I was their healer.

HOSEA 11:1–4

The prophets disturbed the comfortable,
but they also comforted the disturbed.
Hosea did both with delicate balance.

In New Testament times,
Jesus developed Hosea's image of God as father.
Nowhere is it better expressed
than in his Parable of the Prodigal Son.

NARRATOR *While he was still a long way off,*
his father caught sight of him
and was moved deeply.
He ran out to meet him,
threw his arms around his neck,
and kissed him. . . .

FATHER *[to servants]*
Quick! Bring out the finest robe
and put it on him;
put a ring on his finger
and shoes on his feet. . . .

Let us eat and celebrate
because this son of mine was dead
and has come back to life.
He was lost and is found.

LUKE 15:20–24

162

Night

Fire

PHILIP YANCEY

I was in an airplane, 30,000 feet above
Pennsylvania, reading Night, *by Elie Wiesel.*
It's a small book about Elie's teenage years.
He spent them in German concentration camps—
Elie was a Jew in World War II.

The Jews of Elie's town first heard of the German
holocaust through a man named Moche,
a likable fellow
who was physically as awkward as a clown.
Moche, a foreign Jew, was one of the first
to be expelled from the town. . . .
Several months passed before Moche returned.
He was changed.
There was no longer joy in his eyes.
He no longer sang.

Instead, he told of what had happened to him
and the other foreign Jews.
They were freighted far away into Poland,
made to get out and dig huge graves.
Then, one by one they were marched
before the Gestapo and machine-gunned. . . .
Moche was taken for dead and left behind.

Over and over Moche told the story.
The Jews refused to believe him.
Later, they stopped listening to him.

"They take me for a madman,"
Moche would whisper, and tears
like drops of wax, would flow from his eyes.

A whole year passed. It was Spring 1944,
and the German army's outlook appeared bleak.
The Jews' hopes rose. . . . Then came the news
that German units had entered Hungary. . . .

"I warned you," Moche cried to Elie's family.
And he fled.

Police confiscated all valuables in Jewish homes.
Jews were made to wear the yellow star.
Then they moved into a ghetto in the town's center.
Windows were blocked up and a barbed wire fence
separated Jews from the outside world. . . .

One day new faces showed in the ghetto—
two German officers from the Gestapo.
Fear spread among the Jews.
And that night the order was given—deportation.

The Jews were marched to a train station
and shoved into cattle cars—80 people to each car.
Then the cars were sealed. A whistle split the air.
The wheels began to grind. . . .

On the third night,
a piercing cry split the silence in Elie's wagon.
"Fire! I can see a fire! I can see a fire!"

Panic. Everyone awakened.
Madame Schachter was standing in the middle
of the wagon pointing to the window. . . .

Some of the men pressed against the window bars.
They saw nothing but darkness. . . .

Madame Schachter continued screaming "Fire!" . . .

Elie and the other Jews
tried to explain away her behavior,
talking about hallucinations caused by thirst. . . .

Finally they could stand it no longer.
Some of the young men forced her to sit down,
tied her up and put a gag in her mouth. . . .

Toward 11 o'clock, the train moved on slowly.
Elie pressed against the windows.
The train slowed and he could see barbed wire. . . .

And as the train stopped, Elie saw the flames
gushing out of a tall chimney into the black sky. . . .

An abominable odor floated in the air . . .
burning flesh. He had arrived at Birkenau—
reception area for Auschwitz.

I read Elie's story on the horror
he went through at Auschwitz. . . .
I looked up, out of the window
to the rolling countryside below me. . . .

I thought of a street corner in Philadelphia.
That morning, I had watched a man—
a grizzled street preacher—shout and rail . . .
of fire and coming judgment. . . .

Like Moche and Madame Schachter,
he was ignored. The onlookers . . .
thought him a fool.

36
Gloom without Brightness

There comes an hour of reckoning.
There comes a time when we must reap
what we have sown—perhaps unwittingly.

When this moment of truth comes,
we may cry, we may curse.
We may try to blame others,
or we may blame ourselves.
We may wish we could cram a lifetime of change
into a moment, but we can't.

The poet Whittier put it well:

For of all sad words of tongue or pen,
The saddest are these: "It might have been!"

Such a moment of reckoning came for the North.
In spite of Elijah and Elisha,
in spite of Amos and Hosea,
the North did not change its ways.
And so dawned the Day of the Lord,
the day of gloom without brightness (Amos 5:20).

The tool of God's justice was powerful Assyria.
Called the "Romans of Asia,"
the Assyrians conquered
because of superb weapons and organization.
Dominating the Near East from about 900
to 600 B.C., Assyria began intimidating the North
by demanding heavy tribute or taxes.

The North turned to Egypt and was promised
military help. It never came.
Finally, Assyria decided to crush the North.

The siege began under King Shalmaneser V.
It ended in 722, under his successor, Sargon II.

What the prophets tried to avert
was written into the pages of history:
It is the end of the North.

The event is described not only in the Bible,
but also in ancient Assyrian records.
The discovery of these records
came about in an interesting way.

In the 1840s, Paul-Emile Botta, a French diplomat,
bartered with a one-eyed pasha
for an excavating permit.
He got it; and the "dig" turned out to be a bonanza.
It unearthed the palace of Sargon II.
Until this discovery, Sargon was unknown to history,
except for a brief reference in Isaiah 20:1,
which referred to a general sent by Sargon.
Today, it is almost possible to reconstruct
from archaeological discoveries alone
a whole biography of Sargon.

Sargon II (left) conquered the North in 722 B.C.
Buried for 25 centuries beneath tons of desert sand,
this stone carving from Sargon's 209-room palace
was found by Botta at Khorsabad in 1843.
Garbed in ceremonial headdress, robe, and staff,
Sargon receives an official,
possibly one of his army commanders.

Among the palace ruins
were records of Assyria's victory over the North.

One entry says:

I attacked and conquered Samaria,
and led away as booty 27,290 inhabitants. . . .
And I installed over them one of my officers.

LOST TRIBES

Those inhabitants who were led away
were never heard from again.
Historians call them the lost tribes of Israel.

Some northern citizens, for reasons unknown,
were permitted to remain behind.
But their fate has forever fallen under a shadow.
These northerners socialized and intermarried
with the Assyrian occupation forces.
This drew down upon them
the disdain of other Jews forever.
The Samaritans, as they later became known,
were never again held in respect.

Jesus was an exception to the hatred
between Jews and Samaritans.
John records this incident:

NARRATOR   *A Samaritan woman*
                  came to draw water.

JESUS   *Give me a drink.*

WOMAN   *You are a Jew.*
             How can you ask me,
             a Samaritan and a woman,
             for a drink? . . .

NARRATOR   *[Jesus did not respond to her question.*
                  Instead he told her of living water
                  that would lead to eternal life.
                  The woman was amazed.
                  She ran back to the village
                  to report what had happened.]

Assyrian soldiers lead prisoners to labor camps.
This stone relief was dug up at Nineveh
and dates from about the time
Assyria crushed the North.

WOMAN   *Come and see someone*
             who told me everything I ever did!
             Could this not be the Messiah?

NARRATOR   *At that [the villagers]*
                  set out from the town to meet him. . . .
                  So he stayed there two days. . . .

VILLAGERS   *[to the woman]*
                  No longer
                  does our faith depend on your story.
                  We have heard for ourselves,
                  and we know
                  that this really is the Savior of the world.

JOHN 4:7-9, 29-42

Samaritan elder wearing the distinctive white hat. Only a small remnant of this once prominent sect survives today.

Samaritans Today

What is the status of Samaritans today?
A newspaper reporter files this report:

I Met a Samaritan
JANICE ROTHSCHILD

I met a Samaritan,
but it was not on the road to Jericho.
It was at his place of business in Nablus. . . .
My husband and I stopped there
on our way from Jerusalem to Galilee. . . .

The Samaritans . . . are neither Arabs nor Jews,
although in some respects they resemble both.

They have kept to themselves, married only
among their own. . . .

Their number dwindled
from an estimated 40,000 at the time of Jesus
to a mere 152 at the beginning of the twentieth
century. Today improved economy and hygiene
have helped increase their population to 400. . . .

They tell you they are the true Jews . . .
who have the only authentic copy of the Pentateuch
written personally by Moses five days after
he descended Mount Sinai (they showed it to us!).
This is the whole of their Bible.
It differs from the first five books of our Bible
only in certain passages which they use
to support the validity of their beliefs.

Samaritan rites
have not changed since biblical times.
Whereas Judaism abolished the ritual sacrifice,
Samaritans still practice it
as an integral part of their Passover observance.
On Passover eve all the men come
in white garments and red fezzes,
to the house of the high priest on Mount Gerizim.
They then march in procession to a fenced-in area,
in the center of which stands an altar.
Their wives and children remain at a respectable
distance while they themselves
form two circles around the altar.

Twelve sheep are slaughtered. Then the men
break into joyous song and dance, some of them
dabbing blood from the sacrificed animals
onto their foreheads and their children's faces.

The service officially begins with the chanting
of prayers. Next the animals are prepared,
their entrails burned upon the altar,
their carcasses roasted on spits over open fires. . . .
The Samaritans schedule their ceremony so that
the festive meal may begin exactly at midnight.

37

A Holy Remnant

Shock waves rumbled through the South
when they heard of the North's fall.
People clustered in excited groups
outside the temple and around the city gates.

Underlying the talk, however, was a complacency—
a naive belief
that no tragedy like this could strike the South.
Was not Judah ruled by David's successors?
Were they not heirs
to Yahweh's pledge of an unending kingship?

Perhaps this complacency explains
why the South began to drift into the same evils
that plagued the North: idolatry,
religious formalism, and oppression of the poor.

After the North's fall, two southern prophets,
Isaiah and Micah, intensified their preaching.
Both had been preaching reform before the fall.
In fact,
many of their warnings were aimed at the North.

MICAH

Micah is the lesser known of the two prophets.
His unpolished style suggests
that, like Amos, he was of humble origin.
Another prophet says of him:

Micah of Moresheth
used to prophesy in the days of Hezekiah . . .
and he told all the people of Judah:

"Thus says the LORD of hosts:
'Zion shall become a plowed field,
Jerusalem a heap of ruins,
and the temple mount a forest ridge.'"

JEREMIAH 26:18–19

BETHLEHEM PROPHECY

Micah's prophecies, however,
were laced with hope. He said:

But you, Bethlehem-Ephrathah,
too small to be among the clans of Judah,
from you shall come forth . . .
one who is to be ruler in Israel. . . .
His greatness shall reach to the ends of the earth.

MICAH 5:1–3

New Testament writers recalled this prophecy
shortly after Jesus' birth.

NARRATOR *Astrologers from the east*
arrived one day in Jerusalem.

ASTROLOGERS *Where is the newborn king*
of the Jews?
We observed his star at its rising
and have come to pay him homage.

NARRATOR *At this news King Herod became*
greatly disturbed,
and with him all Jerusalem.
Summoning all of the chief priests
and scribes of the people,
he inquired of them
where the Messiah was to be born.

SCRIBES *In Bethlehem of Judea.*
Here is what the prophet has written:
"And you, Bethlehem, land of Judah,
are by no means least
among the princes of Judah,
since from you shall come a ruler
who is to shepherd my people Israel."

MATTHEW 2:1–6

167

ISAIAH

No prophet is more highly esteemed
among Jews and Christians than Isaiah.
Born in Jerusalem, he was qualified
by birth and by education to walk with kings.
In contrast to the unpolished style of Micah,
Isaiah was elegant and aristocratic.

A copy of Isaiah's writings
was found among the Dead Sea Scrolls.
Dating back to the days of Jesus,
it is the world's oldest copy of any biblical book
written in Hebrew.

EXPERIENCE OF GOD

Scholars call Isaiah the prophet of God's holiness.
Throughout his life, Isaiah showed a deep
realization of the total otherness of God.
This resulted from his call in 740 B.C.,
when, for a fractional moment, he was gifted
with an insight into the mystery of God.

The experience produced in him
a feeling of fear and fascination—a paradox
that must be experienced to be understood.
Isaiah described the experience symbolically.

ISAIAH   *I saw the Lord*
seated on a high and lofty throne,
with the train of his garment
filling the temple.
Seraphim . . . hovered aloft.

SERAPHIM   *Holy, holy, holy*
is the LORD of hosts!
All the earth
is filled with his glory!

ISAIAH   *At the sound of that cry,*
the frame of the door shook
and the house was filled with smoke. . . .

Then one of the seraphim flew to me,
holding an ember
which he had taken with tongs
from the altar.
He touched my mouth with it.

SERAPHIM   *See, now that this*
has touched your lips,
your wickedness is removed,
your sin purged.

ISAIAH   *Then I heard the voice of the Lord.*

LORD   *Whom shall I send?*
Who will go for us?

ISAIAH   *"Here I am," I said; "send me!"*

LORD   *Go.*

ISAIAH 6:1-9

Isaiah's experience of God's holiness
affected his entire prophetic career.
No less than 29 times,
he referred to Yahweh as the Holy One of Israel.
And it was to holiness that Yahweh called Israel.
At Mount Sinai, Yahweh said:
"You shall be to me . . . a holy nation" (Exodus 19:6).

The idea of biblical holiness
is not well understood by modern Christians.
It is not something reserved for the saints,
who go off to monasteries or desert hermitages
to spend days in penance and nights in prayer.

Perhaps holiness can be understood best
in terms of its opposite—sinfulness.
When sin entered human life,
it dehumanized people.
It alienated them
from themselves, their neighbor, and God.

The purpose of God's intervention in history
was to restore people to their original integrity.
New Testament writers saw this process
reach a new level of fulfillment in Jesus.

At the Last Supper,
Jesus addressed the Father in these words:

"I pray . . .
that they may be one, as we are one—
I living in them, you living in me—
that their unity may be complete."

JOHN 17:21-23

In the final analysis,
holiness is reconciliation, oneness with oneself,
one's neighbor, and one's God.

Portion of the Isaiah Scroll found at Qumran.

CALL TO CONVERSION

Isaiah's career arched like a great umbrella
over 40 stormy years of Judah's history.
Because of his keen sense of holiness,
Isaiah spoke out repeatedly wherever he found evil.
Condemning religious formalism, he said:

"What care I for the number of your sacrifices?"
says the LORD. . . .
"Trample my courts no more!
Bring no more worthless offerings;
your incense is loathsome to me."

ISAIAH 1:11-13

Isaiah's purpose was not to condemn the people, but to call them to conversion.

The LORD speaks . . .
"Put away your misdeeds. . . .
Redress the wronged, hear the orphan's plea. . . .
Come now, let us set things right. . . .
Though your sins be like scarlet,
they may become white as snow."

ISAIAH 1:2, 16–18

On the other hand, if Judah does not change, Isaiah says: "the sword shall consume you" (Isaiah 1:20).

But what about Yahweh's promise? Will Yahweh reject his people if they reject him? Isaiah gave this answer:

The Lord shall . . .
reclaim the remnant of his people. . . .
The dispersed of Judah he shall assemble.

ISAIAH 11:11–12

REMNANT

This prophecy of Isaiah introduced a new dimension in Old Testament thought: the idea of the remnant. The concept was hinted at by prophets like Amos and Micah. Now, Isaiah develops it.

He warns the people that it is not enough to belong to a chosen nation. Yahweh's covenant is not a blanket pledge to a nation, but only to its faithful members.

From this moment forward, the idea of membership in God's chosen people takes on a qualitative note: it involves more than being born of Jewish parents.

New Testament writers identified the remnant of Judah with the followers of Jesus. Paul wrote:

Has God rejected his people?
Of course not! I myself am an Israelite,
descended from Abraham. . . .

No, God has not rejected his people. . . .
In the present time there is a remnant
chosen by the grace of God.

ROMANS 11:1–5

IMMANUEL PROPHECY

Delivered at a time when Judah's existence was threatened, this prophecy assured the people that Yahweh would rise up a champion to save them. The heart of the prophecy reads:

The Lord himself will give you this sign:
the virgin shall be with child,
and bear a son,
and shall name him Immanuel.

ISAIAH 7:14

Many interpreted this prophecy as referring to Hezekiah, Judah's next king. But New Testament writers interpreted it as being ultimately fulfilled in Jesus. Matthew says of Jesus' birth:

All this happened to fulfill
what the Lord had said through the prophet:
"The virgin shall be with child
and give birth to a son,
and they shall call him Emmanuel,"
a name which means "God is with us."

MATTHEW 1:22–23

Matthew ends his Gospel on the same theme: "God is with us." He reports Jesus' final words as being:

"And know that I am with you always,
until the end of the world!"

MATTHEW 28:20

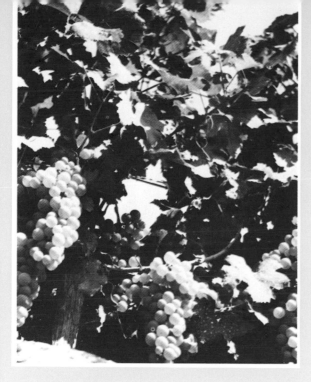

Song of the Vineyard

One of Isaiah's most memorable prophecies
was expressed in song.

Let me now sing of my friend,
my friend's song concerning his vineyard.
My friend had a vineyard
on a fertile hillside;
he spaded it, cleared it of stones,
and planted the choicest vines. . . .
Then he looked for the crop of grapes,
but what it yielded was wild grapes.

Now, inhabitants of Jerusalem . . .
I will let you know
what I mean to do to my vineyard. . . .
I will make it a ruin:
it shall not be pruned or hoed,
but overgrown with thorns and briers;
I will command the clouds
not to send rain upon it.

The vineyard of the LORD of hosts
is the house of Israel,
and the men of Judah are his cherished plant.

ISAIAH 5:1–7

Isaiah's song began on a pleasant note,
but ended with the bitter truth.
Like an arrow, it pierced the hearer's heart.

In New Testament times,
Jesus carried Isaiah's image a step further, saying:

"There was a property owner
who planted a vineyard. . . .
Then he leased it out to tenant farmers
and went on a journey.
When vintage time arrived
he dispatched his slaves to the tenants
to obtain his share of the grapes.

"The tenants responded by seizing the slaves.
They beat one, killed another, and stoned a third.

"A second time
he dispatched even more slaves than before,
but they treated them the same way.

"Finally he sent his son to them, thinking,
'They will respect my son.'

"When they saw the son,
the tenants said to one another,
'Here is the one who will inherit everything.
Let us kill him
and then we shall have his inheritance!'
With that they seized him,
dragged him outside the vineyard, and killed him.

"What do you suppose the owner of the vineyard
will do to those tenants when he comes?"
They replied,
"He will bring that wicked crowd to a bad end
and lease his vineyard out to others. . . ."

When the chief priests and the Pharisees
heard these parables,
they realized he was speaking about them.

MATTHEW 21:33–45

38

Bird in a Cage

In 715 B.C. Hezekiah became king of Judah.
One of the three great kings in Jewish history,
he gave solid backing to the reform efforts
of Isaiah and Micah.
But the South still failed to respond.
It became clear that only a shock
would jolt the people from their apathy.

The shock came in 705 B.C.
News arrived that Sargon II, the Assyrian king
who had crushed the North, was assassinated.
His successor was the dazzling Sennacherib.

Hezekiah began to fear for his people.
He knew that the new king was a warrior at heart.

Modern archaeology
has helped paint a colorful portrait of Sennacherib.
One excavated document records the king's
own reflections about travels with his armies.

Where the countryside was rugged,
I rode my horse and had my chariot carried.
Where it became steep,
I scrambled on foot, like an ox. . . .
When I grew tired,
I sat on a rock and drank from my waterskin.

FALSE FEAR

Hezekiah's fears turned out to be premature.
Sennacherib had other plans for the present.
He drafted slave labor and began making Nineveh,
his capital, the showplace of the Near East.

He even imported Egyptian obelisks
to enhance the grandeur of the city.
The job of transporting these giant stone slabs
must have been staggering,
since they were cut as single blocks
and weighed up to 325 tons.

Modern archaeologists are still exploring
the excavated remains of Nineveh.

SHOCKING NEWS

But Hezekiah's fears eventually materialized.
In 701 B.C. Sennacherib's armies
struck in lightning fashion against Judah.
Town after town fell.
Then came the fateful day when runners brought
the news to Jerusalem: "Sennacherib is coming!"

Warning horns sounded everywhere!
Farmers fled the fields and raced into the city.
The great bronze gates to the city were bolted.
Hezekiah and his generals awaited the inevitable.

When the Assyrians pitched camp outside the city,
they sent peace envoys to negotiate the surrender
of Jerusalem (2 Kings 18:17–37).

When King Hezekiah heard this,
he tore his garments,
wrapped himself in sackcloth,
and went into the temple of the LORD. . . .
"O LORD, our God, save us
from the power of this man,
that all the kingdoms of the earth
may know that you alone, O LORD, are God."

Then Isaiah, son of Amoz,
sent this message to Hezekiah:
"Thus says the LORD, the God of Israel,
in answer to your prayer for help
against Sennacherib, king of Assyria. . . .

"'He shall not reach this city,
nor shoot an arrow at it.'"

2 KINGS 19:1, 19–20, 32

Sennacherib Prism

This hexagonal "Prism of Sennacherib"
was unearthed by archaeologists at Nineveh.
Dating from the seventh century B.C.,
it tells how Sennacherib boasted
of his expedition into Judah.
A portion of it reads:

As for Hezekiah of Judah,
he did not submit to me.
So I laid siege to 46 of his strong cities . . .
and captured them. . . .
I shut him up in Jerusalem . . .
like a bird in a cage.

One of the growing number of examples of ancient records
that confirm events described in the Bible.

Night fell, and in spite of Isaiah's words,
a jittery Jerusalem laid awake in fear of the dawn.
When the sun rose, the people of Jerusalem
could hardly believe what they saw:
the Assyrians were withdrawing.

When the Assyrian armies had gone,
Hebrew patrols went out to the campsite
and found it littered with dead.

Three books of the Bible report the event.
Here's how the Second Book of Kings describes it:

The angel of the LORD went forth
and struck down 185,000 men in the Assyrian camp.
Early the next morning,
there they were, all the corpses of the dead.

So Sennacherib, the king of Assyria,
broke camp, and went back home to Nineveh.

2 KINGS 19:35–36

The Book of Sirach says simply that God struck
the Assyrian camp with a plague (Sirach 48:21).

Ancient historians,
taking their lead from Sirach,
suggest the disaster was triggered by
a sudden outbreak of the bubonic plague.

After the Assyrians pulled out,
Jerusalem breathed a great sigh of relief.
Reluctantly, Hezekiah agreed to pay a tax to Assyria
for the cities that fell
prior to the ill-fated march on Jerusalem.

173

Hour to Remember

The remarkable event
that saved Israel from certain defeat
at the hands of Sennacherib
has been described in poetry by Lord Byron.

The Assyrian came down
like a wolf on the fold,
And his cohorts were gleaming
in purple and gold. . . .

Like the leaves of the forest
when Summer is green,
That host with their banners
at sunset were seen:
Like the leaves of the forest
when Autumn hath blown,
That host on the morrow
lay withered and strown. . . .

And the might of the Gentile,
unsmote by the sword,
Hath melted like snow
in the glance of the Lord!

174

SECRET TUNNEL

A remarkable monument to Hezekiah
remains to this day in Jerusalem.
It is an underground tunnel built by him
to pipe water from the spring of Gihon.
The discovery of the tunnel happened this way.

One hot day in 1880, a student exploring
Jerusalem's Old City came upon it accidentally.
Entering the tunnel, he slipped and fell.
Getting up, he noticed strange writing on the wall.
It turned out to be an inscription,
in ancient eighth-century B.C. Hebrew script,
telling how Hezekiah hastily built the tunnel
to insure a water supply for the city.
Part of the inscription reads:

Quarry men cut through the rock,
each man toward his fellow, axe against axe.

Water still flows in the tunnel
and venturesome tourists
still explore its near-1,800-foot length.

Equipped with a flashlight and hip boots,
you can make out how the two rows of workmen
advanced toward each other.
In the middle of the tunnel, you can see
the exact place where the work parties met.

The Bible mentions the tunnel in three different places
(2 Kings 20:20; 2 Chronicles 32:30; Sirach 48:17).
The Sirach text reads:

Hezekiah fortified his city
and had water brought into it;
with iron tools he cut through the rock
and he built reservoirs for water.

Hezekiah's tunnel stretches in an S-shape from the
spring at Gihon (outside the city)
to the pool of Siloam (inside the city).
The original wall inscription was removed in 1890 by Turks
and placed in an Istanbul museum.

This limestone panel inscribed in early cuneiform writing
dates back to the 18th century B.C.
It pictures Hammurabi, whose ancient Babylonian kingdom
stretched from the Persian Gulf to the Mediterranean Sea.

BABYLONIA

When Sennacherib returned to Assyria,
he ran into a storm of internal problems.
They ended in 680 B.C.
when his own sons murdered him (2 Kings 19:37).

The Assyrians enjoyed prosperity until 625 B.C.
Then things began to decline.
As the Assyrian star faded,
another nation began its rise to power: Babylonia.
The change took place in 612 B.C.
Babylonian troops invaded and crushed Assyria.
Clay tablets, called the Babylonian Chronicles,
describe the event.

Babylonia was not a newcomer among the nations.
It had been around since 2500 B.C.

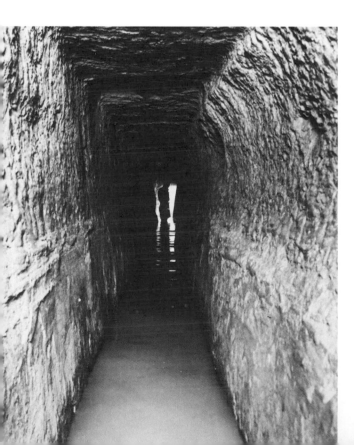

Back in Abraham's time
it had produced the famous lawgiver, Hammurabi.

A stone pillar bearing Hammurabi's Code of Laws
was unearthed by archaeologists in 1902.
It once stood in a Babylonian marketplace,
telling the citizens their rights.
Inscribed in cuneiform, the writing on the pillar
reads from top to bottom—instead of left to right.
Typical of its laws is this one:

*If a citizen has accused a fellow citizen,
and has indicted him for murder,
and has not substantiated the charge,
the accuser himself shall be put to death.*

Babylon, Babylonia's capital, became the dream-city
of its age, dwarfing even Nineveh.
The city was surrounded by walls
decorated with magnificently colored animals.
Dominating the city was a giant ziggurat,
dedicated to the god Marduk.
According to Herodotus, it had seven tiers,
each constructed of different-colored brick.

Even more spectacular
were Babylon's amazing Hanging Gardens.
One of the seven wonders of the ancient world,
these gardens were built on a man-made mountain.
One tradition says the king built them
to please a princess who was homesick
for the mountain scenery of her own country.

175

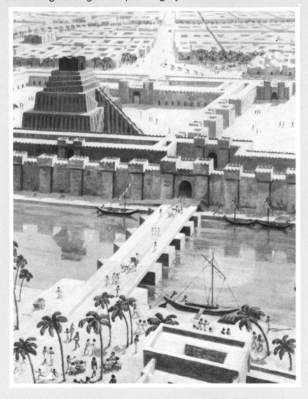

"[Babylon,] your wisdom and your knowledge
led you astray, and you said to yourself,
'I, and no one else!'" (Isaiah 47:10).
Reconstruction of ancient Babylon,
according to Unger. Oil painting by Maurice Bardin.

Star Watchers

The Babylonians were great star watchers.
They pictured the various constellations
as beasts and used them to foretell the future.
From this came our signs of the zodiac.

The Babylonians were also good historians.
They dated all important events
by noting the position of the moon and planets
when the event took place.

This is proving extremely helpful to us today,
as the following news report shows.

"[Babylon,] disaster shall befall you. . . .
Suddenly there shall come upon you ruin
which you will not expect" (Isaiah 47:11).
Ancient Babylon was
exhumed from its grave by modern archaeologists.

At International Business Machines Corp.,
one of the more complicated computers
recently spent 40 hours calculating the motions
of the moon, sun and planets for 600 years
as they cruised over ancient Babylon.

The Babylonians . . .
believed that the motions of the heavenly bodies
had an intimate influence on human affairs.
When they recorded current events . . .
they were likely to include
the position of the moon on that day,
or the location of a couple of planets.

Today, if a scholar
studying the clay tablets of ancient Babylon
wants to know the exact date of a given event,
all he has to do is to calculate the date
when the heavenly bodies were in their positions.

For years, scholars have known about this
dating system, but tracing astronomical motions
backward for more than 2,000 years
is forbiddingly time consuming. . . .

So mathematician Bryant Tuckerman of IBM
got time on a 704 computer.
In 40 hours of electronic calculation the 704 . . .
disgorged 301 tables of figures
showing the positions of the Moon, Venus,
and Mercury at five-day intervals,
and of Mars, Jupiter, Saturn, and the sun
at ten-day intervals between 601 B.C. and A.D. 1. . . .

Scholars who can read the cuneiform writing
of ancient Babylon are already hard at work
with Dr. Tuckerman's tables.
Eventually they may check the dates of such events
as Nebuchadnezzar's deportation of the Jews . . .
perhaps, to the very hour,
Babylonian Standard Time.

39

The Unheeded Prophet

When Isaiah and Hezekiah died,
tragedy struck Judah.
The throne passed to Manesseh, Hezekiah's son.
Historians consider Manesseh
Judah's worst king.

He immolated his son by fire.
He practiced soothsaying and divination,
and reintroduced the consulting of ghosts and spirits.
He did much evil in the LORD's sight,
and provoked him to anger.

2 KINGS 21:6

Good citizens, therefore,
shed few tears when Manesseh died in 638 B.C.

BOY-KING

Eventually, the throne passed to an eight-year-old
boy-king, Josiah.
The youth turned out to be a remarkable ruler.
In his twenties, he ordered the temple remodeled.
During the work, an old book of the law was found.

The high priest Hilkiah
informed the scribe Shaphan,
"I have found the book of the law
in the temple of the LORD."
Hilkiah gave the book to Shaphan,
who read it . . . aloud to the king.
When the king had heard the contents
of the book of the law,
he tore his garments.

2 KINGS 22:8–11

177

New Covenant

For those people who heeded his words,
Jeremiah had a prophecy of hope.

"The days are coming," says the LORD,
"when I will make a new covenant
with the house of Israel and the house of Judah. . . .

"I will place my law within them,
and write it upon their hearts;
I will be their God, and they shall be my people.

"No longer will they have need to teach their friends
and kinsmen how to know the LORD.
All, from least to greatest, shall know me."

JEREMIAH 31:31-33

New Testament writers
recalled Jeremiah's prophecy when Jesus

took bread,
and after he had given thanks,
broke it and said,
"This is my body, which is for you.
Do this in remembrance of me."

In the same way, after the supper,
he took the cup, saying,
"This cup is the new covenant in my blood.
Do this, whenever you drink it,
in remembrance of me."

1 CORINTHIANS 11:23-25

From Jesus' viewpoint
the New Covenant did not destroy the Old Covenant
any more than adulthood destroys childhood.
The one was the outgrowth of the other.

The stress of the New Covenant
was a new law of love,
communicated to each person by the Spirit.
Paul wrote: "We serve in the new spirit,
not the antiquated letter (Romans 7:6).

For Paul, the written law was no longer primary.
Rather, it was subordinated to the law of love.
The Christian should no longer ask:
"How far can I go before I break the law?"
but rather,
"How much more can I do, because I love?"

180

THE STORM BREAKS

Eventually, the day came
when Jeremiah's warnings became a reality.
Babylonian armies crossed the border into Judah.

The battle for Jerusalem took place in 597 B.C.
Quickly, the city was brought to its knees.
The Babylonian king (Nebuchadnezzar)
personally directed its purge.

He deported [the king,] . . . his functionaries,
and the chief men of the land . . .
all 7,000 men of the army,
and a thousand craftsmen and smiths.

2 KINGS 24:15–16

The downfall of Jerusalem in 597 B.C.
is also reported in the Babylonian Chronicles,
found by archaeologists at Babylon.

RUMBLE OF THUNDER

One might think that Babylon's action
would strike fear into the hearts of the people.
But it did not. Some even rejoiced, saying:
"The city and the temple are still untouched;
Yahweh is protecting us."

Jeremiah looked at the situation differently.
He saw it as only the first rumble of thunder.
The real storm may yet lie ahead.
Jeremiah warned Zedekiah, Judah's new king.

Thus says the LORD:
"Do what is right and just.
Rescue the victim from the hand of his oppressor.
Do not wrong or oppress the resident alien,
the orphan, or the widow. . . .
If you do not obey these commands . . .
this palace shall become rubble."

JEREMIAH 22:3–5

The king turned a deaf ear to Jeremiah.
Instead, he secretly began to seek Egypt's help.

40
Day of Drums

Judah's "day of drums" dawned in 586 B.C.
This date is branded on the heart of every Jew.
It marks the fall of the South
and the destruction of Jerusalem and the temple.

Angered by Zedekiah's Egyptian strategy,
Nebuchadnezzar decided to put an end to the South.
His armies marched back to Jerusalem
and reduced the city to rubble—temple and all.
Jeremiah records the tragedy.

In the tenth month
of the ninth year of Zedekiah, king of Judah,
Nebuchadnezzar, king of Babylon, and all his army
marched against Jerusalem and besieged it.
On the ninth day of the fourth month,
in the eleventh year of Zedekiah,
a breach was made in the city's defenses.
All the princes of the king of Babylon
came and occupied the middle gate. . . .

When Zedekiah, king of Judah, saw them,
he and all his warriors fled by night . . .
but the Chaldean army pursued them . . .
and captured Zedekiah in the desert near Jericho. . . .

As Zedekiah looked on, his sons were slain . . .
also all the nobles of Judah.

Nebuchadnezzar then blinded Zedekiah
and bound him in chains to bring him to Babylon.

The Chaldeans set fire to the king's palace
and the houses of the people,

and demolished the walls of Jerusalem.
Nebuzaradan, chief of the bodyguard, deported
to Babylon the rest of the people left in the city,
those who had deserted to him,
and the rest of the workmen.
But some of the poor who had no property
were left in the land of Judah.

JEREMIAH 39:1–10

Contemplating the disaster of Jerusalem,
the Book of Lamentations says:

How lonely she is now,
the once crowded city! . . .
Bitterly she weeps at night,
tears upon her cheeks,
with not one to console her. . . .

The LORD has punished her
for her many sins.
Her little ones have gone away,
captive before the foe.
Gone from daughter Zion is all her glory.

LAMENTATIONS 1:1–6

LOST GLORY

It is impossible for us to imagine
what the fall of Jerusalem meant to devout Jews.
The three great pillars of Judah's existence,
inseparably linked to God's covenant with them,
now lay in smouldering ruins:

> the king,
> the temple,
> the nation.

The king was dethroned, the temple was in ashes,
and the nation was in exile.

The psalmist cried in anguish:

By the streams of Babylon
we sat and wept when we remembered Zion.
On the aspens of that land we hung up our harps,
though there our captors asked of us
the lyrics of our songs,
and our despoilers urged us . . . :
"Sing for us the songs of Zion!"
How could we sing a song of the LORD
in a foreign land?

PSALM 137:1–4

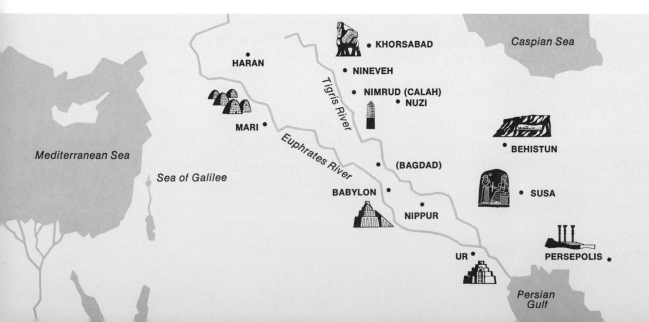

FRAGMENTED CITIZENRY

The fall of Jerusalem split the Jews into three groups.
The overwhelming segment of the citizenry
was deported as prisoners to Babylon.

A handful of poor peasant people,
who had no land or property,
was left behind to fend for themselves.

Another small group, Jeremiah among them,
managed to escape to Egypt.
The Egyptian refugees
began the so-called Jewish diaspora:
Jews dispersed from their homeland
and taking up residence in other parts of the world.

A large colony of these Jews
settled at Alexandria in Egypt.
Centuries later, Alexandrian Jews
translated the Old Testament into Greek.
Called the *Septuagint,* it became the official
Old Testament for Greek-speaking Christians.
Matthew, Mark, Luke, and John
all quoted from it.

Possibly some of the Jews who fled to Egypt
found their way to Elephantine,
an island in the Nile River,
opposite Egypt's modern Aswan Dam.
Archaeologists have found evidence
that a large colony of Jews once lived there.

How the original colony started is uncertain.
Some experts speculate
that the Elephantine Jews may have been part
of the ten lost tribes of the northern kingdom,
who vanished in 722 B.C.

Among the discoveries found at Elephantine
were papyrus scrolls from the fifth century B.C.
Written in Aramaic,
they included business documents
and letters from the colony.
The letters show that the Elephantine Jews
were in touch with the Jerusalem Jews.
They also show
that they celebrated the Passover
and held to Jewish traditions.

KHORSABAD
Giant slabs depicting cherubim (Genesis 3:24)
were found when the palace of Sargon II was excavated.
Records also tell of Assyria's victory over the North in 722 B.C.

NINEVEH
A prism found at this later Assyrian palace site
reports Sennacherib's expeditions against Judah in 701 B.C.
A library of over 20,000 clay tablets was also unearthed.

NIPPUR
Here archaeologists dug up asphalt-sealed jars
containing business records.
These documents
reveal how some Jews adjusted to everyday life in Babylon
after Jerusalem's fall in 586 B.C.

MACEDONIA

Black Sea

PHRYGIA

Mt. Ararat

MESOPOTAMIA

Mediterranean Sea

JERUSALEM

EGYPT

Red Sea

Time Chart

Judah in exile	586 BC	
	562	Nebuchadnezzar dies Others
	557	Cyrus rises in Persia
	555	Nabonidus in Babylon
Judah freed Exiles return	536	Cyrus defeats Nabonidus
	529	Cambyses
Temple reconstruction	522	Darius I
	486	Xerxes
	465	Others
	336	Alexander the Great
	335	Darius III
	331	Alexander rules Judah Alexander defeats Persia
	323	Alexander dies
	275	Egypt rules Judah

EXILE

REMNANT COMMUNITY

Books

Ezra	Joel
Nehemiah	Obadiah
Job	Jonah
Ecclesiastes	Haggai
Wisdom	Zechariah
Isaiah 40–66	Malachi
Ezekiel	

41

Can These Bones Live Again?

With Jerusalem in ashes,
the focus of Jewish history shifted to Babylon.
After the initial shock of exile wore off,
the Jews began to adjust to their new situation.
Many were given considerable freedom;
some even established themselves in trades.
In time, one group of Jews
became completely content with life in Babylon.

A second group, however,
began to think and reflect upon their past.
This group underwent a profound change.
They experienced a reawakening
of a faded, almost lost religious sensitivity.
In short, they experienced a religious conversion.

GOD'S WORD

With the temple miles away and in ruins,
devout Jews turned more and more to God's word
to keep their faith alive.
They gathered to hear it recited from memory,
or to hear read those sections
that had been written out on scrolls.

Two important developments
flowed from these weekly Sabbath meetings.

First, the meetings gave rise to a new worship place,
called the synagogue.
Prior to this time, all public worship took place
in the Jerusalem temple.

Now the synagogue came into being.
Synagogue worship focused on instruction and prayer,
in contrast to temple worship,
which focused on sacrificial offerings.

The second development was that Jewish scribes
began to write out those sections of God's word
that were preserved only in the memory of elders.
These sections were joined with other sections.
Later scribes
would edit them into a continuous whole.

EZEKIEL

The exiled Jews were guided also
by new revelation through new prophets.
One of these prophets was Ezekiel.
Along with Isaiah and Jeremiah,
he now ranks as one of Israel's greatest prophets.

Ezekiel grew up in Jerusalem.
After the first Babylonian invasion of the South,
he was deported to Babylon.
There he received his prophetic call.

Ezekiel's ministry divided into two periods:
before and after the final fall of Jerusalem.
Each period had its own special problems.

During his first days in exile,
Ezekiel warned Jews about their optimism.
Many Jews believed that no harm
could befall Jerusalem or the temple.
Anxiously, they awaited news from home—
news of Egyptian help,
or revolt against the forces of occupation.

Ezekiel warned that such optimism was folly.
As did previous prophets, he pointed out
that Israel's election as God's chosen people
involved moral obligations.
Only repentance would save the nation—
if not the nation, then a remnant of it.

Ezekiel's words fell on deaf ears.
The people persisted in their beliefs.

Finally, in 586 the fateful news arrived in Babylon:
"Jerusalem and the temple are in ashes!"
Refugees started to pour in from the fallen city.
The entire Jewish population
was plunged into unbelievable disillusionment.

Now Ezekiel's task was to save the people
from total despair.
Ezekiel the corrector became Ezekiel the comforter.
Ezekiel's message shifted to one of hope.
First, he prophesied the restoration of the people:

Thus says the Lord GOD . . .
"I will give you a new heart
and place a new spirit within you,
taking from your bodies your stony hearts
and giving you natural hearts. . . .
You shall live in the land I gave your fathers;
you shall be my people,
and I will be your God."

EZEKIEL 36:13, 26–28

Closely related to this prophecy
was Ezekiel's famous allegory of the "dry bones."
Set to music by exiled black slaves in America,
it gave hope to them, as it did to exiled Jews.

EZEKIEL   *The hand of the LORD came upon me,*
           and he led me out in the spirit of the LORD
           and set me in the center of the plain,
           which was now filled with bones. . . .

LORD   *Son of man, can these bones come to life?*

EZEKIEL   *Lord GOD, you alone know that.*

LORD   *Prophesy over these bones,*
           and say to them:
           Dry bones,
           hear the word of the LORD! . . .

EZEKIEL   *I prophesied as I had been told,*
           and even as I was prophesying
           I heard a noise; it was a rattling

as the bones came together,
bone joining bone.
I saw the sinews and the flesh
come upon them,
and the skin cover them . . .
and the spirit came into them;
they came alive. . . .

LORD   *Son of man, these bones*
        are the whole house of Israel.
        They have been saying,
        "Our bones are dried up,
        our hope is lost. . . ."

Therefore, prophesy and say to them:
Thus says the Lord GOD . . .
"I will put my spirit in you
that you may live. . . .
I have promised,
and I will do it, says the LORD."

EZEKIEL 37:1–14

Second, Ezekiel prophesied the restoration
of David's line.

Thus says the Lord GOD . . .
"I will save my sheep
so that they may no longer be despoiled. . . .
I will appoint one shepherd over them . . .
my servant David;
he shall pasture them and be their shepherd.
I, the Lord, will be their God,
and my servant David
shall be prince among them.
I, the LORD, have spoken."

EZEKIEL 34:20–24

Finally, Ezekiel prophesied the return of Yahweh
to the temple.

Then he led me to the gate which faces the east,
and there I saw the glory of the God of Israel
coming from the east.
I heard a sound

like the roaring of many waters,
and the earth shone with his glory. . . .

I fell prone as the glory of the Lord
entered the temple
by way of the gate which faces the east,
but spirit lifted me up
and brought me to the inner court.
And I saw that the temple
was filled with the glory of the Lord.
Then I heard someone speaking to me
from the temple. . . .
The voice said to me:
Son of man, this is where my throne shall be . . .
here I will dwell among the Israelites forever.

EZEKIEL 43:1–7

FULFILLMENT

New Testament writers
interpreted Jesus to be the final fulfillment
of all three of Ezekiel's prophecies.

new nation   Jesus sends the Holy Spirit,
who forms his followers into
a new holy nation of God (Acts 2).

new king   Jesus is the Good Shepherd,
the restored King of Israel
(John 10:11).

new temple   Jesus' followers became
the new living temple of
Yahweh's glory
(1 Corinthians 3:16–17).

Jesus and the New Testament, however,
were 500 years away.
For the present, any fulfillment
of Ezekiel's prophecies lay in the future.

Now, all that Israel could do was to wait
in silence and darkness.

188

Lost City

At the turn of the century,
a group called the German Oriental Society
equipped Professor Robert Koldewey
with a sizable archaeological team
to excavate a huge mound on the Euphrates River.

Eighteen years later,
Babylon, the most famous city of ancient history,
lay exposed in the grave of sand and rubble
that it had occupied for centuries.

42
Suffering Servant

Today, the ancient city of Babylon
has been resurrected from a grave of sand.
For the first time in centuries,
the desert sun shines on its walls and gateways.

Through the city's famous Isthar Gate
once passed Babylon's proud armies.
Carrying trophies of war,
they marched down the long parade street
that led to the center of the city.

An anonymous Jewish prophet of the exile
used to stand along this same street
and watch the great victory parades.
Known to history only as Second Isaiah,

Circling the ancient city
is an 11-mile-long wall.
Soaring to heights of 60 feet in places,
the wall has widths up to 15 feet.
Nearly 600 animals
decorate the wall's surface.

he prophesied in the spirit of the great Isaiah.
Thus, his works were appended to the earlier
prophet's writings.
Forming chapters 40–55,
they are often called the Book of Consolation.

PROPHET OF HOPE

Second Isaiah often walked through Babylon.
He saw its gods of masonry and iron,
and thought to himself:

Idol makers . . . neither see nor know anything;
and they are more deaf than men. . . .

The smith fashions an iron image,
works it over the coals,
shapes it with hammers,
and forges it with his strong arm. . . .
He implores it,
"Rescue me, for you are my god."

ISAIAH 44:9–17

The prophet shook his head: What a tragedy!
How different was Yahweh, the Lord of Israel—
even though he seemed silent now!

The LORD is the eternal God,
creator of the ends of the earth. . . .
They that hope in the LORD
will renew their strength,
they will soar as with eagles' wings;
they will run and not grow weary,
walk and not grow faint.

ISAIAH 40:28–31

With words like these, Second Isaiah
lifted the sagging spirit of Jewish exiles.

DAWN BREAKS

Then came a day of great excitement.
Rumors began filtering through to the exiles
of the spectacular feats of Cyrus, the king of Persia.
As the rumors multiplied,
so did the hopes of the people.

Was it possible?
Would the armies of Cyrus march on the city?
Would Cyrus be the instrument by which Yahweh
would reassert his presence in Israel's history?
Second Isaiah broke the silence.

189

The Isthar Gate
is one of eight passageways
into the city.
It opened onto
a wide parade street.
An inscription
found in Babylon reads:
"In this city
are 53 temples to chief gods,
55 chapels to Marduk,
and 180 altars to Isthar,"
the goddess of love and war.

Comfort, give comfort to my people,
says your God. . . .
Proclaim to her that her service is at an end.

ISAIAH 40:1–2

I say of Cyrus . . .
For the sake of Jacob, my servant, . . .
I have called you by your name,
giving you a title, though you knew me not. . . .

Let justice descend, O heavens,
like dew from above. . . .
Let the earth open and salvation bud forth.

ISAIAH 44:28; 45:4–8

So it happened that, after 50 years of waiting,
Second Isaiah announced
that Yahweh was about to free his people,
as he once freed their ancestors from Egypt.

SOMETHING NEW

The people will soon go forth across the desert
in a new exodus. The prophet says:

A voice cries out:
In the desert prepare the way of the LORD!
Make straight in the wasteland a highway
for our God!

ISAIAH 40:3

Israel's new exodus will culminate
in a new manifestation of God—
a new Sinai experience for all people.

Then the glory of the LORD shall be revealed,
and all mankind shall see it together.

ISAIAH 40:5

All mankind shall know
that I, the LORD, am your savior,
your redeemer, the mighty one of Jacob.

ISAIAH 49:26

SERVANT SONGS

Second Isaiah does more than prophesy
Israel's freedom from Babylon.
He foretells a new Sinai experience for all people,

190

The Isthar Gate and the parade street
as they may have appeared in ancient times.

Proud griffins, fierce bulls,
and snarling lions with red and yellow manes
sparkle against a background of blue glazed tile.

and Israel's role in this great event.
The prophecy is called
"The Suffering Servant Songs."

These songs refer to the servant
sometimes as an individual person
and sometimes as a community of people.
Why this ambiguity?

Scholars say that this was the way the Israelites
saw themselves: sometimes as a community,
and sometimes as an individual,
represented in the person of a single figure,
like the king.

The fourth Servant Song
presents a new concept in Old Testament thought.
It portrays suffering
as the way the servant will reveal God's glory
and become a blessing for all people.

See, my servant . . .
shall be raised high and greatly exalted. . . .
It was our infirmities that he bore,
our sufferings that he endured. . . .

We had all gone astray like sheep,
each following his own way;
but the LORD laid upon him the guilt of us all. . . .
Like a lamb led to the slaughter . . .
he was silent and opened not his mouth. . . .

Through his suffering,
my servant shall justify many. . . .
I will give him his portion among the great.
ISAIAH 52:13; 53:4–12

New Testament writers
interpreted this song as referring to Jesus.

NARRATOR *It happened that an Ethiopian . . .*
was sitting in his carriage
reading the prophet Isaiah. . . .
He invited Philip to get in
and sit down beside him.
This was the passage of Scripture
he was reading:
"Like a sheep
he was led to the slaughter . . .
and opened not his mouth. . . ."

ETHIOPIAN   *Tell me, if you will,*
of whom the prophet says this—
himself or someone else?

NARRATOR   *Philip launched out . . .*
telling him the good news of Jesus.
ACTS 8:27–35

Jesus also identified himself
with the "suffering servant."
On the third day after Jesus was crucified,
two downhearted disciples were returning home.
Jesus intercepted them,
but they failed to recognize him.
The disciples explained to the "stranger"
why they were downhearted.

DISCIPLES   *Our chief priests and leaders*
delivered Jesus up to be condemned
to death, and crucified him.
We were hoping that he was the one
who would set Israel free. . . .

JESUS   *How slow you are to believe*
all that the prophets have announced!
Did not the Messiah have to undergo
all this so as to enter into his glory?
LUKE 24:20–26

REJOICE

Second Isaiah ended his prophecies saying:

Yes, in joy you shall depart,
in peace you shall be brought back;
mountains and hills
shall break out in song before you,
and all the trees of the countryside
shall clap their hands.

ISAIAH 55:12

43
Like Men
Dreaming

As hope mounted among the exiled Jews,
so excitement mounted among Cyrus' troops
massing to attack Babylon.
Informers painted an ideal battle picture.
The popularity of Babylon's king, Nabonidus,
was plunging rapidly.
He was losing the support of his people.

Modern archaeologists
feel a strange kinship toward Nabonidus.
He too was fascinated by antiquity.
Sometimes called the world's first archaeologist,
he loved the past better than he ruled the present.
Excavated records report his interest in rebuilding
old temples.

Among his better-known reconstructions
was the famed Babylonian ziggurat,
which dated from before Abraham. We read:
"I restored this ziggurat to its former state
with mortar and baked bricks."
Twenty-five centuries later,
many of these bricks are still in good condition.
Arabs today occasionally load them on pack mules
and cart them off for use.

CYRUS II

In contrast to the unpopularity of Nabonidus
was the growing popularity of Cyrus.

Under his brilliant leadership,
the star of Persia began to ascend rapidly.
It reached its zenith under Darius the Great,
whose inscription on the cliffs of Behistun
provided the key for deciphering cuneiform.
Still standing in modern Iran are the remains
of the city of Persepolis, built by Darius.

The armies of Cyrus invaded Babylon,
and the city fell easily.
One record, called the Cyrus Cylinder,
says that Cyrus entered the city as a friend.

Unlike conquerors before him,
Cyrus did not deport defeated people for slave labor.
Nor did he suppress their religious traditions.
Rather,
he allowed them to remain in their homeland,
and Cyrus himself honored their gods.

Dating from the fifth century B.C.,
the Cyrus Cylinder was discovered at Babylon.
Speaking in the name of the great Persian king,
it boasts: "I am Cyrus, king of the world,
great king, mighty king."

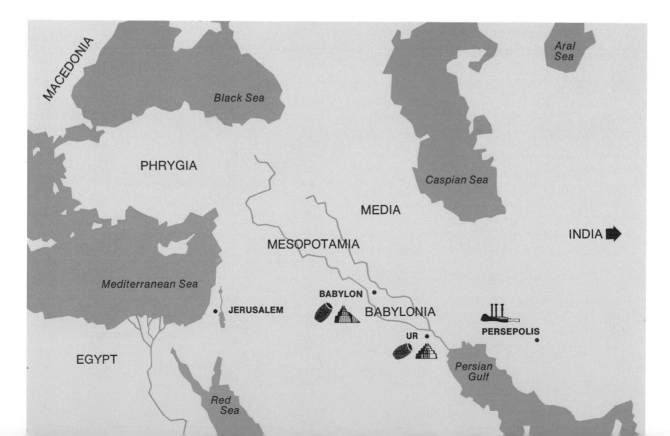

DECLARATION OF FREEDOM

In keeping with his policy toward defeated peoples,
Cyrus issued a proclamation to Jews in Babylon.
The Book of Ezra describes it.

The LORD inspired King Cyrus of Persia
to issue this proclamation
throughout his kingdom,
both by word of mouth and in writing. . . .

"All the kingdoms of the earth
the LORD, the God of heaven, has given to me,
and he has also charged me to build him
a house in Jerusalem, which is in Judah.
Whoever, therefore, among you
belongs to any part of his people, let him go up,
and may his God be with him!"

EZRA 1:1–3

The news of freedom was carried by runners
throughout Babylon.
For Jews who had lost hope and deserted their faith,
the news was embarrassing.
For Jews who had remained faithful to Yahweh,
the news brought joy beyond words.

LIKE MEN DREAMING

Even the former captors of the Jews
were caught up in the spirit.
They came forth with help in every way.
King Cyrus gave the exiles a farewell gift of
"utensils of the house of the LORD . . .
which Nebuchadnezzar had taken from Jerusalem
and placed in the house of his god" (Ezra 1:6–7).

The psalmist recalled Israel's day of freedom:

We were like men dreaming.
Then our mouth was filled with laughter,
and our tongue with rejoicing. . . .
"The LORD has done great things for us;
we are glad indeed."

PSALM 126:1–3

194

"I built Persepolis
beautiful and secure,"
wrote the Persian
King Darius I.

Darius' son, Xerxes, enlarged the city and royal palace.
A portion of the excavated ground plan is shown here.

Persepolis

Neither snow, nor rain,
nor heat, nor gloom of night
stays these couriers
from the swift completion
of their appointed rounds.

This line, adapted from the historian Herodotus and inscribed on the New York City post office, was a tribute to the messenger service established by Darius the Great in ancient Persia. Darius' greatest monument, however, was Persepolis, Greek meaning "Persian City." Its ruins still stand in mute protest to their destruction 2,500 years ago by the armies of Alexander the Great.

The palace at Persepolis ranks among the greatest examples of ancient Persian art and architecture known to modern archaeologists.

When news was announced that the armies of Alexander the Great were not far off, a frightened Darius III fled the palace, leaving behind even his harem.

Alexander's armies carried off
the treasures of the palace
and left the magnificent site
in wreckage and flames.

Twenty-two centuries later,
University of Chicago archaeologists excavated the ruins
buried under the drifting sands of centuries of storms.

44

A Remnant Rebuilds

A plane packed with American POWs
returning home after imprisonment in Vietnam
approached the airport.
On the ground, crowds milled about excitedly.
Then it happened.

Home at Last
NEWSWEEK

*In the control tower, a blip finally appeared
on the traffic controller's radarscope. . . .
"You are cleared for landing on Runway Zero Two,
repeat Zero Two. . . ."*

*When the white and grey Starlifter
settled onto the runway,
a tremendous cheer burst from the crowd—
a cheer echoed by the men on board.
While a phalanx of Air Force police
held back the onlookers,
the airplane taxied into position
and the crowd chanted over and over,
"Welcome home, welcome home."*

DIFFERENT STORY

No such homecoming greeted the Jewish POWs.
All that greeted them was a desolate city
and the charred remains of a once beautiful temple.
Weeds grew where jubilant crowds once walked.
The site of the ghost city ripped open old wounds
and snuffed out homecoming joy.

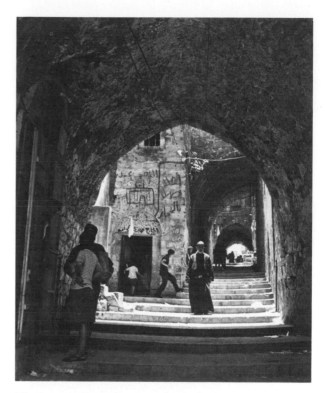

The narrow, stepped streets of today's Jerusalem
still retain some of the flavor of the ancient city.
Inside hole-in-the-wall cafes, old men sit placidly
drawing smoke through the water-filled bowls
of their hookah pipes.

In the months ahead,
the people cleared the rubble and began to rebuild.
Top priority was given to the temple.

As soon as the Jews started working on it,
however, Samaritans from the North
tried to block their efforts.
At times, workmen found themselves
building with one hand and fighting with the other.

To add to the hardship,
farm crops failed during the first season back.
The people found themselves in serious trouble.
Joy and enthusiasm
gave way to depression and discouragement.
Soon, bickering broke out among individuals
and groups.

These stones of the Western (Wailing) Wall
are all that remain of the ancient temple.
Remodeled by Herod in Jesus' time,
it was destroyed by the Romans in A.D. 70.

meek, and riding on an ass. . . .
His dominion shall be from sea to sea,
and from the River to the ends of the earth.

ZECHARIAH 9:9–10

New Testament writers recalled this prophecy
when Jesus rode into Jerusalem on Palm Sunday.

"Tell the daughter of Zion,
Your king comes to you without display . . .
astride a colt, the foal of a beast of burden."

MATTHEW 21:5

NEHEMIAH AND EZRA

Then a big boost to morale occurred.
A second wave of exiles returned from Babylon.
Buoyed in spirit and strengthened in numbers,
the people finished building the temple.

Next, the people turned their attention
to rebuilding the city walls.
Under the dynamic leadership of Nehemiah,
who returned with a third wave of exiles,
the job was completed.

Finally, around 450 B.C.,
the day for celebration came.
Ezra assembled the faithful remnant of Jews
to renew their covenant with Yahweh.

The whole people gathered as one man
in the open space before the Water Gate,
and they called upon Ezra the scribe
to bring forth the book of the law of Moses. . . .

Standing at one end of the open place . . .
he read out of the book from daybreak till midday,
in the presence of the men, the women,
and those children old enough to understand;
and all the people listened attentively. . . .

Ezra blessed the LORD, the great God,
and all the people, their hands raised high,
answered, "Amen, amen!"

NEHEMIAH 8:1–6

Into this critical situation stepped two prophets,
Haggai and Zechariah.
Haggai challenged the people:

Thus says the LORD of hosts:
"Consider your ways! . . .
You expected much, but it came to little;
and what you brought home, I blew away.
For what cause?"

HAGGAI 1:7–9

Zechariah encouraged the people.
He reminded them of Yahweh's promise
that days of glory lay ahead.

Shout for joy, O daughter Jerusalem!
See, your king shall come to you;
a just savior is he,

45

The Reluctant Preacher

A man who is preoccupied with his own problems
tends to see only himself.
His vision shrinks and he forgets
there are other people in the world.

Something like this happened to the Jews
in the years after their return from exile.
They isolated themselves from the world.
The people made Yahweh
into their own image and likeness.
He became a nationalistic God
who was little concerned about the rest of the world
and mainly concerned about his chosen people.

Two prophets emerged to challenge this attitude.
Their words are recorded in the Book of Malachi
and in the Book of Jonah.

MALACHI

The Book of Malachi describes a day
when all nations will worship Yahweh together.

From the rising of the sun, even to its setting,
my name is great among the nations;
and everywhere
they bring sacrifice to my name,
and a pure offering;
for great is my name among the nations,
says the LORD of hosts.

MALACHI 1:11

JONAH

The most forceful challenge to Jewish nationalism
comes in the Book of Jonah.
This book of four short chapters is still hotly debated.
Literalists regard it as a factual report.
Contextualists regard it as a book-length parable
containing an important religious message.

Here is the Book of Jonah in dialogue form.

Chapter One

NARRATOR   *This is the word of the LORD*
that came to Jonah, son of Amittai:

"Set out for the great city of Nineveh,
and preach against it. . . ."

But Jonah . . .
found a ship going to Tarshish . . .
to journey . . . away from the LORD.

The LORD . . .
hurled a violent wind upon the sea,
and . . . the ship was on the point
of breaking up.

Then the mariners became frightened
and each one cried to his god. . . .

Meanwhile, Jonah
had gone down into the hold of the ship,
and lay there fast asleep. . . .

MARINERS   *Let us cast lots to find out*
on whose account
we have met with this misfortune.

NARRATOR   *So they cast lots,*
and thus singled out Jonah. . . .
The sea
was growing more and more turbulent. . . .

Then they took Jonah
and threw him into the sea,
and the sea's raging abated. . . .

Chapter Two

NARRATOR   *But the LORD sent a large fish,*
that swallowed Jonah;
and he remained in the belly of the fish
three days and three nights.
From the belly of the fish Jonah said
this prayer to the LORD, his God:

JONAH   *. . . You cast me into the deep,*
into the heart of the sea. . . .
The waters swirled about me,
threatening my life;
the abyss enveloped me;
seaweed clung about my head.

Down I went
to the roots of the mountains . . .
but you brought up my life
from the pit, O LORD, my God. . . .

NARRATOR   *Then the LORD commanded the fish*
to spew Jonah upon the shore.

Chapter Three

NARRATOR   *The word of the LORD*
came to Jonah a second time:
"Set out for the great city of Nineveh,
and announce to it
the message that I will tell you."

So Jonah made ready
and went to Nineveh,
according to the LORD's bidding.
Now Nineveh
was an enormously large city;
it took three days to go through it.

Jonah began his journey through the city,
and had gone but a single day's walk
announcing, "Forty days more
and Nineveh shall be destroyed,"
when the people of Nineveh believed God;
they proclaimed a fast and all of them,
great and small, put on sackcloth. . . .

When God saw by their actions how they
turned from their evil way, he repented
of the evil that he had threatened to do
to them; he did not carry it out.

Modern Tel Aviv, viewed from adjoining Joppa,
where Jonah boarded a ship for Tarshish.
Centuries later, Crusaders,
commanded by Richard the Lionhearted,
used this same port
to reconquer the Holy Land.

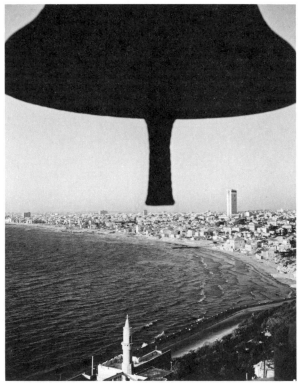

Chapter Four

NARRATOR *But this was greatly displeasing to Jonah,*
and he became angry.

JONAH *I beseech you, LORD,*
is not this what I said
while I was still in my own country?
This is why I fled at first to Tarshish.
I knew that you are a gracious
and merciful God, slow to anger,
rich in clemency, loathe to punish. . . .

NARRATOR *Jonah then left the city for a place*
to the east of it, where he built himself
a hut and waited . . .
to see what would happen to the city.
And when the LORD God provided
a gourd plant, that grew up
over Jonah's head, giving shade
that relieved him of any discomfort,
Jonah was very happy over the plant.

But the next morning at dawn
God sent a worm which attacked
the plant, so that it withered.
And when the sun arose,
God sent a burning east wind;
and the sun beat upon Jonah's head
till he became faint. . . .

JONAH *I would be better off dead than alive.*

GOD *Have you reason*
to be angry over the plant?

JONAH *I have reason to be angry,*
angry enough to die.

GOD *You are concerned over the plant*
which cost you no labor
and which you did not raise;
it came up in one night
and in one night it perished.
And should I not be concerned
over Nineveh, the great city,

in which there are more than
a hundred and twenty thousand persons
who cannot distinguish
their right hand from their left,
not to mention the many cattle?

The point of the Book of Jonah
is contained in its ending.
After the humor subsides,
a serious question is left hanging in the air.
The author has God put it to Jonah this way:

"You are concerned over the plant. . . .
Should I not be concerned over Nineveh?"

The point is clear: God is concerned
not just about Jews, but all people.
Moreover, God's concern
must become the Jews' concern also.

The Book of Jonah
reveals to Jews a new universalism
concerning God's activity in human history.

NEW TESTAMENT TIMES

Jesus referred to the story of Jonah to clarify
his own mission and message. Luke writes:

While the crowds pressed around Jesus
he began to speak to them in these words:
"This is an evil age. It seeks a sign.
But no sign will be given it
except the sign of Jonah.
Just as Jonah was a sign for the Ninevites,
so will the Son of Man be a sign
for the present age. . . .
At the judgment, the citizens of Nineveh
will rise along with the present generation,
and they will condemn it.
For at the preaching of Jonah they reformed,
but you have a greater than Jonah here."

LUKE 11:29–32

201

46

Voice in the Storm

Judah's ghetto years ended
when the armies of Alexander the Great
invaded the Near East.

Alexander was not a power-mad egotist.
A student of the great Aristotle,
he saw himself as a disciple of Hellenic culture.
He wanted to bring its blessings to all the world.

The Roman historian Plutarch
says Alexander's joy of victory was sobered
when he read the inscription on Cyrus' tomb:

O man, whoever you are
and wherever you came from—
for I know you will come—
I am Cyrus, son of Cambyses,
who gave the Persians their empire.
Do not begrudge me
this tiny plot of earth
where my body rests.

Alexander marched his armies to India
before he stopped to solidify his gains.
At the age of 32, he headed the largest empire
ever ruled by one man.

But death, the ultimate tyrant,
closed the door on his brilliant career.
Alexander died without an heir.
Three bickering generals divided his empire.

Two powerful kingdoms developed from it:
the Syrian (Seleucid) and the Egyptian (Ptolemy).
The Jews found themselves controlled first by one,
then the other.

NAGGING INCOMPLETENESS

This pawnlike existence jolted Jewish pride.
It shattered their dreams of political independence.
What chance did a tiny nation have
in a world of giants?

Now, a disturbing sense of incompleteness
began to nag at Jewish hearts. It is reflected
in the Book of Ecclesiastes.

"Tombs are their homes forever . . .
though they have called lands by their names.
Thus man, for all his splendor, does not abide. . . .
But God will redeem me
from the power of the nether world. . . ."

Psalm 49:12–16

This 30-foot-high limestone tomb of Cyrus
is in modern Iran.

But After All That

In a meditation on Alexander the Great
the First Book of Maccabees says:

The earth fell silent before him. . . .
But after all this he took to his bed,
realizing that he was going to die.
He therefore summoned his officers . . .
to divide his kingdom among them. (1:3–6)

This portrait of Alexander
is part of a larger mosaic unearthed at Pompeii.
Containing over a million pieces of marble,
it is patterned after a painting
of Alexander's victory
over the Persian king, Darius III.

The eye is not satisfied with seeing
nor is the ear filled with hearing. . . .
I have seen all things that are done under the sun,
and behold, all is vanity and a chase after wind.

ECCLESIASTES 1:8, 14

Sensing that Judah has reached its day of drums,
the book's author, Qoheleth, writes:

The race is not won by the swift,
nor the battle by the valiant,
nor a livelihood by the wise . . .
for a time of calamity comes to all alike.

ECCLESIASTES 9:11

Repeatedly, the author raises the question:
What is the purpose of life?
His inability to answer the question
gives his work a tinge of sadness—the kind of
sadness that trademarks so many great works.

Classic writers see human moments of joy
and peaks of glory, but deep in their hearts
they know that these things are like the dawn dew—
doomed to disappear.
It is this affirmation of people's fragility
that gives great literature its timeless appeal.

Occasionally Qoheleth counterpoints his sadness
with flights of advice to enjoy life.

Go, eat your bread with joy
and drink your wine with a merry heart.

ECCLESIASTES 9:7

But in the end all things are vanity.
Human life moves in a monotonous, tragic cycle.

Television viewers caught this feeling
as they listened to the reading from Ecclesiastes
during the funeral services for John F. Kennedy
on November 25, 1963.

203

Is It All Useless?

Remember your Creator in the days of your youth,
before the evil days come. . . .

When the guardians of the house tremble . . .

and the grinders are idle because they are few,
and they who look through the windows grow blind;

when the doors to the street are shut,
and the sound of the mill is low . . .

when the almond tree blooms,
and the locust grows sluggish
and the caper berry is without effect . . .

before the silver cord is snapped
and the golden bowl is broken . . .

and the dust returns to the earth as it once was,
and the life breath returns to God
who gave it.

Vanity of vanities, says Qoheleth,
all things are vanity!

ECCLESIASTES 12:1–8
New American Bible

Remember your Creator while you are still young,
before those dismal days and years come. . . .

Then your arms, that protect you, will tremble. . . .

Your teeth will be too few to chew your food,
and your eyes too dim to see clearly.

Your ears will be deaf to the noise of the street.
You will barely be able to hear the mill as it grinds. . . .

Your hair will turn white;
you will hardly be able to drag yourself along,
and all desire will be gone. . . .

The silver chain will snap,
and the golden lamp will fall and break. . . .

Our bodies will return to the dust of the earth,
and the breath of life will go back to God,
who gave it to us.

Useless, useless, said the Philosopher.
It is all useless.

ECCLESIASTES 12:1–8
Today's English Version

There is an appointed time for everything. . . .
A time to be born, and a time to die;
a time to plant, and a time to uproot the plant. . . .
A time to weep, and a time to laugh;
a time to mourn, and a time to dance. . . .
A time to love, and a time to hate;
a time of war, and a time of peace.

ECCLESIASTES 3:1–8

WHAT'S THE ANSWER?

Ecclesiastes contains none of the certainty
of the Book of Proverbs.
The book asks all the big questions,
but comes up only with the admission
that it doesn't know the answers.
"Somewhere out there," the author seems to admit,
"there is an answer, but I don't know what it is."

The Book of Ecclesiastes helps us enter
the heart of a Jew waiting for more revelation.
Early Jews had little or no idea of an afterlife.
True, they believed in a nether world, *Sheol.*
But they thought it was just a place for the dead,
good and bad alike.
What happened there, they did not know.

The question emerged:
If God is good, and if this is man's only home,
why do so many good people go unrewarded?
Worse yet, why do so many suffer so much?

THREE SUGGESTED ANSWERS

One proposal was that such people suffered
because of secret sins.

A second suggestion was that they suffered
because they belonged to the total community
of Israel.
The Book of Deuteronomy seemed to indicate
that God treated Israel as a total community.
Thus, an innocent man might suffer
because he was a member of a guilty whole.

A third proposal was that innocent people suffered
because of the sins of their parents or children.
Thus, one person or the whole community
might suffer because of the sins of another.

A CORRECTION

Later prophets, like Ezekiel, corrected this view.

What is the meaning of this proverb
that you recite in the land of Israel:
"Fathers have eaten green grapes,
thus their children's teeth are on edge"?

"As I live," says the Lord GOD . . .
"there shall no longer be anyone among you
who will repeat this proverb in Israel. . . .

"Only the one who sins shall die.
The son shall not be charged
with the guilt of his father,
nor shall the father
be charged with the guilt of his son."

EZEKIEL 18:2–3, 20

In spite of Ezekiel's revelation,
many Jews
continued to be influenced by the older view,
even in New Testament times.

As Jesus walked along,
he saw a man who had been blind from birth.
His disciples asked him,
"Rabbi, was it his sin or that of his parents
that caused him to be born blind?"
"Neither," answered Jesus.

JOHN 9:1–3

Jews who accepted Ezekiel's new revelation
were forced to examine the question:
Why do good people suffer?
For the answer to this question,
we must turn to the Book of Job.

THE BOOK OF JOB

Cast of Characters

NARRATOR	ELIPHAZ ⎫
LORD	BILDAD ⎬ FRIENDS OF JOB
SATAN	ZOPHAR ⎭
JOB	ELIHU, YOUNG BYSTANDER

NARRATOR *There was a man named Job,*
living in the land of Uz,
who worshiped God
and was faithful to him.
He was a good man,
careful not to do anything evil.
He had seven sons and three daughters,
and owned 7,000 sheep, 3,000 camels,
1,000 head of cattle, and 500 donkeys.
He also had a large number
of servants and was
the richest man in the East.

ACT 1

Scene i

NARRATOR *When the day came*
for the heavenly beings
to appear before the LORD,
Satan was there among them.

LORD *What have you been doing?*

SATAN *I have been walking here and there,*
roaming around the earth.

LORD *Did you notice my servant Job?*
There is no one on earth
as faithful and good as he is.
He worships me and is careful
not to do anything evil.

SATAN *Would Job worship you*
if he got nothing out of it?
You have protected him and his family
and everything he owns.

You bless everything he does,
and you have given him enough cattle
to fill the whole country.
But now suppose
you take away everything he has—
he will curse you to your face!

LORD *All right, everything he has*
is in your power,
but you must not hurt Job himself.

[Exit Satan]

Scene ii

NARRATOR *[Misfortune strikes Job's household.*
Enemies steal his cattle and kill his
servants. Lightning destroys his sheep.
Outlaws carry off his camels.
A wind flattens his house,
killing his sons and daughters.]

Called "ships of the desert," camels
made trade possible across Middle East deserts.
Camel milk delighted the nomad's taste;
camel skin was used for clothing and tent coverings.

Job tore his clothes in grief.
He shaved his head
and threw himself face downward
on the ground.

JOB *I was born with nothing,
and I will die with nothing.
The LORD gave,
and now he has taken away.
May his name be praised!*

NARRATOR *In spite of everything
that had happened,
Job did not sin by blaming God.*

Scene iii

NARRATOR *When the day came
for the heavenly beings
to appear before the LORD again,
Satan was there among them.*

LORD *Where have you been?*

SATAN *I have been walking here and there,
roaming around the earth.*

LORD *Did you notice my servant Job?
There is no one on earth
as faithful and good as he is.
He worships me and is careful
not to do anything evil.
You persuaded me to let you
attack him for no reason at all,
but Job is still as faithful as ever.*

SATAN *A man will give up everything
in order to stay alive.
But now suppose you hurt his body—
he will curse you to your face!*

LORD *All right, he is in your power,
but you are not to kill him.*

[Exit Satan]

Scene iv

NARRATOR *[Severe boils blanket Job's body.
He suffers in deep torment.]*

[Enter three friends of Job]

*[At the sight of Job, his three friends]
began to weep and wail,
tearing their clothes in grief. . . .
Finally Job broke the silence
and cursed
the day on which he had been born.*

JOB *. . . Turn that day into darkness, God.
Never again remember that day;
never again let light shine on it. . . .*

ELIPHAZ *Job, will you be annoyed if I speak? . . .
Evil does not grow in the soil. . . .
Man brings trouble on himself,
as surely as sparks fly up
from a fire. . . .
Do not resent it
when God rebukes you. . . .*

JOB *I have never opposed what God
commands. . . . In trouble like this
I need loyal friends. . . .
Don't condemn me. . . .*

ZOPHAR *Put your heart right, Job.
Reach out to God.
Put away evil and wrong
from your home.
Then face the world again,
firm and courageous. . . .*

JOB *You hit a man who is about to fall. . . .
I am in the right.
Are you coming to accuse me, God?
If you do,
I am ready to be silent and die. . . .
Why do you treat me
like an enemy? . . .*

207

ELIPHAZ   *Can any man be really pure?*
Can anyone be right with God?
Why, God does not trust even
his angels;
even they are not pure in his sight.
And man drinks evil as if it were
water; yes, man is corrupt. . . .

JOB   *The comfort you give*
is only torment. . . .
I want someone to plead with God
for me,
as a man pleads for his friend. . . .

BILDAD   *You are only hurting yourself*
with your anger. . . .

JOB   *Why do you keep tormenting me . . .*
and regard my troubles
as proof of my guilt?
Can't you see it is God
who has done this? . . .
He has taken away all my wealth
and destroyed my reputation.

ZOPHAR   *Job, you upset me. . . .*
What you have said is an insult. . . .

JOB   *Listen to what I am saying;*
that is all the comfort I ask. . . .

ELIPHAZ   *Now, Job, make peace with God*
and stop treating him like an enemy. . . .
Put an end to all the evil
that is done in your house. . . .

JOB   *I will never give up my claim*
to be right; my conscience is clear. . . .
I swear every word is true. . . .

NARRATOR   *Because Job was convinced*
of his own innocence, the three men
gave up trying to answer him.
[Then a bystander, Elihu, spoke up.]

ELIHU   *I am young, and you are old,*
so I was afraid
to tell you what I think. . . .
But I tell you, Job, you are wrong. . . .
Be careful not to turn to evil;
your suffering was sent to keep you
from it. . . .
No one can tell God what to do
or accuse him of doing evil. . . .

[Curtain]

ACT 2

Scene i

NARRATOR   *[Suddenly, a violent storm blows up:*
wind, lightning, and thunder.]
Then out of the storm
the LORD spoke to Job.

LORD   *Answer the questions I ask you.*
Were you there when I made the world?
If you know so much, tell me about it.
Who decided how large it would be?
Who stretched the measuring line
over it?
Do you know all the answers?
What holds up the pillars
that support the earth? Who laid
the cornerstone of the world? . . .

Have you ever visited the storerooms,
where I keep the snow? . . .
Who is the mother of the ice . . .
which turns the waters to stone . . . ?

Have you watched wild deer . . . ?
Do you know how long
they carry their young? Do you
know the time for their birth? . . .

Was it you, Job,
who made horses so strong? . . .
They eagerly paw the ground
in the valley;

The Horse

In ancient times,
horses were reserved mainly for war purposes.
Battle chariots were usually pulled by two steeds,
with a third running alongside for quick change.

they rush into battle
with all their strength.
They do not know
the meaning of fear,
and no sword can turn them back. . . .
Does a hawk
learn from you how to fly?
Does an eagle wait for your command
to build its nest? If so . . .
I will be the first to praise you
and admit
that you won the victory yourself. . . .

JOB   *LORD, I talked about things*
I did not understand. . . .

I knew only
what others had told me,
but now I have seen you
with my own eyes.
So I am ashamed of all I have said
and repent in dust and ashes.

[Curtain]

Epilogue

NARRATOR   *After the LORD had finished speaking . . .*
he blessed the last part of Job's life
even more
than he had blessed the first.

Today's English Version

209

Unfathomable

The God who emerges from the Book of Job
is a God beyond human comprehension.
The greatest blunder a person can make,
the book seems to say,
is to try to reduce God to the level
of human definition and comprehension.

Augustine, the great fifth-century Christian,
put it this way:

God is inexpressible.
It is easier for us to say what he is not
than what he is. . . .
Nothing is comparable to him. . . .
If you could conceive him,
you would conceive something other than God.
He is not at all
what you have conceived him to be.

TRADITIONAL VIEW

If we approach the Book of Job
as *wisdom* literature, several points emerge.

Job's three friends answer Job's questions
in the traditional way,
presupposing that he is being punished for sin.
Their understanding of God,
that he rewards and punishes people in *this* life,
demands that they adopt this view.
To take the opposite view
would be to accuse God of being unjust.

ALTERNATE VIEW

Knowing in his heart that he is innocent,
Job is forced to search for an answer himself.

First, he toys with the idea
that God regards him as some kind of enemy.
But this seems unconvincing, even to Job.

Second, Job speaks the celebrated lines:

In this body I will see God.
I will see him with my own eyes. (19:26–27)

Some Bible readers cite this passage
as one of the first Old Testament indications
of a belief in the resurrection of the body.
Thus, Job will be rewarded in a life to come.

Others say that Job's statement
should not be interpreted
as referring to an afterlife.
For Job himself says earlier:

I will call the grave my father,
and the worms that eat me
I will call my mother and my sisters. (17:14)

In any event, Job continues to search
for an answer to his suffering.
When he can find none, he cries out:
"Let Almighty God answer me." (31:35)

At this point, young Elihu enters the picture.
Some suggest
that Elihu will grant Job's innocence (36:21).
Perhaps God is inflicting pain on Job
to keep him from sinning gravely in the future.

But Job's suffering is so great
that Job cannot accept this explanation.
Punishment for the greatest sin in the world
could not be any worse than his present pain.

Then out of the storm,
the LORD spoke to Job. (38:1)

NEW VIEW

God's words to Job
take the form of a recital of the wonders of nature.
God reminds Job,
in a dramatic series of rhetorical questions,
that Job neither created, manages,
nor understands the universe.

This doesn't answer Job's question directly,
but it does suggest a new line of thought.
It is this:
If Job admits God's wisdom greatly surpasses his,
why does he question God's fairness to him?
If he can't understand other things,
why does he expect to understand this?

Expressed in *wisdom literature* terms,
it comes down to this:
Job's wisdom falls so short of God's wisdom
that it is folly for Job to challenge God.
To challenge God
is the posture of a fool, not a *wise* man.

In any event, Job's experience of God
changes him from a sage into a saint.
It transforms him
from a man who walked by the light of reason
to a man who walked by the light of faith.

The Door Opens

Later Old Testament books
made further inroads into the vexing question
posed in the Book of Job.

The Book of Wisdom
broke new ground in the second century B.C.
It reads:

[The wicked said] . . .
"Brief and troublous is our lifetime. . . .
Haphazard were we born,
and hereafter we shall be
as though we had not been. . . .
Come, therefore . . .
let us have our fill of costly wine and perfumes,
and let no springtime blossom pass us by. . . .
Let no meadow be free from our wantonness. . . .
Let our strength be our norm of justice;
for weakness proves itself useless. . . ."

These were their thoughts, but they erred. . . .
For God formed man to be imperishable;
the image of his own nature he made him. . . .

The souls of the just are in the hand of God,
and no torment shall touch them.
They seemed, in the view of the foolish,
to be dead . . .
and their going forth from us,
utter destruction.
But they are in peace.

For if before men, indeed,
they be punished,
yet is their hope full of immortality;
chastised a little,
they shall be greatly blessed,
because God tried them
and found them worthy of himself.

WISDOM 2:1–3:5

47

Dreams and Visions

The sense of incompleteness in Jewish hearts
exploded into agony in 167 B.C.
The stage was set this way.

Around 200 B.C., Syrian armies conquered Egypt.
Judah passed from Egyptian hands to Syrian hands.
At first, Judah's status remained about the same.
But then a Hellenic-minded tyrant, Antiochus IV,
took over the Syrian throne.

Calling himself Epiphanes, he fancied himself
an incarnation of the Greek god Zeus.
Coins bearing his name
were found by American archaeologists in 1931,
in a dig west of the Dead Sea.
It was this king who decided
to make Greeks out of his Jewish subjects.

The king sent messengers with letters
to Jerusalem and to the cities of Judah,
ordering them to follow customs
foreign to their land: to prohibit . . . sacrifices . . .
to profane the sabbaths and feast days,
to desecrate the sanctuary and the sacred ministers,
to build pagan altars and temples and shrines. . . .

He appointed inspectors over all the people. . . .
Any scrolls of the law which they found
they tore up and burnt.
Whoever was found with a scroll of the covenant,
and whoever observed the law,
was condemned to death by royal decree.

1 MACCABEES 1:44–57

This decree created an impossible situation.
Those who disobeyed it were persecuted brutally.
Typical was the martyrdom of seven brothers,
while their mother looked on (2 Maccabees 7).

FAITH CRISIS

This reign of terror shook Judah's faith to the roots.
Devout Jews cried out to God:

How long, O LORD?
Will you hide yourself forever? . . .
Where are your ancient favors, O Lord,
which you pledged to David by your faithfulness?

PSALM 89:47–50

Into this crisis
stepped the unknown prophet of the Book of Daniel.
Like prophets before him, he faced the problem
of communicating a profound religious message
to a simple, uneducated people.
He had decided upon two literary devices to do it:
folktales and visions.
These he centered around a Jewish hero, Daniel.

BOOK OF DANIEL

The Book of Daniel divides into two parts:
the first half narrates a series of folktales;
the second half describes a series of visions.

The book opens on the eve of Jewish exile in 586 B.C.,
just after Babylon destroys Jerusalem.
The king of Babylon
instructs his army officer to take prisoners:

Israelites of royal blood and of the nobility,
young men without any defect, handsome,
intelligent and wise, quick to learn . . .
such as could take their place in the king's palace;
they were to be taught
the language and literature of the Chaldeans;
after three years' training
they were to enter the king's service.

DANIEL 1:3–5

The Syrian (Seleucid) ruler
Antiochus I.

The god Zeus
poised to hurl a thunderbolt
with his mighty right arm.

Antiochus IV

This 2,000-year-old coin portrays Antiochus I.
From his line came Antiochus IV,
who called himself Epiphanes (god-manifest).
In mocking hatred,
Jews dubbed him Epimanes (madman).

Antiochus thought himself
to be a manifestation of the Greek god Zeus,
pictured on the fifth-century B.C. coin
at the right, above.

He ordered Zeus' statue to be erected
in the place of honor in the Jerusalem temple.
Jews condemned the act,
calling it the "abomination of desolation"
or the "terrible sin" (Daniel 8:13).

It is interesting to note
that it was in honor of the same god, Zeus,
that the Olympic games were begun in 776 B.C.
and celebrated thereafter at four-year intervals.

FOLKTALES

The first tale describes
Daniel's fidelity to Jewish laws and customs
during his first days in Babylon.

NARRATOR *The king allotted the young men*
a daily portion of food and wine
from the royal table. . . .
But Daniel . . .
begged the chief chamberlain
to spare him this defilement. . . .

CHAMBERLAIN *I am afraid of my lord the king;*
it is he
who allotted your food and drink.
If he sees that you look wretched
by comparison with
the other young men of your age,
you will endanger my life
with the king.

DANIEL *Please test your servants for ten days.*
Give us vegetables to eat
and water to drink.
Then see how we look in comparison
with the other young men. . . .

NARRATOR *The chief steward*
acceded to this request . . . ;
after ten days they looked healthier
and better fed. . . .
So the steward continued to take away
the food and drink they were to
receive, and gave them vegetables.

To these four young men
God gave knowledge and proficiency
in all literature and science,
and to Daniel the understanding
of all visions and dreams.

DANIEL 1:5–17

215

UNHEWN STONE

A second tale concerns a disturbing dream
that the king had.
When the king's wise men show ignorance about it,
Daniel is called in.

KING   *Can you tell me the dream that I had,*
and its meaning? . . .

DANIEL *In your vision, O king,*
you saw a statue,
very large and exceedingly bright,
terrifying in appearance
as it stood before you.

The head of the statue was pure gold,
its chest and arms were silver,
its belly and thighs bronze,
the legs iron,
its feet partly iron and partly tile.

While you looked at the statue,
a stone which was hewn from a mountain
without a hand being put to it,
struck its iron and tile feet,
breaking them in pieces . . .
and the wind blew them away
without leaving a trace.
But the stone that struck the statue
became a great mountain
and filled the whole earth.

This was the dream;
the interpretation we shall also give. . . .

You are the head of gold.
Another kingdom shall take your place,
inferior to yours,
then a third kingdom, of bronze,
which shall rule over the whole earth.

There shall be a fourth kingdom,
strong as iron;

it shall break in pieces
and subdue all these others,
just as iron breaks in pieces
and crushes everything else.
The feet and toes you saw,
partly of potter's tile and partly of iron,
mean that it shall be
a divided kingdom. . . .

In the lifetime of those kings
the God of heaven will set up a kingdom
that shall never be destroyed
or delivered up to another people;
rather, it shall break in pieces all these
kingdoms and put an end to them,
and it shall stand forever.

That is the meaning of the stone
you saw hewn from the mountain. . . .
The great God has revealed to the king
what shall be in the future;
this is exactly what you dreamed,
and its meaning is sure.

DANIEL 2:26–45

The four kingdoms are the great empires
(Babylonian, Median, Persian, Greek)
that dominated the Near East
from the time of the Jewish exile
to the era of Jewish persecution.

Daniel's message is one of hope.
God will soon destroy the last of these empires.

New Testament writers
interpreted Jesus to be the unhewn stone,
rejected by human builders (Luke 20:18).

New Testament writers also
interpreted the kingdom of God, preached by Jesus,
to be the eternal kingdom foretold in this vision.

216

Darius and the Lion

King Darius I of Persia
takes aim at the head of a wounded lion.
Once the target
of a popular, ancient sport,
the lion is now extinct in the Near East.

The winged emblem above the carving
symbolizes Ahurmazka,
the national god of ancient Persia.

Made from a fifth-century B.C. cylinder,
this seal measures
two inches by four inches.

Darius' name appears to the right in three languages.
It was this same Darius whose Behistun inscription
(same three languages) solved the riddle of cuneiform.

LIONS' DEN

A third tale concerns Daniel's fidelity to prayer.
As Daniel grew older, King Darius the Mede
made him one of his chief administrators.
The other administrators grew jealous of Daniel.
They connived to have the king issue a decree
forbidding prayer to anyone but the king.
Daniel ignored the decree.

NARRATOR *Daniel continued his custom*
of going home to kneel in prayer
and give thanks to his God. . . .

So the administrators rushed in
and found Daniel praying. . . .
They then went to remind the king
about the prohibition.

MEN *Did you not decree, O king,*
that no one is to address a petition
to god or man for thirty days,
except to you . . . ?

KING *The decree is absolute, irrevocable*
under Mede and Persian law.

MEN *Daniel, the Jewish exile,*
has paid no attention to you. . . .

NARRATOR *The king was deeply grieved. . . .*
He ordered Daniel to be brought
and cast into the lions' den.

KING *[to Daniel] May your God,*
whom you serve so constantly,
save you. . . .

NARRATOR *Then the king returned to his palace*
for the night; he refused to eat
and he dismissed the entertainers.

Since sleep was impossible for him,
the king rose very early
the next morning
and hastened to the lions' den. . . .

KING	*O Daniel, servant of the living God,* *has the God whom you serve* *so constantly* *been able to save you from the lions?*
DANIEL	*O king, live forever!* *My God has sent his angel* *and closed the lions' mouths* *so that they have not hurt me. . . .*
NARRATOR	*This gave the king great joy.* *At his order* *Daniel was removed from the den,* *unhurt because he trusted in his God.*

DANIEL 6:11-24

The message, again, is one of hope.
Yahweh will save his people
just as he saved Daniel from the jaws of the lions.

VISIONS

The visions of Daniel
begin in the second half of the book.
They are filled with strange images and symbols.
This kind of colorful writing style
is often referred to as apocalyptic writing.
The author's purpose is to communicate,
in a veiled (apocalyptic) way, things to come.

Apocalyptic writing is similar to prophetic writing,
but there are differences.
Prophetic writing
stresses human cooperation with God's plan;
apocalyptic writing
stresses God's final control over his plan.
Prophetic writing calls for action;
apocalyptic writing calls for patience.

The apocalyptic writer tells his readers
that God's action in the present is nothing
compared to what will happen in the future.
People must therefore be patient and trust in God.

THE SON OF MAN

Daniel's first vision is regarded by many experts
as the most important.
Daniel sees four beasts emerge from the sea.

Thrones were set up
and the Ancient One took his throne. . . .
Thousands upon thousands
were ministering to him. . . .
The court was convened,
and the books were opened.

DANIEL 7:9-10

The Ancient One and the court then pass judgment
on the four beasts.
After the judgment is passed, the visions continue.
Daniel says:

As the visions during the night continued,
I saw one like a son of man coming,
on the clouds of heaven;
when he reached the Ancient One
and was presented before him,
he received dominion, glory, and kingship;
nations and peoples of every language serve him. . . .
His kingship shall not be destroyed.

I, Daniel, found my spirit anguished . . .
and I was terrified by the visions of my mind.

I approached one of those present
and asked him what all this meant in truth;
in answer, he made known to me
the meaning of the things:

"These four great beasts stand for four kingdoms
which shall arise on the earth.
But the holy ones of the Most High
shall receive the kingship,
to possess it forever and ever."

DANIEL 7:13-18

INTERPRETATION

For most readers these verses
reaffirm Nathan's prophecy to David
of an eternal kingship.

A new image, however, is the "son of man."
Daniel's vision equates the "son of man" (king)
with the "holy ones" (nation).
Thus, the king and nation
are combined in one figure.

New Testament writers referred to Jesus
as the "Son of Man" no less than 69 times.
The most striking reference
came when Jesus stood trial for his life.

HIGH PRIEST *Are you the Messiah,*
the Son of the Blessed One?

JESUS *I am;*
and you will see the Son of Man
seated at the right hand
of the Power and coming
with the clouds of heaven.

HIGH PRIEST *What further need do we have*
of witnesses?
You have heard the blasphemy.

MARK 14:61–64

For New Testament writers,
the descriptive expression "the Son of Man
seated at the right hand of the Power"
captured the mysteriousness of Jesus' personality.

On the one hand,
it recalled that he was David's offspring.
On the other hand,
it recalled that he was Yahweh's servant.

In other words,
the expression captured the polarity of Jesus:
related to David,
and related to Yahweh.

Both the humble and the exalted aspects
of Jesus' personality were served.

No other title could have identified better
Jesus' person and mission.
He is both,
a humble member of the "holy ones" (nation)
and the exalted servant
of the "mighty one" (Yahweh).
His suffering will establish an eternal kingdom
not just for Israel, but for all peoples.

Referring to Jesus
as Son of Man and Suffering Servant, Paul said:

Christ is head of his body the church,
as well as its savior.

EPHESIANS 5:23

DAY OF JUDGMENT

The Book of Daniel ends dramatically.
Concerning the day of Yahweh's final judgment,
Daniel is told in a final vision:

At that time your people shall escape,
everyone who is found written in the book.

Many of those who sleep
in the dust of the earth shall awake;
some shall live forever,
others shall be an everlasting horror and disgrace.

But the wise shall shine brightly
like the splendor of the firmament,
and those who lead the many to justice
shall be like the stars forever.

As for you, Daniel,
keep secret the message and seal the book.

DANIEL 12:1–4

Esther

Three other pieces of Old Testament literature
belong to this era: Tobit, Judith, and Esther.
Each of these books centers around a Jewish hero
who remains faithful to Yahweh in time of trial.
As such, the books exhort persecuted Jews
to hold fast to their faith.

The Book of Esther is typical.
It is named after a beautiful Jewish girl
who was raised in exile by her uncle, Mordecai.
A Persian king, not knowing her nationality,
makes her his wife and queen.
Haman, an ambitious Persian leader,
convinces the king
to destroy the Jews of the kingdom.
Esther intervenes to outwit the evil Haman
and save her people.

Modern Jews celebrate the event on Purim.
The holiday is also known as the Feast of Lots,
after the way Haman chose the day
for exterminating all the Jews.

Ancient caves still honeycomb the rugged ravine
country of Palestine.
The Maccabees launched
their counteroffensive from sites like this.
Heroines like Esther inspired them.

THE MACCABEES

Fired with the spirit of the Book of Daniel,
loyal Jews came alive.

Soon a resistance movement was mounted
under the leadership of three Jewish brothers:
Judas, Jonathan, and Simon.

Called the Maccabees, they formed a guerrilla army.
From rocky ravines and hills,
they set in motion a counteroffensive.

Coming unexpectedly upon towns and villages,
Judas would set them on fire.
He captured strategic positions,
and put to flight a large number of the enemy.
He preferred the nights . . .
for such attacks.
Soon the fame of his valor spread everywhere.

2 MACCABEES 8:6–7

Jewish poetry recalls Judas this way:

In his actions he was like a lion,
like a young lion roaring for prey. . . .
The lawbreakers were cowed by fear of him,
and all evildoers were dismayed. . . .
He made Jacob glad by his deeds,
and his memory is blessed forever.

1 MACCABEES 3:4–7

The revolt gained momentum
when the ragged freedom fighters
stormed the temple and reclaimed it.
Modern Jews still celebrate the event
with the Feast of Lights, known as Hanukkah.

The tide finally turned in favor of the revolutionaries
when Antiochus overextended his army on other
battlefronts and ran into economic problems.

Typical of so many leaders, Judas and Jonathan
were killed in the process of bringing victory
to their people. It fell to their brother, Simon,
to bring the revolt to a successful conclusion.

Life after Death

Taking cue from the Book of Daniel,
a new attitude toward life after death emerged
among many Jews in this period.
We see it reflected in the martyr stories
of the seven brothers.
The first brother says to his tormentors:

You are depriving us of this present life,
but the King of the world
will raise us up to live again forever.
It is for his laws that we are dying.

2 MACCABEES 7:9

The fourth brother echoes the same idea:

It is my choice to die at the hands of men
with the God-given hope
of being restored to life by him;
but for you, there will be no resurrection to life.

2 MACCABEES 7:14

Similarly, a new attitude about the relationship
between the living and the dead emerged.

On one occasion Judas had his men
pray for the dead and took up a collection
to offer sacrifice for them.

In doing this
he acted in a very excellent and noble way,
inasmuch as
he had the resurrection of the dead in view;
for if he were not expecting the fallen to rise again,
it would have been . . . foolish
to pray for them in death. . . .
Thus he made atonement for the dead
that they might be freed from this sin.

2 MACCABEES 12:43–46

48
Threat from Within

The Persecution Era
was followed by the Hasmonean Era.
Simon, the last of the Maccabees brothers, died
and leadership passed to his son John.

If Jewish existence was threatened from without
during the Persecution Era,
it was now threatened from within.
The Hasmoneans (probably named for John's
grandfather) used the office of high priest
for political purposes.

During this era, three religious groups polarized:
Sadducees, Pharisees, and Essenes.

SADDUCEES

All three groups claimed loyalty to the Torah,
but took different religious stances.
The Sadducees, composed of priestly
and wealthy families, supported the Hasmoneans.

Opposing the Sadducees
were Jews of very strict observance, called Hasidim.
From this group emerged the Essenes and Pharisees.

ESSENES

The Essenes were so opposed to Hasmonean rule
that they broke with conventional Jewish society
and lived apart in the desert.
They believed that God's great intervention
in human history was close at hand.

221

Greek customs became widespread
among Near Eastern nations during this period.
Baths and gymnasiums appeared in Jerusalem.
Pharisees and Essenes found Greek customs offensive,
especially the cult of the body
and nudity in athletic games.

Thus, marriage meant little to them
and most of them lived as "monks."

It was their scrolls
that were found in the Dead Sea caves.
Some scholars speculate
that John the Baptist once belonged to this group.

PHARISEES

The Pharisees remained within the mainstream
of Jewish society.
Unlike the conservative Sadducees,
they accepted later prophetic revelation
concerning immortality, judgment after death,
and the resurrection of the body.

On the other hand,
they so stressed the letter of the law
that legalism became a constant threat in their lives.
In New Testament times,
this brought them into open conflict with Jesus.

ROMAN EAGLE

The clock began to strike midnight
for the Hasmonean Era in 63 B.C.
Then, Roman armies occupied Jerusalem.
A vivid story is told in connection with the event.

Witnesses to God
LEONARD JOHNSTON

When the Roman general Pompey
captured Jerusalem in 63 B.C.
he determined to see its famous temple.
It was widely known
that the Jews would not worship any of the gods
which Rome received . . .
but there was some mystery
about the sort of God they did worship.
Now he would find out.

So he made his way up the hill
on which the Temple stood,
and crossed the courtyard which surrounded it.
Passing under the great doors
and through an outer hall,
he found himself in a long room with,
at the far end, shut off by a curtain,
a little secret room.

This was the sanctuary of the god.
And as he advanced toward it,
with no sound but the echo of his footsteps,
even the conqueror
could not prevent a feeling of awe.
What lay beyond those curtains?
Some strange and terrible animal?
A mysterious presence aglow with flame?

Pompey swept back the curtains and gazed in—
and burst into a bellow of laughter.

For there was nothing there.
This was the famous secret of the Jews.
No wonder they made a mystery of it;
no wonder no one had seen their god.
There was nothing to see.

The curtain finally fell on the Hasmonean Era around 40 B.C., when the Romans installed Herod the Great as king of Judah.

Herod catered to the Romans and used terror tactics to control Jews who opposed him.
Here's how one writer described him:

The Years of Galilee
HOWARD LAFAY

He murdered members of his own family—
yet scrupulously observed Mosaic dietary laws
and would eat no pork.
This provoked his Roman master Augustus
into jesting:
"I would rather be Herod's pig than Herod's son."

Another writer completed the portrait of Herod this way:

Who Was the Man Jesus?
ROBERT COUGHLAN

Herod was a brilliant, scheming, ruthless,
bloody man who reigned from 40 to 4 B.C. . . .

One of the few things
that recommended him to his subjects was . . .
that he began rebuilding the Temple
according to the grandiose plans of Solomon.

It was this ruler who served as the bridge between the Old and the New Testament periods.

Augustus Caesar

After occupying Jerusalem in 63 B.C.,
Pompey returned to Rome
and struck up a political friendship
with a young military genius, Julius Caesar.

But Pompey's ties with Julius were doomed.
A corrupt Roman Senate
turned the two leaders against each other.
Pompey met death in Egypt in 48 B.C.

By 44 B.C., Julius was Rome's undisputed boss;
but his days were numbered, also.
On March 15, Julius Caesar was assassinated.

Into his shoes stepped Octavian (photo),
his 18-year-old adopted son.
In 27 B.C., Octavian became Rome's first emperor,
taking the name Augustus Caesar.
It was during his reign that Jesus was born.

49
The Unfinished Story

The early American writer
Nathaniel Hawthorne was dead.
On his desk lay the outline to a play
that he never got a chance to write.

The play centered around a person
who never appeared on stage.
Everyone talked excitedly about the person,
everyone dreamed about him,
everyone wanted to meet him,
everyone waited eagerly for his arrival.

All kinds of minor characters
discussed the arrival of the main character.
But the play ended without the main character
ever putting in an appearance.

The Old Testament
is something like Hawthorne's unfinished play.
It, too, ends
without the main character appearing.

The Book of Sirach
rings down the curtain on ancient literature
from Old Testament times.
Fitting the category of *wisdom* literature,
it divides into two main themes:

    meditations on how to live
    and eulogies of Old Testament heroes.

MEDITATIONS

The tone of the meditations reminds us
of a departing parent addressing a child.

When you come to serve the LORD,
prepare yourself for trials. (2:1)

With all your strength, love your Creator. . . .
To the poor man also extend your hand. . . .
Be generous to all the living,
and withhold not your kindness from the dead. . . .
In whatever you do, remember your last days,
and you will never sin. (7:30–36)

EULOGIES

Next, the Book of Sirach contains a review
of Old Testament history.
It does this in the form of eulogies to the giants
of Israel's past.
One by one, it parades before the reader
the great persons who peopled its pages.

ABRAHAM

Abraham, father of many peoples . . .
observed the precepts of the Most High,
and entered into an agreement with him. . . .
God promised him with an oath
that in his descendants
the nations would be blessed. . . .
From him was to spring
the man who won the favor of all. (44:19–21; 45:1)

MOSES

God wrought swift miracles at his words. . . .
He gave him the commandments for his people,
and revealed to him his glory. . . .
God selected him from all mankind . . .
that he might teach his precepts to Jacob,
his judgments and decrees to Israel. (45:3–5)

Meditation on God

He sprinkles the snow like fluttering birds;
it comes to settle like swarms of locusts.
Its shining whiteness blinds the eyes,
the mind is baffled by its steady fall.

He scatters frost like so much salt;
it shines like blossoms on the thornbush.
Cold northern blasts he sends
that turn the ponds to lumps of ice.
He freezes over every body of water,
and clothes each pool with a coat of mail. . . .

Let us praise him the more,
since we cannot fathom him,
for greater is he than all his works. . . .
It is the LORD who has made all things,
and to those who fear him he gives wisdom.

SIRACH 43:18–35

Meditation on Friendship

A faithful friend is a sturdy shelter;
he who finds one finds a treasure.
A faithful friend is beyond price,
no sum can balance his worth.

He who touches pitch blackens his hand;
he who associates with an impious man
learns his ways. . . . How can the earthen pot
go with the metal cauldron?
When they knock together,
the pot will be smashed.

Who insults a friend breaks up the friendship.
Should you draw a sword against a friend,
despair not, it can be undone. . . .
But from him who brings harm to his friend
all will stand aloof who hear of it.

SIRACH 6:14–15; 13:1–2; 22:20–26

A tenth-century frieze of David and Goliath from church near Lake Van, Turkey.

*You are destined, it is written, in time to come
to put an end to wrath before the day of the LORD,
to turn back the hearts of fathers toward their sons,
and to re-establish the tribes of Jacob. (48:4–10)*

HEZEKIAH AND ISAIAH

*During his reign Sennacherib led an invasion,
and . . . shook his fist at Zion. . . .
The people's hearts melted within them,
and they were in anguish like that of childbirth.
But they called upon the Most High God . . . ;
he heard the prayer they uttered,
and saved them through Isaiah. . . .
For Hezekiah did what was right
and held fast to the paths of David. . . .
Isaiah looked into the future
and . . . foretold what should be till the end of time,
hidden things yet to be fulfilled. (48:18–25)*

JOSIAH AND JEREMIAH

*The name Josiah is like blended incense. . . .
Precious is his memory,
like honey to the taste, like music at a banquet. . . .
He turned to God with his whole heart. . . .
Except for David, Hezekiah and Josiah,
the kings all were wicked. . . .
So he gave over their power to others . . .
who burned the holy city and left its streets desolate,
as Jeremiah had foretold;
for they had treated him badly
who even in the womb had been made a prophet,
to root out, pull down, and destroy,
and then to build and to plant. (49:1–7)*

EZEKIEL AND OTHERS

*Ezekiel beheld the vision
and described the different creatures of the chariot;
he also referred to Job,*

DAVID

*As a youth he slew the giant
and wiped out the people's disgrace. . . .
With his every deed
he offered thanks to God Most High,
in words of praise.
With his whole being he loved his Maker. . . .
The LORD forgave him his sins . . .
and established his throne in Israel. (47:4–11)*

ELIJAH

*How awesome are you, Elijah! . . .
You sent kings down to destruction. . . .
You were taken aloft in a whirlwind,
in a chariot with fiery horses.*

who always persevered in the right path.
Then, too, the Twelve Prophets—
may their bones return to life
from their resting place!—
gave new strength to Jacob
and saved him by their faith and hope. (49:8–10)

NEHEMIAH

Extolled be the memory of Nehemiah!
He rebuilt our ruined walls,
restored our shattered defenses,
and set up gates and bars. (49:13)

SIMON

Like the sun shining upon the temple,
like the rainbow appearing in the cloudy sky . . .
Simon ascended the glorious altar
and lent majesty
to the court of the sanctuary. . . .
All the people of the land
would shout for joy,
praying to the Merciful One. (50:7–19)

CONCLUSION

The Book of Sirach ends with these thoughts:

Happy the man
who meditates upon these things,
wise the man who takes them to heart!

If he puts them into practice,
he can cope with anything,
for the fear of the LORD is his lamp. (50:28–29)

Let your spirits rejoice in the mercy of God,
and be not ashamed to give him praise.

Work at your tasks in due season,
and in his own time
God will give you your reward. (51:29–30)

ISRAEL IN WAITING

By its own admission
the Old Testament is an unfinished story.
It ends with faithful Jews
waiting for the return of Elijah,
waiting for the "Day of the Lord,"
waiting for "hidden things yet to be fulfilled."

The Old Testament drama closes with old Jews,
like Zechariah and Simeon,
watching, praying—waiting!
(Luke 1:67; 2:25)

Perhaps the most appropriate signature
to our study of God's chosen people is this image
by a modern novelist.

The Source
JAMES A. MICHENER

Rabbi Asher
wandered among the gnarled olive trees;
his attention was arrested
by one so ancient that its interior was rotted away,
leaving an empty shell
through which one could see;
but somehow the remaining fragments
held contact with the roots,
and the old tree was still vital,
sending forth branches that bore good fruit;
and as he studied this patriarch of the grove
Asher thought that it well summarized
the state of the Jewish people:
an old society
much of whose interior had rotted away,
but whose fragments
still held vital connection with the roots of God,
and it was through these roots of law
that Jews could ascertain the will of God
and produce good fruit.

REFERENCE NOTES

Part One

John T. Scopes, "The Trial That Rocked the Nation," *Reader's Digest,* March 1961, pp. 136–44.

"The Lutheran Pope," *Newsweek,* July 23, 1973, p. 50.

Charles Clayton Morrison, "Protestant Misuse of the Bible," *The Christian Century,* June 5, 1946.

Robert E. Gentet, "Dinosaurs Before Adam?" *Tract #670* (Pasadena, Calif.: Ambassador College, 1963).

Watch Tower Bible and Tract Society, *Is the Bible Really the Word of God?* (Watch Tower Bible and Tract Society of Pennsylvania, 1969), pp. 21–22.

William F. Dankenbring, "Why the New Creation-Evolution Controversy?" *Plain Truth,* June 1973, pp. 24–27.

Loren Eiseley, "In Darwin's Century," from *Adventures of the Mind* in *The Saturday Evening Post,* April 26, 1958.

Ronald Kotulak, "Deadend for Expanding Universe?" *Chicago Tribune,* 1973.

Ronald Kotulak, "End Only 100 Billion Years Away," *Chicago Tribune,* May 1, 1979.

D. J. Wiseman, *Illustrations from Biblical Archaeology* (Grand Rapids, Mich.: Wm. B. Eerdmans Publishing Co., 1959).

Feodor Dostoevski, *The Brothers Karamazov,* trans. by Constance Garnett (New York: Random House, Modern Library, 1950), pp. 436–37.

James Weldon Johnson, "Creation," from *God's Trombones* (New York: Viking Press, 1955).

Nikos Kazantzakis, *The Last Temptation of Christ* (New York: Simon & Schuster, 1960), pp. 391–92.

Watch Tower Bible and Tract Society, *Is the Bible Really the Word of God?* pp. 30–32.

Bill Barry, "Carbon Copy Man," *Chicago Sun-Times Midwest Magazine,* March 11, 1973.

"The Mind," *Time,* April 19, 1971, pp. 46–47.

Albert Rosenfeld, *The Second Genesis: The Coming Control of Life* (Englewood Cliffs, N.J.: Prentice-Hall, 1969), p. 135.

Ronald Kotulak, ". . . Half Plant, Half Animal," *Chicago Tribune,* March 21, 1976.

William Hines, "Fierce DNA Debate . . . ," *Chicago Sun-Times,* March 13, 1977.

Martin Luther King, Jr., *Strength to Love* (New York: Harper & Row, 1963).

Arthur J. Snider, "Man's a Born Killer . . . ," *Chicago Daily News,* September 1–2, 1973.

Paul Horn, "A Visit with India's High-Powered New Prophet," *Look,* February 6, 1968.

Thomas Merton, *The Seven Storey Mountain* (New York: Harcourt, Brace & Co., 1948), p. 111.

James T. Farrell, *Studs Lonigan* (New York: Vanguard Press, 1962), p. 385.

James Weldon Johnson, "Noah Built the Ark," from *God's Trombones* (New York: Viking Press, 1955).

Werner Keller, *The Bible as History: A Confirmation of the Book of Books,* trans. by William Neil (New York: William Morrow & Co., 1956), pp. 35–36.

Watch Tower Bible and Tract Society, *Is the Bible Really the Word of God?* pp. 35–36.

Editors, *Science News,* March 26, 1977.

John J. Dougherty, *Searching the Scriptures* (New York: Doubleday & Co., 1959), p. 52.

George Higgins, "Sin Comes Back on the Scene" (Washington, D.C.: National Catholic News Service, 1974).

Dorothy Thompson, "The Lesson of Dachau," *Ladies' Home Journal,* September 1945.

Edith Sitwell, "Still Falls the Rain," from *Street Song* (New York: A. Watkins, 1940).

Avery Corman, *Oh, God!* (New York: Simon & Schuster, 1971), pp. 21, 22, 24–25.

Part Two

Samuel Noah Kramer, "The World of Abraham," in *Everyday Life in Bible Times* (Washington, D.C.: National Geographic Society, 1967), p. 44.

James A. Michener, *The Source* (New York: Random House, 1965), pp. 112–13.

Morris West, *The Devil's Advocate* (New York: William Morrow & Co., 1959), p. 294.

Carlo Carretto, *Letters from the Desert,* trans. by Rose Mary Hancock (New York: Pillar Books, 1976), pp. 12–15, 30, 121–22, 125–26.

Sholem Asch, *Moses* (New York: G. P. Putnam Sons, 1951).

Bernhard W. Anderson, *Understanding the Old Testament* (Englewood Cliffs, N.J.: Prentice-Hall, 1966), p. 37.

National Geographic Society, *Everyday Life in Bible Times,* p. 179.

David N. Nichol, "Biblical Eighth Plague Hits Again," *Chicago Daily News,* March 7, 1969.

Mordecai Kaplan, Eugene Kohn, and Ira Eisenstein, eds., *The New Haggadah* (New York: Behrman House, 1941), pp. 11–13.

John Putnam, "To Sinai and the Promised Land," in *Everyday Life in Bible Times,* pp. 178–204.

David S. Boyer, "Geographical Twins a World Apart," *National Geographic Magazine,* December 1958, p. 852.

Gordon Gaskill, "Which Mountain Did Moses Climb?" *Reader's Digest,* June 1973, pp. 209–16.

Will Herberg, "Jewish Existence and Survival: A Theological View," *Judaism,* Vol. I (1952), p. 20.

Herodotus, *Histories IV,* The Penguin Classics, p. 264.

Barnabas Ahern, "The Biblical Way of Life," *The Critic,* September 1965, pp. 38–46.

Carl Sandburg, as quoted by Ralph McGill in "The Most Unforget-table Character I've Met," *Reader's Digest,* May 1954, p. 110.

Philip S. Bernstein, "What the Jews Believe," *Life,* September 11, 1950.

George Kent, "Happily Ever After with the Brothers Grimm," *Reader's Digest,* January 1965.

Roland de Vaux, "The Qumran Story," *The Bible Today Reader* (Collegeville, Minn.: The Order of St. Benedict, Inc., 1973), p. 42.

"Geiger Counters Prove Age of Biblical Scrolls," *Catholic Universe Bulletin,* December 7, 1951.

Robert Aron, *The Jewish Jesus* (Maryknoll, N.Y.: Orbis Books, 1971), p. 83.

Part Three

Werner Keller, *The Bible as History,* p. 74.

G. Ernest Wright, "The World of David and Solomon," in *Everyday Life in Bible Times,* pp. 209–13.

Charlotte D. Lofgreen, "From the Volunteer's Viewpoint: History by the Bucketful," *The Biblical Archaeology Review,* March 1976, pp. 35–37.

James A. Michener, *The Source,* pp. 281, 284–87.

Stuart E. Rosenberg, *Judaism* (New York: Paulist Press, 1966), pp. 61–63, 147–49.

Robert Wallace, "Kingly Glory and Ordeal," *Life,* December 25, 1964, p. 63.

Philip Yancey, "Ordeal on Mt. Hood," *Campus Life,* February 1978, pp. 77–78.

James Daniel, "The Psalms: Hymnbook of Humanity," *Christianity Today,* April 15, 1966.

George W. Cornell, "Salvation: PWs Say God Didn't Help—He Pulled Them Through," *Chicago Daily News,* March 10–11, 1973, p. 24.

Part Four

James Fitzgerald, "Grim Poverty Stalks the Land of Red Cloud," *Our Sunday Visitor,* May 19, 1968, pp. 4–5.

Roy Larson, "Reform Rabbis Will Vote on New Seder Celebration," *Chicago Sun-Times,* April 21, 1973, p. 14.

Emil G. Kraeling, "The Prophets," *Life,* December 25, 1964, p. 75.

Eamonn O'Doherty, "Ezekiel Today," *The Bible Today,* April 1963, p. 387.

Philip Yancey, "Fire," *Campus Life,* September 20, 1970.

Janice Rothschild, "I Met a Samaritan," *The Atlanta Journal-Constitution,* September 20, 1970.

Lord Byron, "The Destruction of Sennacherib."

"History by Computer," *Time,* April 27, 1962.

Part Five

"Home at Last," *Newsweek,* February 26, 1973, p. 26.

Part Six

Leonard Johnston, *Witnesses to God* (New York: Paulist Press, 1963), p. 109.

Howard LaFay, "The Years in Galilee," in *Everyday Life in Bible Times,* p. 328.

Robert Coughlan, "Who Was the Man Jesus?" *Life,* December 25, 1964, p. 92.

James A. Michener, *The Source,* p. 431.

Persepolis 194–96
Pithom 69
Pompeii 203

Qumran 93–97, 169, 179

Raamses (Tanis) 69, 70, 74
Ras Shamra 149
Rosetta (Rashid) 67, 74

Samaria 150, 158
Susa 46

Tanis (Raamses) 69, 70, 74
Tell el Amarna 74, 102
Thebes 74

Ugarit 149, 150
Ur 46–50 passim

Biblical Persons

Aaron 75
Abel 35
Abraham 36, 46–47, 50–55, 102, 103, 118, 224
Abishai 116, 124
Absalom 126
Adam 15, 31–33, 36, 53, 57
Adonijah 126
Ahab 149
Amaziah 160–61
Amos 158, 159–61, 170
Antiochus IV 214–15

Baruch 178
Bathsheba 124–26
Bildad 208
Boaz 112–13

Cain 35
Cyrus 189, 192–94, 202

Daniel 158, 214–19
David 112–27 passim, 158, 187, 219, 226
Delilah 112

Elihu 208, 211
Elijah 149, 151–53, 226
Eliphaz 207–8

Elisha 149, 153, 154
Esau 60–61
Esther 220
Eve 15, 30–33
Ezekiel 158, 186–88, 205, 226–27
Ezra 198

Goliath 115–16, 226

Habbakuk 158, 178
Hagar 46, 51, 53
Haggai 158, 198
Haman 220
Herod the Great 223
Hezekiah 170, 172–74, 226
Hilkiah 177
Hosea 158, 161–62

Isaac 53–55, 57, 60–61, 102, 118
Isaiah 92, 97, 158, 168–71, 226
Isaiah (Second) 188–92
Ishmael 51, 53
Ittai 123–24

Jacob 60–61, 63–65, 102
Jehu 154–56
Jephthah 111
Jeremiah 158, 178–81, 226
Jeroboam I 149
Jeroboam II 157, 160
Jesse 112–13
Jezebel 149
Joab 124, 126
Job 206–10
Joel 158
John the Baptist 91, 152, 222
John Hyrcanus I 221
Jonah 158, 199–201
Jonathan 117
Jonathan (Maccabees) 220
Joseph (son of Jacob) 64–69
Joseph (foster father of Jesus) 123
Joshua 102, 103, 106–8, 110
Josiah 177–78, 226
Judah 64
Judas (Maccabees) 220, 221

Lot 46, 50

Maccabees 220–21
Malachi 158, 199

Manesseh 177
Mary (mother of Jesus) 123
Matthew 24
Mesha 149, 154
Micah 158, 167, 170
Mordecai 220
Moses 57, 70–71, 74–75, 78–91 passim, 102, 138, 166, 224

Naaman 153
Nabonidus 192
Nahum 158, 178
Naomi 112
Nathan 120–21, 125–26, 158, 219
Nebuchadnezzar 181
Nebuzaradan 182
Nehemiah 198, 227
Noah 36–39 passim

Obadiah 158
Obed 112–13
Omri 149, 154

Paul (letters) 10
Philip (apostle) 191–92

Qoheleth 203–4

Rameses II 69–75 passim
Rebekah 60–61
Rehoboam 148–49
Ruth 112–13

Samson 112
Samuel 113–15
Sarah 46, 50, 51, 53
Saul 113, 115–17
Sennacherib 172–75
Shaphan 177
Shem 36
Shimei 124
Simeon 227
Simon (Maccabees) 220, 221, 227
Solomon 126, 133, 136–38, 148

Terah 36, 46

Uriah 124

Zechariah 158, 198, 227
Zedekiah 181

Zephaniah   158, 178
Zophar   207–8

Nonbiblical Names

Ahern, Barnabas   90
Alexander the Great   202–3
Anderson, Bernhard W.   71
Augustine of Hippo   13, 62, 210

Basil   161
Botta, Paul-Emile   34, 35, 164–65
Bryan, William Jennings   8–9
Byron, Lord   174

Caesar, Julius   223
Caesar, Augustus   223
Carnarvon, Lord   69
Carretto, Carlo   58–59
Carter, Howard   69
Champollion, Jean-Francois   66, 67
Chardin, Teilhard de   14
Coleridge, Samuel Taylor   25
Confucius   141
Corman, Avery   43

Darrow, Clarence   8–9
de Vaux, Roland   93
Dostoevski, Feodor   22

Eiseley, Loren   13

Frankl, Viktor   42
Franklin, Benjamin   132, 145

Hammurabi   175
Hawthorne, Nathaniel   224
Herberg, Will   85
Herodotus   64, 70, 86, 175

Jerome, Saint   99
Johnson, James Weldon   24, 37
Johnston, Leonard   222

Kazantzakis, Nikos   24
Keller, Werner   38, 105
King, Martin Luther   29
Koldewey, Robert   188
Kramer, Samuel Noah   49–50

Layard, Austen   155
Libby, Willard F.   97
Luther, Martin   10

Maharishi Mahesh Yogi   31
Menninger, Karl   42
Merton, Thomas   32
Michener, James A.   54–55, 118–19, 227

Napoleon   66, 123

Pius XII, Pope   15, 94
Plutarch   202
Pompey   222, 223
Putnam, John   79–80

Rawlinson, Henry   49
Richard the Lionhearted   200
Rickenbacker, Eddie   134

Sandburg, Carl   91
Scopes, John T.   8–9
Shakespeare, William   36
Sitwell, Edith   43

Thompson, Dorothy   42
Toynbee, Arnold   148

West, Morris   57
Whittier, John Greenleaf   164
Wiesel, Elie   162–63
Wiseman, D. J.   16
Woolley, Leonard   38, 48
Wright, G. Ernest   108

Zwingli, Ulrich   10

INDEX OF BIBLICAL CITATIONS AND PASSAGES

ACKNOWLEDGMENTS (Continued from page 2)

Excerpts from *The Bible as History: A Confirmation of the Book of Books* by Werner Keller, trans. by William Neil. Copyright 1956 by Werner Keller. Reprinted by permission of William Morrow & Co., Inc.

Excerpt from *Searching the Scriptures* by John T. Dougherty. Copyright 1959 by Doubleday & Co., Inc. Reprinted by permission of Doubleday & Co., Inc.

Excerpt from "Still Falls the Rain" by Edith Sitwell. Copyright 1942 by Edith Sitwell. Reprinted from *Street Song* by permission of A. Watkins, Inc. Reprinted from *Collected Poems* (Macmillan) by permission of David Higham Associates Limited, London.

Excerpt from "Sin Comes Back on the Scene" by George Higgins. Copyright 1974, by the National Catholic News Service. Reprinted with permission.

Excerpt from *Oh, God!* by Avery Corman. Copyright © 1971 by Avery Corman. Published by Simon & Schuster. Reprinted by permission of Avery Corman.

Excerpts from "The World of Abraham" by Samuel Noah Kramer, "To Sinai and the Promised Land" by John Putnam, "The World of David and Solomon" by G. Ernest Wright, "The Years in Galilee" by Howard LaFay, from *Everyday Life in Bible Times* by the National Geographic Society. Copyright 1967. Reprinted by permission of the National Geographic Society.

Excerpts from *The Source* by James A. Michener. Copyright © 1965 by Marjay Productions, Inc. Reprinted by permission of Random House, Inc., and Martin Secker & Warburg Limited, London.

Excerpt from *The Devil's Advocate* by Morris West. Copyright © 1959 by Morris West. Reprinted by permission of William Morrow & Co., Inc., and William Heinemann Ltd., London.

Excerpts from *Letters from the Desert* by Carlo Carretto, trans. by Rose Mary Hancock. Published and © 1972 by Orbis Books and Darton Longman & Todd Ltd. Reprinted by permission of Orbis Books and Darton Longman & Todd Ltd.

Excerpt from "Biblical Eighth Plague Hits Again" by David N. Nichol, *Chicago Daily News*, March 7, 1969. Reprinted with permission from Field Enterprises, Inc.

Excerpt from *The New Haggadah* by Mordecai Kaplan, Eugene Kohn, and Ira Eisenstein, eds., on page 77, reprinted with permission of the Publisher, Behrman House Inc., 1261 Broadway, New York, N.Y.

Excerpt from "Geographical Twins a World Apart" by David S. Boyer, *National Geographic Magazine*, December 1958. Reprinted by permission.

Excerpt from "Which Mountain Did Moses Climb?" by Gordon Gaskill, *Reader's Digest*, June 1973. Reprinted by permission.

Excerpt from "The Biblical Way of Life" by Barnabas Ahern, *The Critic*, September 1965. © *The Critic*, September 1965. Published by the Thomas More Association, Chicago, Illinois. Reprinted by permission of the Thomas More Association.

Excerpt from "The Qumran Story" by Roland de Vaux, *The Bible Today Reader*. Copyright 1973 by The Order of St. Benedict, Collegeville, Minnesota. Used with permission.

Excerpt from *The Jewish Jesus* by Robert Aron. Copyright © 1971 by Orbis Books. Reprinted by permission of Orbis Books.

Excerpt from "From the Volunteer's Viewpoint: History by the Bucketful" by Charlotte D. Lofgreen, *Biblical Archaeology Review*, March 1976, pp. 35–37. Reprinted by permission of *Biblical Archaeology Review*.

Excerpts from *Judaism* by Stuart E. Rosenberg. Copyright © 1966 by the Missionary Society of St. Paul. Reprinted by permission of Paulist Press.

Excerpt from "Grim Poverty Stalks the Land of Red Cloud" by James Fitzgerald, *Our Sunday Visitor*, May 19, 1968. Reprinted by permission of *Our Sunday Visitor*.

Excerpt from "Reform Rabbis Will Vote on New Seder Celebration" by Roy Larson. Excerpted with permission from the *Chicago Sun-Times*, April 21, 1973.

Excerpt from "Fire" by Philip Yancey. Used by permission from *Campus Life* Magazine, September 20, 1970. Copyright 1970, Youth for Christ International, Wheaton, Illinois.

Excerpt from "I Met a Samaritan" by Janice Rothschild, *The Atlanta Journal-Constitution*, September 20, 1970. Reprinted by permission of Janice Rothschild Blumberg.

Excerpt from "History by Computer," *Time*, April 27, 1962. Reprinted by permission from *Time*, The Weekly Newsmagazine; Copyright Time Inc. 1962.

Excerpt from "Home at Last," *Newsweek*, February 26, 1973. Copyright 1973 by Newsweek, Inc. All rights reserved. Reprinted by permission.

Excerpt from *Witnesses to God* by Leonard Johnston. Published by Paulist Press. Reprinted by permission of the author.